RED STATE, BLUE STATE, RICH STATE, POOR STATE

Red State, Blue State, Rich State, Poor State

WHY AMERICANS VOTE THE WAY THEY DO

EXPANDED EDITION

*Andrew Gelman, David Park, Boris Shor,
and Jeronimo Cortina*

PRINCETON UNIVERSITY PRESS

PRINCETON AND OXFORD

Published by Princeton University Press, 41 William Street,
Princeton, New Jersey 08540

In the United Kingdom: Princeton University Press, 6 Oxford Street,
Woodstock, Oxfordshire OX20 1TW

Expanded paperback edition, 2010
Paperback ISBN: 978-0-691-14393-4

The Library of Congress has cataloged the cloth edition of this book as follows

Gelman, Andrew.
  Red state, blue state, rich state, poor state : why Americans vote the way they
do / Andrew Gelman ; with David Park ... et al.
      p. cm.
  Includes bibliographical references and index.
  ISBN 978-0-691-13927-2 (hardcover : alk. paper)
1. Elections—United States.   2. Political parties—United States.
3. Politics, Practical—United States.   4. Presidents—Election.
I. Park, David, 1967–   II. Title.
  JK1976.G45 2008
  324.973—dc22   2008013737

British Library Cataloging-in-Publication Data is available

This book has been composed in New Baskerville
Printed on acid-free paper. ∞
press.princeton.edu

Printed in the United States of America

10   9   8   7   6   5   4   3   2   1

Contents

PART I

THE PARADOX

Introduction

> OK, but here's the fact that nobody ever, ever mentions—
> Democrats win rich people. Over $100,000 in income, you are
> likely more than not to vote for Democrats. People never point
> that out. Rich people vote liberal. I don't know what that's all
> about.
> —*Tucker Carlson, 2007*

CARLSON was half right. Nowadays the Democrats win the rich
states, but rich people vote Republican, just as they have for
decades.

What makes the statement interesting, though, is that it sounds
as if it could be right. Consider the 2000 and 2004 elections, where
George W. Bush won the lower-income states in the South and middle of the country, while his Democratic opponents captured the
richer states in the Northeast and West Coast. As we shall discuss,
this pattern is not an illusion of the map—the Democrats really
have been doing better in richer parts of the country, and this
pattern has become more noticeable in recent elections.

The paradox is that, while these rich states have become more
strongly Democratic over time, rich voters have remained consistently more Republican than voters on the lower end of the income
scale. We display this graphically in figure 1.1. Tucker Carlson's
statement sounds reasonable given the voting patterns in states,
but it doesn't match what individual voters are doing. If poor people were a state, they would be "bluer" even than Massachusetts; if
rich people were a state, they would be about as "red" as Alabama,
Kansas, the Dakotas, or Texas.

The point of this book is to explain where the red–blue paradox
comes from and what it means for American politics. To answer
these questions, we first ask who votes for whom. It seems that there

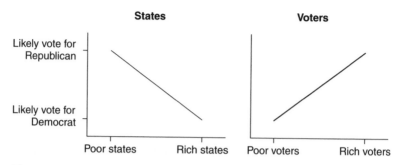

Figure 1.1: The red–blue paradox: Rich *states* vote for the Democrats, but rich *people* vote Republican.

are a lot of well-off urbanites who are voting for Democrats, but how do we square this with poll data showing that George W. Bush in 2004 received over 60% of the votes of people with incomes over $200,000?

Rich people in rich states are socially and economically more liberal than rich people in poor states. But only in recent decades has this translated into Democratic dominance in the coasts. What's new is polarization—the increasingly ideological nature of politics. Both parties are now more cohesive on issues than they were in the days of Richard Nixon, Gerald Ford, Jimmy Carter, and even Ronald Reagan. Liberal Democrats face off against conservative Republicans in Congress with little middle ground, and voters within each party are also more likely to agree with each other on issues ranging from taxes to gay rights to foreign policy. Again, the paradox is that polarization is going in one direction for voters and the other direction for states.

The resolution of the paradox is that the more polarized playing field has driven rich conservative voters in poor states toward the Republicans and rich liberals in rich states toward the Democrats, thus turning the South red and New England and the West Coast blue and setting up a national map that is divided by culture rather than class, with blue-collar West Virginia moving from solidly Democratic (one of the ten states that went for Michael Dukakis in 1988) to safely Republican and suburban Connecticut going the other way.

Income varies much less among states than within states—the average income in the richest state is only about twice that of the poorest (only one-and-a-half times after adjusting for cost of living), but, at the level of individual households, the top 20% have incomes that are more than ten times larger, on average, than the bottom 20%. What this means is that the political differences among states are driven by cultural issues, but within states, the traditional rich–poor divide remains.

States differ in other ways, too, both socially and economically. Conservative born-again Christians are concentrated in the relatively low-income states of the South where the split between rich and poor also overlaps with a racial divide. Another dividing line is immigration, which is concentrated in states with some of the largest differences between high- and low-income families.

In this book, we explore the red-state, blue-state paradox, starting with the basic facts on income and voting and then moving backward through the past several decades to identify when the now-familiar patterns began, with the breakup of the Democratic coalition of urban northerners and rural southerners. We also explore the ways in which race and religion intersect with income. Churchgoing predicts vote choice much more for the rich than the poor, but this pattern has only become prominent since 1990—it took a while for the mobilization of the religious right to appear in national voting patterns.

Now more than ever, Democrats and Republicans disagree on issues as varied as abortion and the Iraq War, on factual judgments about the economy, and even on assessments of their personal finances. Americans have not become ideological extremists by any means, but they are more coherently sorting themselves by party label.

Finally, we consider the political implications of the new red–blue divisions. We discuss how Republicans have consistently won elections with economically conservative policies that might arguably seem inherently unpopular with the majority of the voters, and why we don't think the Democrats would gain votes by shifting to the left on economic policy. We also show why congressmembers of both parties can remain in office even while holding ideological and policy positions that are more extreme than most of the voters in their districts. And, in a world where the two parties do have distinct policy positions, we show how the different patterns of income and voting in rich and poor states can influence the directions in which the Democrats and Republicans might go.

This book was ultimately motivated by frustration at media images of rich, yuppie Democrats and lower-income, middle-American Republicans—archetypes that ring true, at some level, but are contradicted in the aggregate. Journalists are, we can assume, more informed than typical voters. When the news media repeatedly make a specific mistake, it is worth looking at. The *perception* of polarization is itself a part of polarization, and views about whom the candidates represent can affect how political decisions are reported. And, as we explore exhaustively, the red–blue culture war does seem to appear in voting patterns, but at the high end of income, not the low, with educated professionals moving toward the Democrats and managers and business owners moving toward the Republicans.

After a study of Mexico and a comparison of voting patterns around the world—in which we find that the rich–poor gap in conservative voting is greater in the United States than in many other countries—we wrap things up by considering the factors that have polarized American politics and keep the parties divided. As historians and political scientists have noted, the political consensus of the 1950s and early 1960s was undone during the civil rights revolution, ultimately switching the political alignments of the North and South and freeing the Democrats and Republicans to become more consistently liberal and conservative parties. In the meantime, political divisions have become cultural for upper-income voters, who can afford to live in places suitable to their lifestyles.

We're looking at a landscape of politicians trying to stay alive, voters searching for a party that feels like home, and journalists and scholars sifting through the polls to figure out what it all means. The red–blue map represents real divisions among Americans, especially at the high end of income, but not the simple contrast of rich Democrats and poor Republicans as sometimes imagined by pundits.

Rich State, Poor State

MILLIONS of Americans stayed up past midnight on November 7, 2000, staring at the map showing the deadlocked election, with its blue states on the coasts and red states in the South and middle of the country. During the weeks in which the election was undecided, the split between red and blue states was on the news every night,

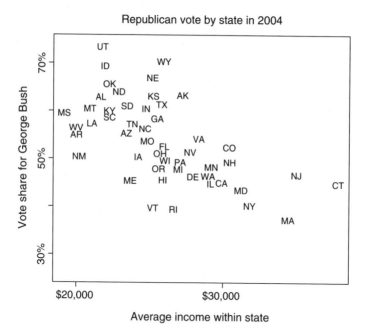

Figure 2.1: For each state, Bush's share of the two-party vote in 2004, plotted with the average income of people in the state, ordered from poorest (Mississippi) to richest (Connecticut). Republicans won the poor states and Democrats won the rich states. (Most of the states are above the 50% line, but Kerry won most of the larger states so that the national vote was close to evenly divided.) The red–blue map of the states won by each candidate in the 2004 election is shown in plate 1.

with evenly divided Florida acting as the microcosm of the country. The Democrats did best in the states with most of the big cities (New York, Los Angeles, Chicago, and so forth), and the Republicans did better elsewhere.

And yes, the Democrats did better in the states with higher average income. Plate 1 in the center of the book shows the 2004 red–blue map, and figure 2.1 shows the Republicans' vote proportions in that election by state, as ordered by per capita income: Bush won the fifteen poorest states (on the left side of the graph), starting with nearly 60% of the vote in Mississippi, the poorest state. At the other end, Kerry (and Gore before him) won in Connecticut and in eight of the ten next richest states. If the Republicans represent the rich and big business and Democrats traditionally represent poorer people, why do wealthy states vote for the Democrats? These patterns, along with blue-collar Reagan Democrats, the decline of organized labor, and the rise of the Sunbelt, motivate recent discussions of yuppie Democrats in the coastal cities and poorer Republicans elsewhere in the country. We'll use poll data to get inside the states and compare rich and poor voters directly.

Rich Voters Continue to Support Republicans

> For more than thirty-five years, American politics has followed a populist pattern . . . the average American, humble, long-suffering, working hard, and paying his taxes; and the liberal elite, the know-it-alls of Manhattan and Malibu, sipping their lattes as they lord it over the peasantry with their fancy college degrees and their friends in the judiciary.
> —*Thomas Frank, 2005*

Who gets the votes of the rich and the poor? Amid all the noise about red and blue states, rich voters continue to support the Republicans. Figure 2.2 shows exit-poll results: In 2004, Bush received 62% support among voters making over $200,000, compared to only 36% from voters making less than $15,000. The geographic bases of the two parties have changed over the years,

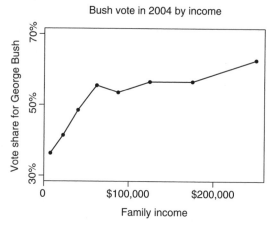

Figure 2.2: From exit-poll data, voting patterns by income. Despite all the talk of latte Democrats and NASCAR Republicans, Bush won among the rich voters and Kerry won in the lower-income brackets.

but at the individual level, income continues to be an important predictor of Republican vote.

The income differential between voters for the two parties has persisted for decades—and since there are more poor and middle-income voters than rich voters, the Democrats would seem to have it made. Democrats outnumbered Republicans in voter registration and self-identification from the 1930s to the 1990s. During this period, however, the patterns of support for the two parties have shifted, even reversing in some places, with California, New Jersey, and New England moving from the Republican to the Democratic column and the southern states decisively going in the other direction. This has led to vigorous discussion about how this could happen and what it means.

THE PUNDITS SPEAK

Like upscale areas everywhere, from Silicon Valley to Chicago's North Shore to suburban Connecticut, Montgomery County [Maryland] supported the Democratic ticket in last year's presidential election, by a margin of 63 percent to 34 percent.
—*David Brooks, 2001*

Exploring the new geography of liberal and conservative America is a prime task for political journalists. Two of the most influential recent explorations of political and cultural divisions come from David Brooks, the *New York Times* columnist and author of *Bobos in Paradise* and *On Paradise Drive*, and Thomas Frank, left-leaning cultural critic and author of *The Conquest of Cool* and other studies of the ideology of corporate America.

David Brooks gave his take on the differences between red and blue America in an influential article, "One Nation, Slightly Divisible," in the *Atlantic Monthly* shortly after the 2000 election. Sometimes described as the liberals' favorite conservative, Brooks embodies the red–blue division within himself. He has liberal leanings on social issues but understands the enduring appeal of traditional values—"today's young people seem happy with the frankness of the left and the wholesomeness of the right"—and his economic views are conservative but he sees the need for social cohesion between rich and poor. His *Atlantic* article compared Montgomery County, Maryland, the liberal, upper-middle-class suburb where he and his friends live, to rural, conservative Franklin County, Pennsylvania, a short drive away but distant in attitudes and values, with "no Starbucks, no Pottery Barn, no Borders or Barnes & Noble," plenty of churches but not so many Thai restaurants, "a lot fewer sun-dried-tomato concoctions on restaurant menus and a lot more meatloaf platters."

In Brooks's home state of Maryland, there is no clear relationship between county income and Republican vote, and it was not difficult for him to go from Montgomery County, the prototypical wealthy slice of blue America, to a poorer, more Republican-supporting county nearby; see figure 2.3.

Brooks lives in a liberal, well-off part of the country. It is characteristic of the Northeast and West Coast that the richer areas tend to be more liberal, but in other parts of the country, notably the South, richer areas tend to be more conservative. A comparable journey in Texas would go from Collin County, a wealthy suburb of Dallas where George W. Bush received 71% of the vote, to rural Zavala County in the southwest, where Bush received only 25%

11

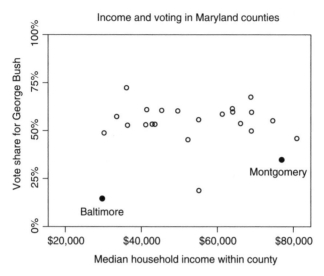

Figure 2.3: Income and voting in the twenty-three counties of Maryland and the city of Baltimore. Highlighted are Baltimore and Montgomery County, a rich suburb of Washington, D.C., which pundit David Brooks compared to a poorer, more conservative rural county nearby in Pennsylvania. Unlike Texas, Maryland's counties do not show a consistent pattern of voting by rich and poor.

of the vote; see figure 2.4. Collin and Zavala are the richest and poorest counties in Texas: many of the poor counties in the state supported the Democrats, while the Republicans won everywhere else. Rich and poor counties look different in blue America than in red America.

When we showed our graph of Texas counties to another political scientist, he asked about the state capital, noted for its liberal attitudes, vibrant alternative rock scene, and the University of Texas: "What about Austin? It must be rich and liberal." We looked it up. Austin is in Travis County and makes up almost all of its population. Travis County has a median household income of $45,000 and gave George W. Bush 53% of the vote in 2000, about midway between Bush's vote shares in Collin and Zavala counties. (Austin has its own red–blue divide, with a highly Democratic university area and urban center, and strongly Republican suburbs.)

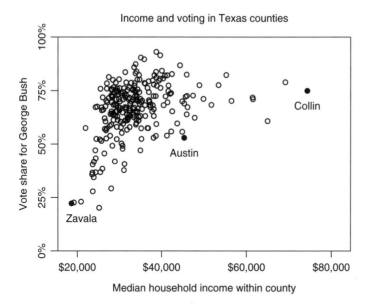

Income and voting in Texas counties

Figure 2.4: Voting and income in the 254 counties in Texas in the 2000 election. Collin, the richest county, is a white suburb of Dallas, and Zavala is a rural Latino county in the southwest of the state. The capital city of Austin fell in between. Overall, the richest counties supported Bush and the poorest supported Gore.

David Brooks reported on the lifestyles of Democratic and Republican areas in the Northeast. From the other side of the political fence, Thomas Frank wrote *What's the Matter with Kansas?*, a study of the struggles and successes of the conservative movement that asked why voters of low and moderate income were not supporting the Democrats. Beyond this, though, exit-poll results reveal that the real strength of Republicans in Kansas is among upper-income voters; see figure 2.5.

Throughout the twentieth century and even before, the Democratic Party in the United States has been considered the party of the lower classes and the average person. Americans consistently have viewed and continue to view the Democratic Party as the party that protects the economic interests of the poor and middle class. In a 2006 poll, 66% of respondents agreed that the

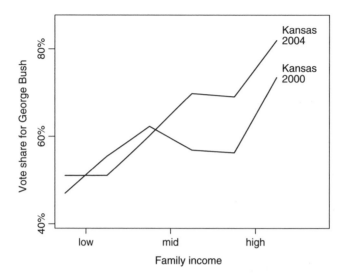

Figure 2.5: George W. Bush's share of the vote in 2000 and 2004 (as estimated from exit polls) among different income groups in Kansas. As in most other states, richer people are more likely to vote Republican.

Democratic Party "looks out for the interest of the average American," while only 37% said this about the Republican Party. In much of the political discourse, however, the Democrats are portrayed as representing the elites rather than the masses. There is often an assumption that populist political stances appeal to lower- and middle-income Americans, but it depends on what populist message is being sent.

Returning to Kansas: conservative attitudes there are not new, as can be seen in figure 2.6, which shows the Republican share of the two-party vote in the state over the past several decades. The raw vote total jumps around from election to election, ranging from 45% to 70% over the past half century. But when you look at the Republicans' performance in Kansas compared to the national vote for each election, the pattern is stable. Throughout the national vote swings over the decades, including Lyndon Johnson's landslide in 1964 and Ronald Reagan's in 1984, Kansas has consistently supported the Republicans by about 10% more

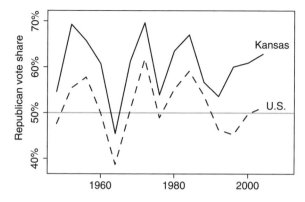

Figure 2.6: Republican share of the presidential vote in Kansas over the past sixty years, with the national vote share as a comparison. Kansas is about 10% more Republican than the national average, and it's been this way for a long time. Thus, it is not clear that recent economic and political developments are needed to explain the Republicans' strength in Kansas.

than the national average (with a little jump in 1996 when Kansas senator Bob Dole ran on the Republican ticket).

DEMYSTIFYING THE PARADOX

> Tax and tax, spend and spend, elect and elect.
> —*attributed to presidential adviser Harry Hopkins, 1930s*

> [It's] the economy, stupid.
> —*James Carville, 1992*

From different perspectives, David Brooks and Thomas Frank are addressing a key puzzle in the study of politics: why are lower-income areas bastions of support for economic policies that benefit the rich? Frank's answer is that poor and middle-class voters are driven by identification and resentment: many Kansans (rich and nonrich) are unhappy with the direction the country has been going and have a screw-the-hippies, nuke-the-whales attitude toward liberals and irresponsible hedonists—people not like

15

them who they feel are taking their tax dollars and spending them on welfare, degenerate art, and so forth. Others don't trust the Democrats on economics or other issues. How you vote is partly a matter of what kind of person you see yourself as and who you want to identify with.

Frank's argument is consistent with other critiques of American politics from the left and older notions of false consciousness—that voters are distracted or disillusioned into voting against their economic interests; for example, choosing a president based on an essentially symbolic issue such as the death penalty.

In contrast, pundits who are economically conservative claim that low- and middle-income Americans are, compared to the upper classes, closer to economic reality and thus more supportive of the Republicans' philosophy of tax cuts and minimal government. If the economy is working the way it is supposed to, poor people won't be poor forever, and if they support free-market policies, they have an easier path up.

The key difference between the analysts on the left and right is whether poor and middle-class voters ultimately prefer economic redistribution (and are frustrated because neither party, including the Democrats, offers a coherent version of this) or a traditionally business-friendly policy such as that offered by the Republicans (in which case the lower-income people who happen to vote for the Democrats are either greedy for government cash—essentially being bribed from tax dollars—or are voting out of ignorance).

We think both sides on this argument are trying too hard to explain something that's simply not true. Lower-income Americans don't, in general, vote Republican—and, where they do, richer voters go Republican even more so. As we've already seen from poll data, poorer voters voted for Kerry, and for Gore before him, and for Clinton before that, and so on. Bush got enough votes from all income levels to put him over the top in 2004, but he did not do particularly well with low-income voters.

Before answering why Democrats win richer states while Republicans get the support of richer voters, we need to settle the more descriptive puzzle of how it is possible for the rich–poor pattern to go in opposite directions between individuals and states. We begin to piece the puzzle together with some statistics from exit polls in Mississippi (the poorest state) and Connecticut (the richest state).

Bush won Mississippi, but he didn't do it with the votes of the poor. Kerry won among low-income Mississippians, but Bush dominated among middle- and upper-income voters, enough to win the state handily. On the other side, Kerry didn't win Connecticut by piling up the votes of richer people in the state; instead, he won equally among all income groups. In between, in middle-income states such as Ohio, Bush did better among the rich and Kerry did better among the poor, with the balance tipping based on the partisanship of the state.

INCOME MATTERS MORE IN POOR STATES THAN IN RICH STATES

> There is, for example, this large class of affluent professionals who are solidly Democratic. DataQuick Information Systems recently put out a list of 100 ZIP code areas where the median home price was above $500,000. By my count, at least 90 of these places—from the Upper West Side to Santa Monica—elect liberal Democrats.
> —David Brooks, 2004

> A lot of Bush's red zones can be traced to wealthy enclaves or sun-belt suburbs where tax cuts are king.
> —Matt Bai, 2001

There is still a rich–poor divide in voting, in popular perceptions of the Democrats and Republicans, and in the parties' economic policies. But voting patterns have been changing, and the red–blue map captures some of this. The economic battles have not gone away, but they intersect with cultural issues in a new way. In low-income states such as Mississippi and Alabama, richer people were far more likely to vote for Bush. But in richer states such as New York and California, income is not a strong predictor of individual votes.

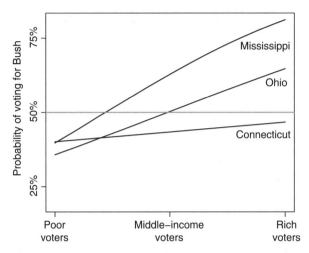

Figure 2.7: The resolution of the red–blue paradox and the introduction of a new puzzle. Within any state, Republican support is flat or increasing with income. At the same time, the Democrats do better in richer states. (The three lines show the estimated pattern of income and voting in 2004 in the poorest state, a middle-income state, and the richest state.) The new puzzle is that the relationship between income and vote choice is much stronger in poor states such as Mississippi than in rich states such as Connecticut.

How can it both be true that rich people vote Republican and rich states vote Democratic? Figure 2.7 graphically shows the resolution of the red–blue, rich–poor voting paradox, using survey data from the 2004 election. (For details on our data sources and statistical models, see the Notes at the end of the book.) In Mississippi, rich people were much more likely than poor people to vote for Bush. The pattern was weaker in middle-income states such as Ohio, and in the richest state, Connecticut, there was barely any relationship between income and vote choice.

When we saw the graph showing different relationships between income and voting in rich, middle-income, and poor states, we were stunned. We weren't looking for this sort of pattern. Our original thinking was that some states are more Republican than others, but that there would be a consistent pattern of income and voting within each state, in which case figure 2.7 would show three parallel lines (still upward-sloping) with Mississippi on the top, then Ohio, then Connecticut. The graph as a whole was intended to show how increasing income could be predictive of Republican vote in each state, even while, on average, richer states supported Democrats. But when we looked more carefully, we found that the simple parallel-line pattern was not what was happening in the data. It turned out that support for Bush among low-income voters in Connecticut and other rich states was much higher than expected. We then generalized our model to allow for income to predict voting differently in each state, revealing the dramatic pattern shown here.

Is there something special about the Mississippi-Ohio-Connecticut comparison? No. Looking at all fifty states confirms the pattern. Plate 3 in the color insert maps the election winner for each state in 2004 among rich, middle-income, and poor voters. Rich voters show the familiar red–blue pattern, with Democrats clinging to a majority in California, New York, and a few other states. Going down to the lower end of the income scale, we see a much different pattern, with Democrats also doing well in the South and center of the country.

In summary, who's been voting for Democrats in recent presidential elections? Most of the poor people in most of the country (except for Texas and some of the plains and mountain states), as shown in the bottom of the three maps in plate 3. Democrats also have the support of the middle class in the West Coast, the Northeast, and some of the upper Midwest. Among the rich, Democrats win only in California, New York, Massachusetts, and Connecticut.

Conversely, Republicans have been winning the votes of most of the upper-income voters in almost all of the states, middle-income voters in most of the states, and lower-income voters in only a few states. In fact, if only rich people's votes were counted, Republicans would win an electoral landslide, and if only poor people's votes were counted, Democrats would win overwhelmingly.

So, yes, affluent city dwellers are voting Democratic—as we discuss in the next chapter, the richer states are, in general, more urban. But most of the affluent Americans—in particular, those living outside of California and the Northeast—support the Republicans. Democrats are doing well in the richest, highly urban states and among the rich voters in these states, but Republicans are getting the support of rich voters elsewhere.

The difference in voting between richer blue America and poorer red America is clear for rich voters, and to a lesser extent among the middle class, but does not appear at all among the poor. It is middle- and upper-income voters who drive the political culture war, and it is in this upper stratum of society where rich states and poor states have their political differences, at least when it comes to national politics.

WHY DOES INCOME MATTER MORE IN POOR STATES THAN IN RICH STATES?

The electoral map of the United States captured the imagination of political junkies during the 2000 and 2004 presidential elections. Influential journalists have evoked powerful images and archetypes of voters, and there has been a parallel discussion among academic political scientists studying the changes in political attitudes between rich and poor. As we discuss in chapter 8, Americans have relabeled themselves over the past few decades so that people with more conservative issue positions are identifying with the Republican Party, and Democrats are more likely to be more liberal—but there has been little overall movement toward extreme positions on the issues themselves.

The configuration of red and blue states isn't fixed in stone. Some of the places that strongly supported the Democrats a generation ago have moved to the Republican column and vice versa. Plate 2 shows the states won by Jimmy Carter and Gerald Ford in 1976. Carter won the South and some midwestern and eastern states, while Ford took much of New England along with the now strongly Democratic West Coast, winning states such as California and New Jersey that George W. Bush didn't even seriously contest in 2000 and 2004. Figure 2.8 shows that in 1976 there was no correlation between voting pattern and state income.

The divisions we associate with American politics—north and south, rich and poor, differences in religion and ethnicity—occur

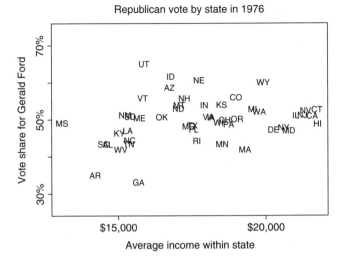

Republican vote by state in 1976

Average income within state

Figure 2.8: As recently as 1976, the pattern of election results looked much different from what we've seen in recent years. Plate 2 shows the states won by Ford and Carter; the graph here shows that, unlike in recent years, there was little correlation between state income and vote. (The graph excludes Alaska, which had a very small population and huge average income at that time.)

throughout the world. Mexico, for example, is divided into a richer, more industrial north and a poorer south, although unlike in the United States, it is the north that is more politically conservative. Canada is divided into west, center, Quebec, and maritime areas, each with its own politics. Britain has a rich south and poorer north; in Italy the geographic pattern goes the other way. In India, too, different parties do better among rich and poor voters and in rich and poor states. Within the United States, too, each state has its own story. High-income liberal Democrats in San Francisco have different concerns than middle-income liberal Democrats in Cleveland and low-income liberal Democrats in south Texas.

Geography matters politically. States are not merely organizational entities—mere folders that divide individuals for convenience. Nor are the differences cosmetic: a y'all here, a Hahvahd Yahd there. States have real, significant cultural and political differences. And despite the homogenizing tendencies of national

21

media, drastically lower transportation costs, and a franchised consumer economy, regional political differences have not gone away. We can understand the difference between voters in rich and poor states as one of context. The Mississippi electorate is more conservative than that of Connecticut, so much so that the richest segment of Connecticutians is only barely more likely to vote Republican than the poorest Mississippians. In poor states, rich people are very different from poor people in their political preferences. But in rich states, they are not.

Why is this happening?

Part of the story is race. In poor southern states such as Mississippi, the rich–poor divide coincides with a racial divide, which, given the differences between the two parties on racial issues, will lead to a bigger difference between the voting patterns of rich and poor. Beyond this, race is tied into economic issues and policies: given the high correlation of income and race, redistribution often looks like a racial policy.

Religion also plays a role. In poor states, richer people are more likely than the poor to attend religious services, but in rich states, it is poor people who are churchgoers, often in evangelical denominations. By virtue of their religiosity, richer voters in Mississippi and other poor states are even more likely to vote Republican. In contrast, richer voters in Connecticut and other poor states have a conflict between their economic status and their relative lack of religiosity.

Differences between rich and poor states can also be considered historically. The rich states in the Northeast, Midwest, and West Coast generally have higher rates of unionization, with large cities or near large cities, often with a tradition of immigration, which has perhaps led them to be more politically liberal on social issues. In recent years, the two parties have more sharply locked social issues into their orbits—in most of the country, liberal Republicans and conservative Democrats are endangered, if not extinct, species—and this has coincided with more cosmopolitan states moving toward the Democrats and rural states moving in the opposite direction.

Finally, the political differences between Democratic and Republican voters are greatest among the middle-class and rich, and these are the people who can more easily afford to live where they would like. Increasingly, culture and religion are more important predictors of vote choice among the rich than the poor, and in that sense the country is polarized in two ways: *economically* between the rich and the poor, and *culturally* between upper-income Americans in red and blue areas.

How the Talking Heads Can Be So Confused

> One of the Republican Party's major successes over the last few decades has been to persuade many of the working poor to vote for tax breaks for billionaires. . . . One problem is the yuppification of the Democratic Party.
> —*Nicholas Kristof,* New York Times *columnist, 2004*

> Who are the trustfunders? People with enough money not to have to work for a living, or not to have to work very hard. . . . These people tend to be very liberal politically. Aware that they have done nothing to earn their money, they feel a certain sense of guilt. . . . They are citizens of the world with contempt for those who feel chills up their spines when they hear "The Star Spangled Banner."
> —*Michael Barone, author of the* Almanac of American Politics, *2005*

IT MAY very well be that the leadership and activists of the Democratic Party are mostly well-off financially. But, as we have discussed relentlessly, Democratic *voters* have, on average, lower incomes. Given these statistics, it seems highly unlikely that trustfunders—in Barone's words, "people with enough money not to have to work for a living, or not to have to work very hard"—are mostly liberal. It's possible, but the data strongly support the statements that (1) richer people tend to vote Republican, but (2) voters in richer states (and, to some extent, counties) tend to support Democrats. There definitely are differences between richer and poorer states—but the evidence is that, within any state, richer voters tend to go for the Republicans.

Michael Barone has been editing the respected *Almanac of American Politics* for decades and knows more about American political geography than just about anyone. When an expert makes this sort of mistake, it's worth exploring further. The conceptual confusion between patterns among states and among individuals (in quantitative social science, the practice of inferring individual behavior from aggregate data is sometimes called the "ecological fallacy") has led commentators to confusion even at the state and county levels. For example, Barone joked:

> Where Democrats had a good year in 2004 they owed much to trust-funders. In Colorado, they captured a Senate and a House seat and both houses of the legislature. Their political base in that state is increasingly not the oppressed proletariat of Denver, but the trustfunder-heavy counties that contain Aspen (68 percent for Kerry), Telluride (72 percent) and Boulder (66 percent).

But Kerry got 70% of the vote in Denver, so the story of Democratic trustfunders and Republican commoners doesn't quite fit. It's worth understanding what makes this story so compelling.

Barone might be right when he cites trustfunders as a source of *money* for the Democrats (as they also are for the Republicans). And, as a political matter, it might very well be a bad thing if both political parties are being funded by people from the top of the income distribution. There's a wide spectrum of political participation, ranging from voting, to campaign contributions, to activism, and the demographics of these contributors and activists is potentially important. But you're not going to find it by looking at state-level or county-level vote returns.

WHY DO WE CARE WHAT THE JOURNALISTS SAY?

As a result of the electoral college system and also, perhaps, because of the appeal of colorful maps, state-level election results are widely presented and studied. After seeing the pattern of richer coastal states supporting the Democrats and poorer states in the South and middle of the country supporting the Republicans—a pattern that has intensified in recent years—it is natural to personify the states and assume that the Democrats also have the support

25

of richer voters. Psychologists have studied the human tendency to think of categories in terms of their typical members; for example, a robin and a penguin are both birds, but robins are perceived of as typical members of the bird category and penguins are not. The image of the typical Democrat seems to have moved from a unionized laborer to a Starbucks-sipping yuppie, while the image of the typical Republican is perhaps in an unstable balance between a religious Wal-Mart shopper and a smug banker.

Political scientists have also noted that the division into two bright colors is itself unnatural, considering that most voters have moderate views on a range of issues. Here we are making a slightly different point, which is that a typical Republican (or Democratic) state does not look like an aggregation of typical Republican (or Democratic) voters.

We are not claiming that journalists are unaware of poll data and election results but rather that they are often working in a conceptual framework that allows them to make mistakes. Sometimes it is the errors that we don't even notice that reveal our preconceptions.

Different Sorts of Income Divisions

> Shop at Wal-Mart? You're likely a social conservative and pro-gun. A Target habitue? You're both style- and price-conscious, a swing voter. Bloomingdale's? Upscale, urban, liberal. Those are just some of the ways political strategists are slicing and dicing the electorate, as "microtargeting" puts a new twist on the age-old chore of getting out the vote.
> —*Thomas Fitzgerald,* Houston Chronicle, *2006*

Setting aside qualms about anecdotal evidence, we recognize that political journalists are reacting to real changes in how Americans vote, and some of these changes are masked by a narrow focus on income.

Rich and poor continue their historic pattern of voting for Republicans and Democrats—but, as we see in figure 3.1, these are not the same sorts of rich and poor as before. Professionals

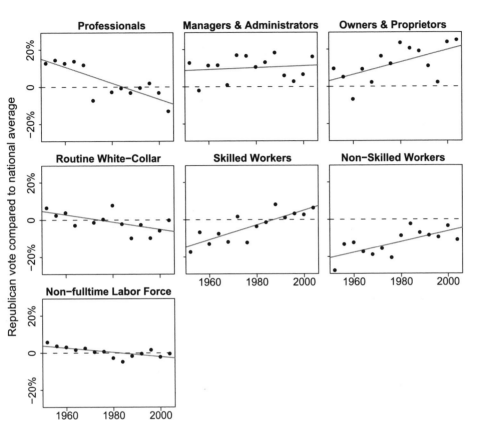

Figure 3.1: Trends in support for Republican presidential candidates over time, by occupation. For each category, the plot shows the percentage who voted Republican compared to the national vote in each year. Professionals such as doctors and lawyers and routine white-collar workers used to lean Republican but have moved toward the Democrats; business owners and skilled and unskilled workers have moved in the opposite direction.

(doctors, lawyers, and so forth) and routine white-collar workers (clerks, etc.) used to support the Republicans more than the national average, but over the past half century they have gradually passed through the center and now strongly support the Democrats. Business owners have moved in the opposite direction, from being close to the national average to being staunch

27

Republicans, and skilled and unskilled workers have moved from strong Democratic support to near the middle.

These shifts are consistent with oft-noted cultural differences between red and blue America. Doctors, nurses, lawyers, teachers, and office workers seem today like prototypical liberal Democrats, while businessmen and hardhats seem like good representatives of the Republican Party. The dividing points were different fifty years ago. The Republicans still have the support of most of the high-income voters, but these are conservatives of a different sort. As E. J. Dionne notes, the Democrats' strength among well-educated voters is strongest among those with household incomes under $75,000—"the incomes of teachers, social workers, nurses, and skilled technicians, not of Hollywood stars, bestselling authors, or television producers, let alone corporate executives."

To get a rough sense of what is being talked about in political campaigns, we did a count of mentions of various political phrases in the news and display the result in figure 3.2. The terms "red

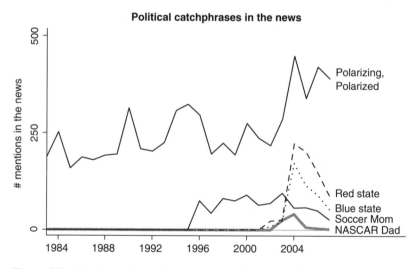

Figure 3.2: Number of mentions per year of several political catchphrases in *Time, Newsweek,* and the *Washington Post.* All these expressions get used more during election years, with "red state" and "blue state" becoming especially popular during and after the 2004 campaign.

state" and "blue state," and particular terms such as "soccer mom" and "NASCAR dad," are relatively recent. "Polarization" has been cited frequently in the news for decades but has come up more often since the 2004 campaign.

One way that people connect geography to politics is through patterns of consumption. For example, figure 3.3 maps the frequency of Starbucks and Wal-Mart stores in each state. There are 100 Starbucks outlets per million people in Washington State, the home of the franchise, and only a tenth as many per person in latte-starved West Virginia, Mississippi, and Vermont. Wal-Mart has a different pattern, with over twenty-five per million in its home state of Arkansas and neighboring Oklahoma, down to one-seventh as many in New York, New Jersey, and California. But we don't really know how different the Wal-Mart and Starbucks voters are, or how these differences vary geographically.

Could political science microtarget populations and trends as effectively as political campaigns do? Bill Wetzel, who spent three years traveling the country with a sign that read "Talk to Me," asks, "How can you track or study the culture war in a way that is slightly more rigorous than newspaper editorials and slightly less aggregated than state-by-state analysis? Tracking consumer habits could be a great place to try to get an actual pulse of the culture war, with organic turnip fritters on one end and, well, black powder and bullets on the other. Perhaps there is a metropolitan region in the U.S. that would have at least one of [each of] the following stores: Cabela's, Wal-Mart, Target, and Whole Foods. There could be exit polls done at each store regarding political preferences."

MOM AND APPLE PIE

> Pat doesn't have a mink coat. But she does have a respectable Republican cloth coat.
> —*vice presidential candidate Richard Nixon, 1952*

Starbucks per capita

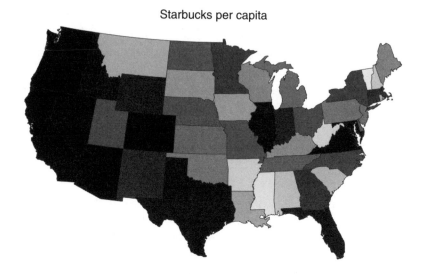

Wal–Marts per capita

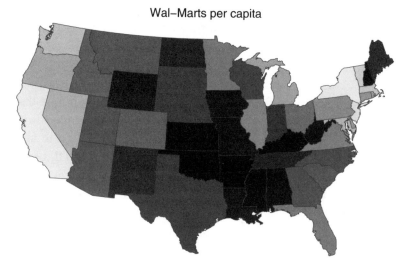

Figure 3.3: States ranked by number of Starbucks and Wal-Marts per person. Dark colors show states with more stores per capita. Correlations of store densities with political preferences are difficult to separate from the geographic pattern of Starbucks spreading out from Seattle and Wal-Mart expanding from Arkansas.

I come from Huntington, a small farming community in
Indiana. I had an upbringing like many in my generation—
a life built around family, public school, Little League,
basketball, and church on Sunday. My brother and I shared a
room in our two-bedroom house.
—*Vice President Dan Quayle, 1992*

Clinton displays almost every trope of blackness: single-parent
household, born poor, working-class, saxophone-playing,
McDonald's-and-junk-food-loving boy from Arkansas.
—*Toni Morrison, 1998*

Income is not the single driving factor in politics in the United
States. However, income is important in political perceptions, is
relevant to a wide range of policies such as minimum-wage regulation, tax rates, and Social Security, and is also correlated with
many measures of political participation. Geography, too, is not
all-important: red–blue maps of elections are appealing, but most
of the states are not far from evenly divided. Once again, though,
geography is highly relevant to decisions on government spending,
among other policies.

As the previous quotations illustrate, both income and geography are relevant to politicians' claims of authenticity, just as the
income and geography of a candidate's supporters are used to signify political legitimacy. Being middle class or lower middle class is
part of the so-called mom and apple pie story in American politics.
Abraham Lincoln grew up in a log cabin, Harry Truman was a plain-
speaking man from Missouri, and George H. W. Bush enjoyed pork
rinds. Even nonpoliticians play this game; for example, television
journalist Tim Russert identifies himself as a blue-collar guy from
Buffalo, and Michael Moore is the regular guy in a baseball cap
from industrial Flint, Michigan.

We're so used to these populist claims that they barely register
anymore—if anything, they often appear more as defensive tactics,
assuring the rest of us that the rich and successful Quayles and
Russerts are just like us. But, looked at another way, there is something odd about all this poor-mouthing. It didn't have to be this

31

way. Imagine a world in which politicians bragged more about their elite backgrounds rather than their regular-guy authenticity. For example, what if Dan Quayle had said, "As an heir to a multimillion-dollar newspaper empire, I understand from the inside out how this country works." In his celebrated eagerness to link himself with John Kennedy, why not emphasize the elite background they had in common? Similarly, instead of eating meals at McDonald's, why didn't Bill Clinton advertise the sophisticated tastes he may have developed while at Yale and as a Rhodes Scholar?

There are many reasons why modern political players feel the need to establish credentials as ordinary Americans in a way that their upper-class predecessors such as the two Roosevelts, Woodrow Wilson, and the Kennedys have not. How is it that John Kerry, that patrician windsurfer from Massachusetts, outpolled regular-guy Texan George Bush among lower-income voters? Presumably it was their parties and the policies they stood for, not their personalities, that led Bush and Kerry to get similar patterns of rich and poor votes as previous Republican and Democratic candidates. To put it another way, maybe there were some people who voted against Kerry because he was a windsurfer—or against Bush because he was a cheerleader in college, rather than a football star in the mold of Gerald Ford or former vice-presidential candidate Jack Kemp—but we know of no evidence that lower-income people are more likely to vote on this basis.

MISPERCEIVING OTHERS

> The governor of Massachusetts, he lost his top naval adviser last week. His rubber ducky drowned in the bathtub.
> —*vice-presidential candidate Dan Quayle, 1988*

In 1995, the *Washington Post* reported on a survey in which Americans were asked to estimate the percentage of different racial and ethnic groups in the U.S. population. As reported in the article: "Most whites, blacks, Hispanics and Asian Americans said the black population, which is about 12 percent, was twice that size." Survey respondents similarly overestimated the percentage of Hispanics and Asians in the country.

Americans also show systematic misperceptions about the economic status of different groups. Once again, from the *Post* article: "A majority of white Americans have fundamental misconceptions about the economic circumstances of black Americans, according to a new national survey, with most saying that the average black is faring as well or better than the average white in such specific areas as jobs, education and health care. That's not true. Government statistics show that whites, on average, earn 60 percent more than blacks, are far more likely to have medical insurance and more than twice as likely to graduate from college."

Survey questions on economic views seem more complicated in that they would naturally be tied in with political ideology. It may be that a lot of whites don't want to answer Yes to the question, "Are blacks worse off than whites?" because they associate the question with specific policies, such as affirmative action, that they don't like. Some of the quotes in the *Post* article seem relevant to this point. It can be difficult to get accurate responses, even on a factual question, if people associate it with a political position.

Americans are not alone in misperceiving minorities. Similar surveys in European countries find nearly universal overestimation of the percentage of immigrants; see figure 3.4. Political scientist John Sides analyzed these data and writes that "overestimation is associated with more opposition to immigration. However, misperception's effect is conditional: only if you think that your country receives about the same, more, or far more immigrants than other countries is the absolute level of misperception significant. In other words, it's both this relative perception and the absolute (mis)perception that matter."

Sides continues: "At the individual level, misperceptions are driven by several factors. Not surprisingly, education and political engagement tend to render estimates more accurate. This suggests that misperceptions derive in part from an availability bias: the more prominent are immigrants in one's immediate environment or social networks, the greater the overestimate. Misperceptions

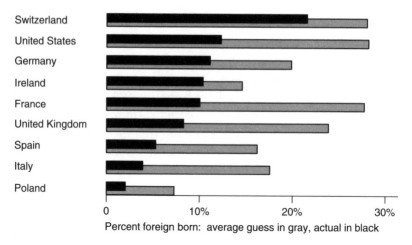

Percent foreign born: average guess in gray, actual in black

Figure 3.4: John Sides and Jack Citrin's graph of actual and estimated percent of immigrants in the United States and several European countries. The estimates are average survey responses in each country. People consistently overestimate the percent who are foreign born.

are positively related to economic dissatisfaction as well, which implies that estimates are driven not only by availability but also by anxiety."

Misperceptions can drive policy preferences. To use a well-known example, Americans overwhelmingly support reducing the share of the federal budget that goes to foreign aid, but they also vastly overestimate the current share of the budget that goes to this purpose (average estimate of 15%, compared to an actual value of 0.3%).

IT'S NOT SO EASY TO READ A MAP

> The margin (Poizner beat the Democrat, 51% to 39%, with more than 10% favoring other candidates) suggests that Bustamante's TV ads highlighting the rotund lieutenant governor's weight loss failed to build voter confidence in his qualifications to regulate insurers.
> —*Michael Finnegan*, Los Angeles Times, *2006*

One of the themes of political science over the past several decades is that voters are often more predictable than they themselves realize. During the campaign season, you may believe yourself to be carefully evaluating what the candidates offer, but when the election arrives, you—like most people—will probably vote in the way that could be predicted from your political ideology and partisan affiliation. Political journalists are well aware of the stability of voting patterns, which is a good reason for them to focus on maps. By and large, the battleground states of one election also will be crucial states in the next.

Nonetheless, there are statistical, political, and psychological reasons that people get confused about red states and blue states. States are not uniformly red or blue—in fact, some state elections are almost evenly divided. In plate 4, we display a map with continuous color variation with solidly Democratic and Republican states in red and blue and closer states in different shades of purple. Plate 5 shows a similar map at the county level. In plate 6 we show more elaborate red–blue maps—one by state, one by county— made by computer scientists Michael Gastner, Cosma Shalizi, and Mark Newman that distort so that areas are proportional to population rather than land area. The usual maps show vast swathes of red in the middle of the country; in contrast, the population-based maps show that each candidate won in areas containing approximately half the people in the country. Yet another way to display the votes is with a map that contains a red dot for each thousand Bush voters and a blue dot for each thousand Kerry voters. Such a graph conveys the information from state or county maps but without distracting distortions.

The polarization into red and blue America has different implications when looked at from different political perspectives. From the left, geographic divisions are often seen as a distraction from a more appropriate battle of rich versus poor: if only the masses could rise above their petty local concerns, they could unite and elect a more progressive government.

Looking at it another way, however, red and blue represent legitimately different philosophies of politics, going beyond immediate issues of rich and poor to larger concerns about the role of government and traditional social structures in guiding American life. If the standoff between conservatives and liberals is simply a struggle between rich and poor, this suggests a traditional battle of economic interests; if income does not so clearly line up with political preference, then other issues would seem to be relevant. Looking forward to the 2008 election and beyond, we expect to see a continuation of the current pattern where economic divisions are more important in the poor states and cultural issues matter more in richer areas.

IMPUTING HOW THE OTHER HALF LIVES: AVAILABILITY BIAS

> I can't believe Nixon won. I don't know anybody who voted for him.
> —*attributed (in error) to Pauline Kael, movie critic for the* New Yorker, *1972*

> It evidently irritates many liberals to point out that their party gets heavy support from superaffluent "people of fashion" and does not run very well among "the common people."
> —*Michael Barone, 2005*

Cognitive scientists use the term "availability bias" to refer to the human tendency to generalize based on nearby information. In this case, we could speak of first-order and second-order availability biases. A national survey of journalists found that about twice as many are Democrats as Republicans. Presumably their friends and acquaintances are also more likely to support Democrats, and a first-order availability bias would lead a journalist to overestimate Democrats' support in the population—as in the notorious quote misattributed to movie critic Pauline Kael.

Political journalists are well aware of the latest polls and election forecasts and are unlikely to make such an elementary mistake. However, they can easily make the second-order error of assuming that the correlations they see of income and voting are representative of the population. The aforementioned survey found that 90%

of journalists are college graduates and their incomes are mostly above the national average—so it is natural for them to think that they and their friends represent Democrats as a whole. It is easy for elite journalists to falsely project an incorrect correlation of income and Democratic voting on the general population. Again, we are using Michael Barone as an example precisely because he is so well informed but is still vulnerable to the cognitive traps that affect us all.

Another form of availability bias is that the centers of national journalistic activity include the relatively rich states of New York, California, Maryland, and Virginia. Once again, journalists—and, for that matter, academics—avoid the first-order availability bias: they are not surprised that the country as a whole votes differently from the residents of big cities. But they sometimes make the second-order error of too quickly generalizing from the correlations in their states. Richer counties tend to support the Democrats within the media center states of Maryland, Virginia, New York, and California but not, in general, elsewhere. And richer voters support the Republicans just about everywhere, but this pattern is much weaker—and thus easier to miss—within these richer states.

Much has been written in the national press about the perils of ignoring red America, but these second-order availability biases have done just that, in a more subtle way. Journalists' focus on red–blue maps has been somewhat misguided, but the differences between states are real, and indeed have changed in recent decades.

Despite all of this, we would not claim that all of the misrepresentation and mistakes in journalists' accounts come from statistical misunderstanding. It is often just a different way of looking at the world. Consider David Brooks and Thomas Frank, both of whom have been attacked for oversimplifying complex voting patterns into simple, appealing stories. On one level, we differ with both Brooks and Frank on demographic analysis because both present a picture—of deeply conservative ordinary, lower- and middle-income Americans who vote Republican—that contradicts patterns of who's voting for whom in presidential

37

elections. On another level, however, both Brooks and Frank supply a lot of information on groups that are important, even if they do not represent a majority of voters in their income categories. Brooks, Frank, and other analysts give insight into the recent trend toward upscale Democratic areas and lower-income Republican strongholds.

HAPPY CONSERVATIVES AND GLOOMY LIBERALS

Some 45% of all Republicans report being very happy, compared with just 30% of Democrats and 29% of independents. This finding has also been around a long time; Republicans have been happier than Democrats every year since the General Social Survey began taking its measurements in 1972.
—*Pew Research Center, 2006*

Fifty-eight percent of Republicans report having excellent mental health, compared to 43% of independents and 38% of Democrats. This relationship between party identification and reports of excellent mental health persists even within categories of income, age, gender, church attendance, and education.
—*Gallup Poll, 2007*

Just as the labour movement had never been quite sure whether the capitalist system was on its last legs and needed only a final push to be toppled, or was healthy enough to be milked over and again, so the cultural-intellectual left had never quite decided whether it liked increasing prosperity or not.
—*Geoffrey Wheatcroft, 2005*

Parallel to the culture war is a debate on the economy, with conservatives arguing that Americans are happy versus liberals who say that, no, even if people have more televisions and refrigerators than they used to have, they're really not so happy as all that. In political terms, this seems to us a continuation and elaboration of the debates between Democrats and Republicans in the Carter-Mondale-Reagan era. Reagan could certainly be serious about the problems facing the country, but he was basically pro-happiness and anti-gloom-and-doom.

It hasn't always been this way. From the 1920s through the 1960s, it was the Democrats who were the happy party, favoring prohibition repeal, easy credit, and federal spending, whereas the Republicans were the grouches. Look at the Barry Goldwater campaign, for example, for some serious grouching. Why have the terms of debate changed? One explanation is the implicit rivalry with the European social model of higher taxes and services compared to the United States. The high-tax, low-tax dispute gets transferred to the question, Are people happier in the United States than in Europe? But we've only been able to have this battle since 1970 or so; before that, Europeans were still much poorer than the average American. There is a logic to the happiness debate, but it's still not clear to us how general the arguments are, beyond a disagreement about tax rates.

For some historical perspective on views of happiness and material progress, here's what the Catholic conservative G. K. Chesterton had to say in 1910 in response to George Bernard Shaw's socialist program of human improvement through technological and moral progress:

> I know it is all very strange. From the height of eight hundred years ago, or of eight hundred years hence, our age must look incredibly odd. We call the twelfth century ascetic. We call our own time hedonist and full of praise and pleasure. But in the ascetic age the love of life was evident and enormous, so that it had to be restrained. In a hedonist age pleasure has always sunk low, so that it had to be encouraged. How high the sea of human happiness rose in the Middle Ages, we now only know by the colossal walls that they built to keep it in bounds. How low human happiness sank in the twentieth century our children will only know by these extraordinary modern books, which tell people that it is a duty to be cheerful and that life is not so bad after all. Humanity

never produces optimists till it has ceased to produce happy men. It is strange to be obliged to impose a holiday like a fast, and to drive men to a banquet with spears.

Shaw, on the left, associated progress with material advances, while Chesterton, on the right, said that people were happier in the Middle Ages. Nowadays, the debate seems to usually go in the other direction, with liberals being less positive about material progress and conservatives tending to say that things are great now and are getting better.

Current debates about income and happiness link, directly or indirectly, to ideological and policy disagreements about the role of government in a mixed economy: Is the United States correctly taking the lead in a globalizing world with lower taxes and fewer business regulations, or should we be copying some features of the European model, with higher taxes and unemployment but shorter working hours and universal health care?

In the following chapters, we explore how voting in America has become more ideological, with Democrats and Republicans developing distinct positions on a range of economic and social issues, and with changing geographic bases of support for the two parties.

PART II

WHAT'S GOING ON

Income and Voting over Time

HAVING ruled out the most obvious explanation—that rich and poor states represent the preferences of rich and poor voters—it makes sense to consider systematic differences among states, which are particularly interesting given Americans' mobile lifestyle, the possibilities of self-stratification in exposure to news media and choosing where to live, and the increasing polarization of states and counties.

Political stories are often written in the continuous present tense (for example, "Republicans can't win in California") without a full historical perspective. In the 1970s and 1980s, much was written about why the Republicans were winning presidential elections while the Democrats retained control of Congress, but all this had to be rewritten in the 1990s when Bill Clinton was elected, followed by a Republican Congress. Regions and states are important for understanding American politics, but the story is not static.

Graphs of the presidential vote by state show countervailing trends in different regions of the country. New England used to be solidly Republican in presidential voting and the South used to favor the Democrats, but this has reversed. From a position of favoring neither party, the mid-Atlantic states have now become solidly Democratic and the mountain west solidly Republican. Figure 4.1 shows each state plotted relative to the U.S. average because we are interested in the relative partisanship of each state and region.

RICH STATE, POOR STATE

Richer states now support the Democrats. It makes sense that the "red–blue" issue has been more widely discussed in recent

Republican vote for president by state, relative to the national vote in each year

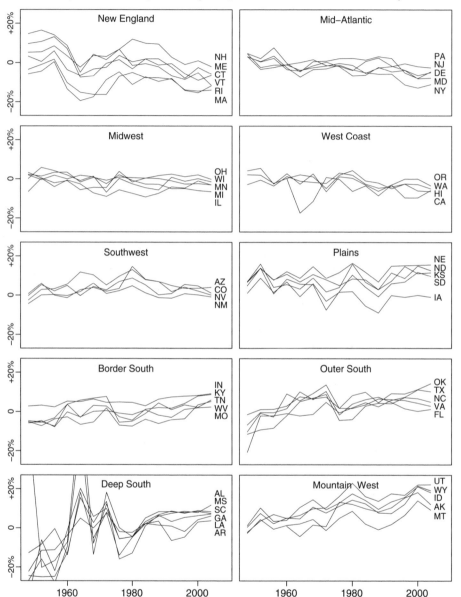

Figure 4.1: Republican vote share for president compared to the national average, plotted for each state over the past sixty years. States are grouped by regions, revealing which areas have moved toward the Democrats and which have trended Republican.

years because this pattern has become increasingly clear since the Bush–Gore contest. In the 2000 and 2004 presidential elections, rich states supported the Democrats 10% more, on average, than did poor states, a pattern that has developed gradually since 1980. We compared 1976 and 2000 in chapter 2. We now broaden our perspective to look at the Republican vote share in rich and poor states in every presidential election since 1940. The top graph in figure 4.2 shows the current red-state, blue-state pattern in historical context.

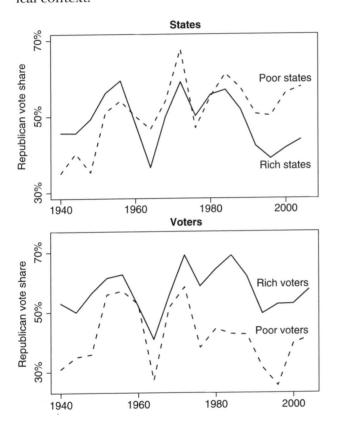

Figure 4.2: Top: Republican vote for president since 1940 for states in the upper third and lower third of per capita income. Since the 1980s, rich and poor states have diverged politically. Bottom: Republican presidential vote for individuals in the upper and lower thirds of family income. The difference between rich and poor has been large for decades.

45

From this historical perspective, what is new about the current political difference between rich and poor states is not just its magnitude but also its persistence and gradual increase over a twenty-year period, giving it the feel of a political realignment rather than a blip.

Dividing the country into north and south makes no difference, as shown in the top row of graphs in figure 4.3. Since 1980, both regions have exhibited the same trend: increasingly, the richer the state, the more that state is likely to support Democratic presidential candidates. These trends arise from people within these states changing their attitudes (for example, Mississippians being unhappy with the Democratic Party's positions on issues ranging from welfare to gay rights, or New Yorkers disliking the evangelical Christian tone of Republican leaders), generational change, and people moving to places that feel more compatible with their political values.

RICH VOTER, POOR VOTER

In 2004, the richest third of the population supported George W. Bush by over ten percentage points more than the poorest third. The pattern of richer voters supporting the Republicans is not new, as shown in the bottom graph in figure 4.2.

The gap between how the rich and poor vote was large in the 1940s, declined to near zero in the 1950s (a period in which there was little difference between the two parties on economic issues), increased during the 1960s and 1970s, and has been wide ever since, with the Republicans typically doing about 20% better among high-income voters than low-income voters. The rich–poor gap in recent decades has been large in elections such as in 1976 (when Gerald Ford and Jimmy Carter offered relatively moderate economic platforms) as well as in years such as 1984 (when there was a clear distinction between Walter Mondale and Ronald Reagan).

It is difficult to get survey data from before the 1940s, but the available information suggests that the gap between the votes of

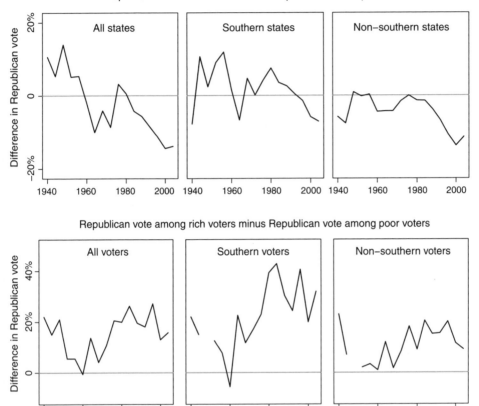

Figure 4.3: Top: Rich *state*, poor *state* difference in Republican presidential votes over time. Separate plots show the entire United States, the South, and the rest of the country. When the lines are above zero, richer states vote more Republican. In recent years, the lines have gone below zero: rich states are supporting the Democrats, in the South and in the country as a whole.

Bottom: Rich *voter*, poor *voter* difference in Republican presidential votes over time. (For 1948 we had no survey data with state and income.) When the lines are above zero (which has generally been the case), richer individuals vote Republican.

rich and poor increased during the Depression and New Deal periods. In the words of political scientist V. O. Key: "The rankings from 'wealthy' to 'poor' assigned by the interviewers are doubtless not measures of precision; nevertheless, of the 'wealthy' 1936

Democratic voters, in the neighborhood of four of ten deserted to the Republicans in 1940. At the other extreme, less than one in seven persons on relief took this step."

A related factor is income inequality. Since the 1970s the income and wealth differences between rich and poor have been steadily increasing. In addition, Democrats and Republicans in Congress are further apart than they used to be on economic issues (a point to which we return in chapter 8).

So, if income-based voting differences were strictly based on personal finances, we might expect the gap in voting patterns between rich and poor to have increased during the past three decades. Actually, this gap has been steady during this period, as we see in the bottom graphs of figure 4.3. Rich voters favor the Republicans and poor voters support the Democrats, but no more than in the 1980s and 1990s (or, for that matter, the 1940s). Why hasn't the rich–poor voting gap been increasing? One reason is that, according to political surveys, economic issues are less important to voters than they used to be. In that sense, the continued importance of income-associated voting, given the diversity of Americans' political views and interests, is all the more striking.

DIFFERENCES IN INCOME AND VOTING WITHIN AND BETWEEN STATES

To visualize the changing voting patterns of rich and poor within states, we return to the visualization tool we call the *superplot* that we introduced in figure 2.7. The graph has three lines, showing the chance that a voter in each of five income categories supports the Republican candidate within each of three states—Connecticut (the richest state), Ohio (an intermediate state), and Mississippi (the poorest state).

Recall figure 2.7 and the statistical resolution of the red–blue paradox: the pattern of income and voting is different within Republican-leaning and Democratic-leaning states. Within each state, income is positively correlated with Republican voting, but average income varies by state in the opposite way. Republican-leaning states have more lower-income people, and as a result, there is a negative overall correlation between average income and support for Bush, even with the positive slope for each state. The poor people in most Republican-leaning states tend to be Democrats; the rich people in most Democratic-leaning states tend to be Republicans. Income matters, but context—geography—also matters. Individual income is a positive predictor and state average income is a negative predictor of Republican voting.

We estimate the pattern of income and voting within each state (we display three states in figure 4.4 for illustrative purposes). In each state, the pattern can be described by the degree of Republican support among high- and low-income voters. The level of the line (in statistical jargon, the intercept) can be mapped to the probability that a middle-income voter in the state votes Republican. In our example, Connecticut has a lower level than Mississippi. The slope of the line for each state maps to the difference in Republican vote share, comparing high- and low-income voters. Where the slope is high, rich people are much more likely than poor people to support the Republicans; where the slope is low, there is not much connection between income and vote choice. Again, from our example, Connecticut has a lower slope than Mississippi.

What about previous elections? Do we see the same pattern? Figure 4.4 shows results from exit polls back to 1984. These charts summarize our analyses with a display of the estimated Republican vote share by income in rich, middle-income, and poor states in each election from 1984 to 2004. Since the 1990s, income has predicted vote preference more strongly in poor states than in rich states. This difference in voting patterns has arisen during the same period that the red and blue states have diverged.

So far, so good for these three states. But what about the remaining forty-seven? We can unpack things further and see what's going on in each state. Figures 4.5 and 4.6 display the estimated levels and slopes for all fifty states, revealing a consistent pattern, with high coefficients (steep slopes) in poor states and low coefficients (moderate slopes) in rich states. Income matters more in red America

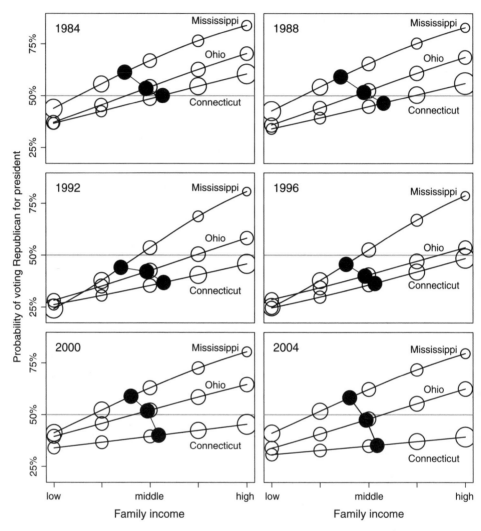

Figure 4.4: Probability of Republican vote as a function of income in poor, middle-income, and rich states for the past six presidential elections. Since the 1990s the lines have had much steeper slopes in poor states than in rich states. Income is more strongly associated with Republican voting in Mississippi than in Connecticut.

The open circles on the plot show the relative size of each income group in each state (thus, Mississippi has more poor people than average, and Connecticut has more rich people). The solid circles show the average Republican vote and average income in each state.

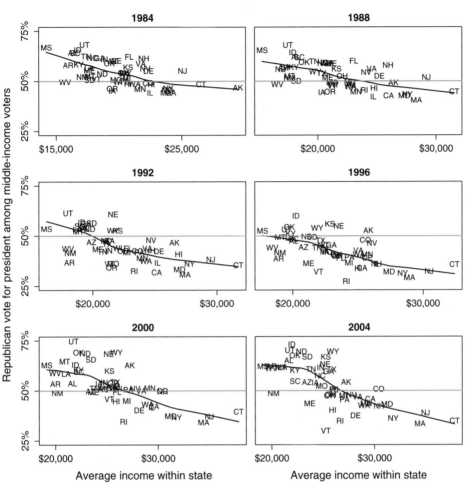

Figure 4.5: From the model predicting presidential vote preference given individual income by state: estimated level (the Republican strength in the state among middle-income voters) plotted versus state per capita income. For each year, states that are above the line are more Republican (among their middle-income voters) and states that are below the line support Democrats.

than in blue America. Or, to put it another way, being in a red or blue state matters more for rich than for poor voters.

We did not have access to exit-poll data from before 1984, so we used the National Election Study since 1952, combining data over twenty-year periods to get a large enough sample during each period to estimate the difference between the voting patterns of

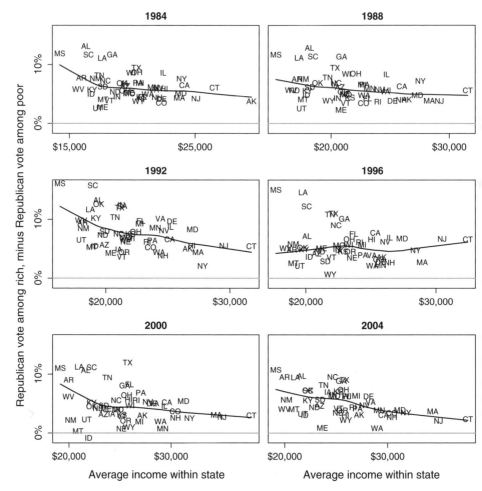

Figure 4.6: From the model predicting presidential vote preference from individual income by state: estimated slope (the importance of income in predicting Republican vote within the state) plotted versus state per capita income. For each year, the states that are higher in the graph are those where the relationship between individual income and Republican voting is strongest.

rich and poor Americans separately in high-, middle-, and low-income states. As we have already seen on the bottom graph of figure 4.2, in the 1950s–1960s, high-income voters preferred the Republicans by only a small amount. Figure 4.7 breaks the data

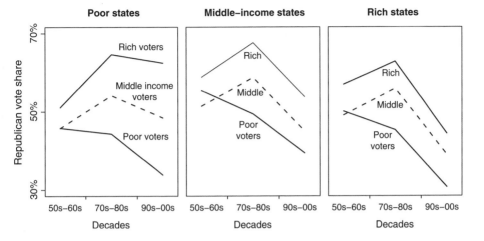

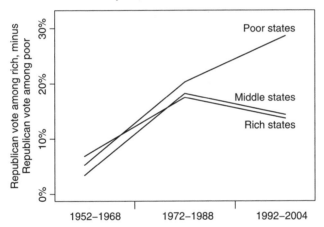

Figure 4.7: Top: Average Republican share of the presidential vote, for each two-decade period, among different income groups. Separate graphs show trends among high-, middle-, and low-income voters. The left graph shows that, in poor states, there is an increasing difference between how rich and poor people vote.

Bottom: Differences between the Republican share of the presidential vote, comparing rich and poor voters in states in the lower, middle, and upper thirds, of per capita income in each period. Rich voters are much more Republican than poor voters, especially in poor states, a pattern that emerged after 1990.

down by income and state, revealing that when the rich–poor voting gap increased during the 1970s and 1980s, there were no systematic differences between high- and low-income states. Since 1992, though, rich and poor have diverged in low-income states.

Our analysis has redefined the puzzle. In asking why the patterns within states differ from those among states, we are specifically interested in why rich and poor have diverged so much in poor states and so little in rich states. In short, what's the matter with Connecticut?

VOTES FOR CONGRESS

We have focused on presidential elections, which is where there is the most attention and the most voter interest—about 20% more people vote in presidential election years than in off years such as 2002 and 2006—but we see similar patterns in votes for other offices.

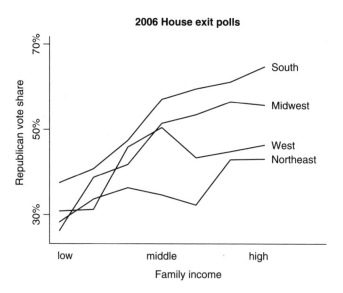

Figure 4.8: Voting by income and region for the 2006 congressional elections. The lines for the South and Midwest have steeper slopes, which tells us that income was associated with Republican vote more strongly in these regions than in the Northeast and West.

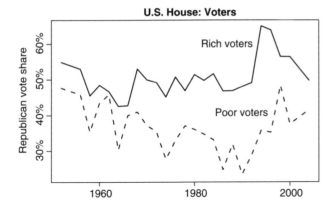

Figure 4.9: Estimated Republican share of the vote for the House of Representatives among voters in the upper and lower third of family income, estimated from pre-election poll data for each election from 1952 to 2006. As with presidential voting (see the bottom graph of figure 4.2), rich people continue to vote Republican.

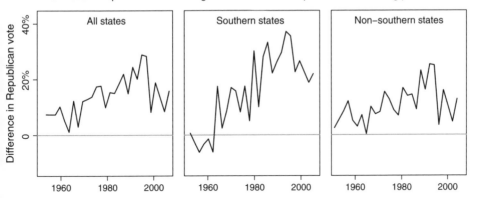

Figure 4.10: Estimated rich–poor difference in Republican vote share for the House of Representatives (comparing voters in the upper and lower third of family income), displayed for each election from 1952 to 2006: the entire United States, the South, and the rest of the country. The lines are above zero, indicating that Republican candidates do better among the rich than the poor.

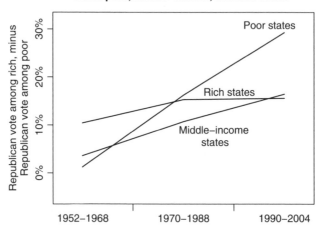

Figure 4.11: Differences between the Republican share of the vote for the House of Representatives, comparing rich and poor voters in high-, middle-, and low-income states in each period. In recent years, rich voters have been consistently more Republican than poor voters, especially in poor states.

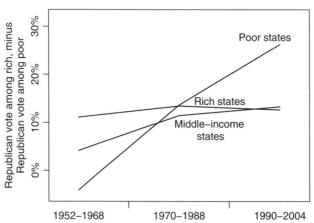

Figure 4.12: Differences between the Republican share of the vote for the Senate, comparing rich and poor voters in high-, middle-, and low-income states in each period. In recent years, rich voters have been consistently more Republican than poor voters, especially in poor states.

Exit polls for the 2006 congressional elections showed that the Republicans do best in the South and among high-income voters, with the pattern of income being strongest in the South and weakest in the Democratic-leaning West and Northeast; see figure 4.8. As with presidential voting, the distinctive regional voting patterns occur among the middle- and upper-income voters but not among the poor.

Trends in congressional voting are also similar to what we have seen with presidential elections: rich states used to favor the Republicans but have switched to the Democrats and poor states have gone in the opposite direction. And, as shown in figures 4.9 and 4.10, at the individual level, income has been correlated with Republican voting for decades.

Finally, figures 4.11 and 4.12 reveal that income differentials in congressional voting have been larger since 1990 in poor states than in rich states, again following a similar pattern to presidential voting. This is no surprise, but it is good to review these other elections to rule out the possibility that the familiar red–blue maps are simply artifacts of particular presidential candidates and campaigns. Elections for governor show similar patterns, with richer voters favoring Republicans in recent years, especially in poor and Republican-leaning states.

Inequality and Voting

IN THEIR book *Polarized America: The Dance of Ideology and Unequal Riches,* political scientists Nolan McCarty, Keith Poole, and Howard Rosenthal point to the dramatic increase in income inequality as a reason for the new polarization in American politics. As figure 5.1 shows, in the past the United States was not more economically stratified than other countries, but the last thirty years have seen exceptional growth in the incomes of the richest Americans.

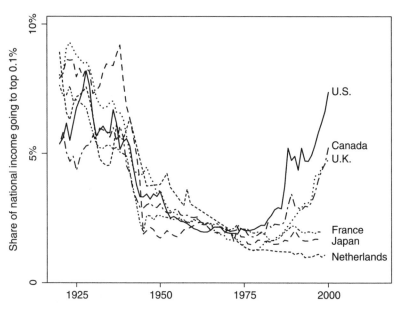

Figure 5.1: Graph by Thomas Piketty and Emmanuel Saez showing the share of income received by the richest tenth of a percent of households in the United States and several other developed countries during the twentieth century. Up to about 1975, the countries showed similar patterns of income concentration, but in the past thirty years the distribution of income in America has become more unequal than in these other places.

This increasing inequality has occurred within, not among, states. (In fact, as we discuss shortly, the income gap between rich and poor states steadily declined over most of the past century.) To the extent that the Democratic and Republican parties represent the rich and poor differently, it makes sense that, as the income gap between rich and poor grows, we would see a corresponding increase in the voting gap as well. The general increasing trend of inequality is consistent with the increasing importance of income in determining vote choice.

To explore this in more depth, look at figure 5.2, which shows trends in income of the upper and lower tenths of the population within each state. Until about 1975, the tenth percentile of income in many of the poor states increased sharply, as many of the less economically developed areas of the country pulled out of poverty. The more recent period has seen divergent patterns in different areas of the country. The poor have been getting richer faster in the poor states and the rich have been getting richer faster in the rich states; see figure 5.3. The increase at the lower end can be attributed to decades of economic growth in the Sunbelt as well as the building up of the social safety net. Welfare benefits per recipient are higher in rich states, but even so, policies designed to benefit the poorest Americans end up having the most noticeable effect in the poorer states. During the same period, income inequality has increased among sectors of the economy, with the largest gains occurring in metropolitan areas in the Northeast and West Coast.

Income inequality has been increasing in Democratic-leaning states and decreasing in Republican-leaning states. Tax cuts and deregulation (which have been championed by Republicans and reluctantly accepted by Democrats) have increased inequality in the richest states, while poverty-relief programs (largely instituted in Democratic administrations but generally left standing by Republicans) have decreased inequality in poor states.

One would expect different sorts of income-biased policies from the two parties on different issues. For example, in tax policy, one can target individuals, and it makes sense that we see Democrats favoring their poorer supporters and Republicans favoring those higher on the income scale. But on issues that affect

Trends in 90th and 10th percentile of income within each state, 1963–2004

Figure 5.2: Forty-year trends in incomes of ninetieth and tenth percentiles within each state. The graphs are all on a common logarithmic scale (so that changes at the low end remain clear) running from $2,000 to $125,000 in inflation-adjusted dollars, with states ordered from poorest to richest. In poor states such as Mississippi, there have been sharp income gains among the poor (especially in the first decade), whereas in rich states such as Connecticut, the poor started at a high level but have not improved. The upper quartiles of income have gone up everywhere, but most dramatically in the Northeast.

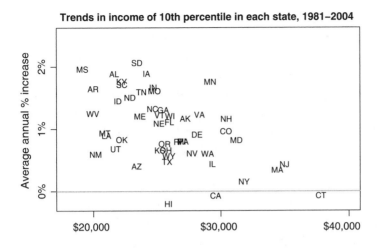

Trends in income of 10th percentile in each state, 1981–2004

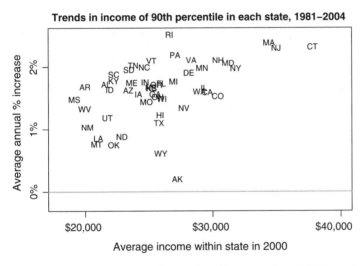

Trends in income of 90th percentile in each state, 1981–2004

Figure 5.3: Average annual growth of income since 1981, at the low and high ends within each state, plotted against current average state incomes. The bottom tenth of income has increased in almost all of the states, but most dramatically in poorer states. At the high end, incomes have generally increased faster, especially in the richest states.

states or regions rather than individual voters (for example, transportation policy or military spending), one might see Democrats favoring richer localities and Republicans favoring poorer areas. Continuing from there, one might see certain policy areas where

Democratic officeholders, as friends of the rich areas, become friends of the rich people, for example, in supporting the federal tax deduction for state income tax (which benefits taxpayers, especially upper-income taxpayers, in New York and California).

At the state level, Democrats' willingness to tax high earners and Republicans' motivation to spend in poor states combine to yield large transfers from mostly Democratic states in the Northeast, Midwest, and West Coast to mostly Republican states in the South and middle of the country. According to the Tax Foundation, the poorest ten states (all of which George W. Bush carried in 2004) receive an average of $1.60 in federal spending for every $1.00 they spend in federal taxes, while the richest ten states (nine of which were won by John Kerry) receive only $0.80 on average.

Income inequality is a distinctive feature of the American political landscape and it does not appear to be going away anytime soon. That said, it does not explain the differences in voting between red and blue states. Figure 5.4 maps the areas with high and low within-state inequality, revealing high-inequality Democratic states such as California and New York but also high-inequality Republican states such as Texas and Arizona, with the most unequal states being those with high immigration. Overall, the Democrats' vote share by state is slightly correlated with income inequality, but much less than the correlation with income itself. It is in the rich states, but not consistently the unequal states, that Democrats are doing best.

INTERSTATE INCOME INEQUALITY

A natural question, then, is when did the rich states become rich and the poor states become poor? The political leanings of different states have changed dramatically in recent decades (as illustrated in figure 4.1), but figures 5.5 and 5.6 reveal that the rankings of states by income have remained stable over the past century, with rural southern states such as Mississippi being the poorest and northeastern industrial and suburban states having the highest per capita incomes.

States with high and low income inequality

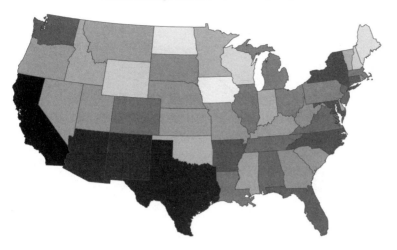

Figure 5.4: Map of income inequality by state, based on 2004 census figures. Dark colors correspond to greater inequality, as measured by the ratio between the ninetieth and tenth percentiles of pre-tax income within each state. The ratios range from 7.2 in California and 6.7 in Texas to 4.3 in North Dakota and 4.2 in Iowa.

Thus, any discussion of rich and poor states is potentially as much about each state's history as peripheral and rural or as metropolitan and urban. As economists Edward Glaeser and Bryce Ward write, "the share of the labor force in manufacturing in 1920 and the share of the population that was foreign born in 1920 strongly predict liberal beliefs and voting for John Kerry."

The steady positions of states' relative incomes (see figure 5.7) also bring into focus the changes in the red-state, blue-state maps. Something has happened in the past twenty years that has aligned rich and poor states with the Democrats and Republicans. The realignment of the South is part of this but not the complete story: the correlation of Democratic vote with state income is prominent in the rest of the country as well.

Could the labels of rich and poor states merely reflect differences in the cost of living? Incomes in Connecticut are higher than in Mississippi, but it is more expensive to live in Connecticut. Perhaps, after adjusting for the cost of living, Connecticut is not a

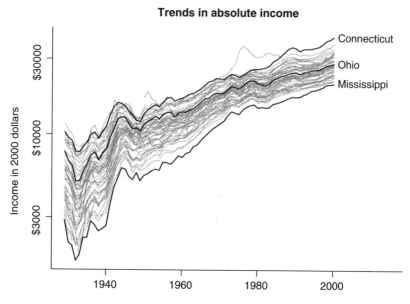

Trends in absolute income

Figure 5.5: Average income by state (adjusted for inflation) over most of the past century. Each line on the graph shows a different state. Incomes have increased dramatically in all states, but the relative positions of the states have changed little. Connecticut, Ohio, and Mississippi are highlighted to show the trajectories of rich, middle-income, and poor states.

rich state at all. There is no perfect adjustment for living costs—you have to balance food, housing, and many other items—but the standard adjustment leaves the states pretty much in the same positions; see figure 5.8. The scale is shrunk: after adjustment, the average income in Connecticut is only one-and-one-half times that of Mississippi, reduced from more than twice as large before adjustment. Cost of living does not explain the differences between red states and blue states.

Rich County, Poor County

One of the more glaring differences between the two groups is income. The average per capita income in the Blue states was $27,899 in 1998, versus $23,722 for the Red states, per the

Bureau of Economic Analysis. Of the top 10 metropolitan areas with the highest per capita income, eight were from Blue states; the other two were from the highly contested state of Florida. Similarly, eight of the top 10 metro areas with the lowest income levels were from Red states.
—*Todd Wasserman, 2002*

Where can you find trustfunders? Not scattered randomly around the country, but heavily concentrated in certain areas.... Trustfunders stand out even more vividly when you look at the political map of the Rocky Mountain states. In Idaho and Wyoming, each state's wealthiest county was also the only county to vote for John Kerry.
—*Michael Barone, 2005*

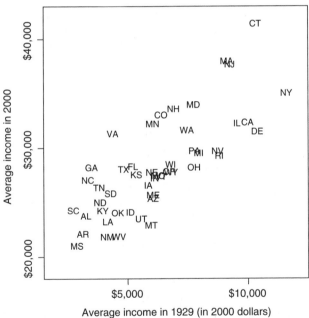

Little change in ranking of state incomes

Figure 5.6: State incomes then and now. Even after all that has happened since 1929—the Great Depression, World War II, the postwar expansion, oil shocks, and the rise of the Sunbelt—the states that were rich or poor at the beginning of the twentieth century are similarly situated now.

65

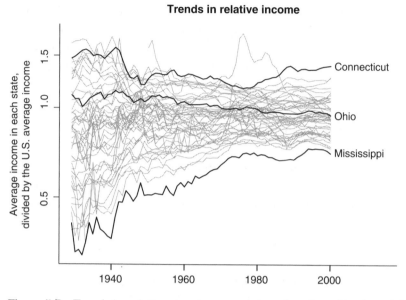

Figure 5.7: Trends in relative state incomes (plotted on logarithmic scale). The gap between rich and poor states narrowed until about 1980 but has remained steady or widened since then. (The state whose per capita income jumped so high in the 1970s is Alaska.)

If states go one way and voters go the other, maybe we can understand where the income and voting pattern changes by looking at intermediate levels. Richer counties used to support Republicans, but this pattern has steadily declined during the past forty years, and in the 2000 and 2004 presidential elections there was little difference between how rich and poor counties voted, in aggregate. But the complete pattern is more complicated than implied by the previous quotations.

In most southern states, rich counties voted for Republicans in the past and continue to do so. In contrast, in the rest of the country, the patterns are not so strong. We can also look within individual states. Some regions have shifted toward the Democrats and some toward the Republicans in the past few decades, and there are also trends in the differences between rich and poor counties.

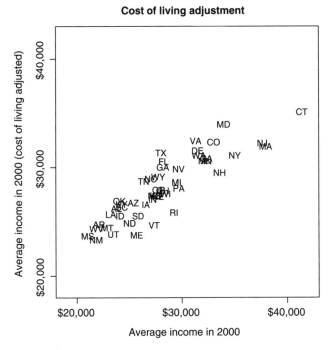

Figure 5.8: State incomes with and without cost of living corrections. Adjusting for cost of living narrows the gap among states but does not significantly change their rankings.

Figures 5.9–5.12 display regional patterns in the trends in the voting difference between rich and poor counties. In most southern states, rich counties vote Republican. An additional pattern is revealed by the ordering of our plots by the percentage of the vote received by George W. Bush in 2004. The most-Republican leaning of the southern states show the strongest correlations between county income and Republican support. In contrast, in western states, richer counties once tended to vote Republican but now increasingly vote for Democrats. Trends in the Midwest and Northeast are more mixed.

In deep-red southern states such as Oklahoma, Texas, and Mississippi, richer counties support Republicans and poorer counties support Democrats. In contrast, consider the states that are

67

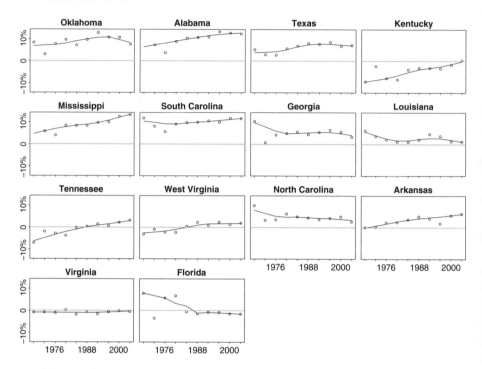

Figure 5.9: South only. Difference in Republican vote for president comparing rich and poor counties in each state from 1968 to 2004. Within the region, the states are in decreasing order of support for Bush in 2004. In each graph, points that are above the zero line correspond to states where the Republicans did better in richer counties.

located near major national media: New York, Maryland, Virginia, and California. There, richer counties were more likely to go for the Democrats. Thus, amusingly, journalists noticed a pattern (richer counties having more liberal voting patterns) that is concentrated in the states where the journalists live. (For example, as we discussed in chapter 2, David Brooks compared a rich county in Maryland to a poor county in Pennsylvania.) If journalists had compared counties within states such as Oklahoma, they would have noticed a completely opposite pattern.

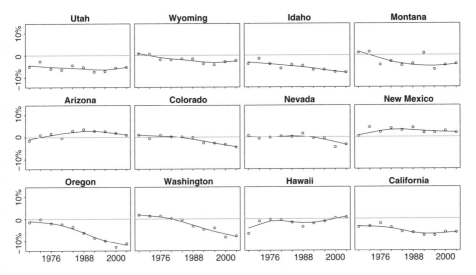

Figure 5.10: West only. Difference in Republican vote for president comparing rich and poor counties in each state from 1968 to 2004. Within the region, the states are in decreasing order of support for Bush in 2004. In each graph, points that are above the zero line correspond to states where the Republicans did better in richer counties.

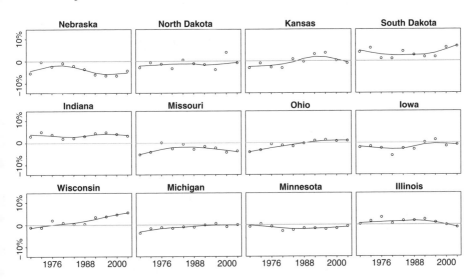

Figure 5.11: Midwest only. Difference in Republican vote for president comparing rich and poor counties in each state from 1968 to 2004. Within the region, the states are in decreasing order of support for Bush in 2004. In each graph, points that are above the zero line correspond to states where the Republicans did better in richer counties.

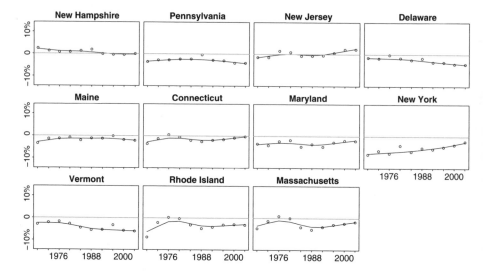

Figure 5.12: Northeast only. Difference in Republican vote for president comparing rich and poor counties in each state from 1968 to 2004. Within the region, the states are in decreasing order of support for Bush in 2004. In each graph, points that are above the zero line correspond to states where the Republicans did better in richer counties.

RICH–POOR DIFFERENCES AT THE LOCAL, STATE, AND REGIONAL LEVELS

> Pennsylvania is Philadelphia on one end, Pittsburgh on the other, and Alabama in the middle.
> —*attributed to James Carville, campaign manager for Bill Clinton, 1992*

We have already learned that the rich vote much differently than the poor in Mississippi but not so much in Connecticut. What about rich and poor regions within states? We separately analyzed rural, suburban, and urban voters and, by replicating our analysis in this way, revealed similar patterns to our comparison of poor, middle-income, and rich states.

Our next step was to separately analyze survey data within each state, analyzing voting using income within each county of a state (instead of predicting within each state of the country). We then estimated a level of Republican support and a slope for the predictive power of income within each county.

Our analysis revealed that, within any county, the higher your income, the more likely you are to vote Republican. However, richer counties tend to have higher levels of Democratic support. Comparing two voters of the same income level within a state, the resident of the poorer county was more likely to vote for Bush in 2000 and 2004.

These patterns to some extent mask each other when combined in a statewide analysis. For example, consider income and voting in California, looking at the entire state and then separately at poor, middle-income, and rich counties. Within any county, rich people were quite a bit more likely to vote for George W. Bush, but in the state as a whole, the pattern is weak.

A similar pattern occurs when we compare the votes of rich and poor people within congressional districts: the pattern between income and voting is stronger within individual districts than in entire states or the nation as a whole. Figure 5.13 shows the pattern and sheds light on the polarization in Congress: within any district, the voters tend to be lined up politically as upper versus lower income, which motivates the Democratic and Republican congressional candidates to similarly take strong positions.

Blacks and Whites, North and South

> Instead of being seen as advancing the economic well-being of all voters, including white mainstream working and middle-class voters, liberalism and the Democratic party came to be perceived, in key sectors of the electorate, as promoting the establishment of new rights and government guarantees for previously marginalized, stigmatized, or historically disenfranchised groups, often at the expense of traditional constituencies.
> —*Thomas and Mary Edsall, 1991*

71

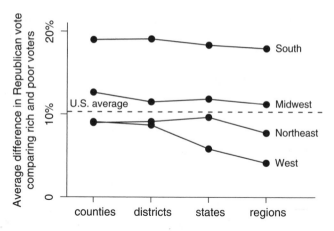

Figure 5.13: Average income gap in voting within counties, congressional districts, states, regions, and the entire country. Each line traces a different region of the country; for example, the top line shows the average difference between rich and poor voters within southern counties, southern congressional districts, southern states, and the entire South. All the lines are well above zero, which tells us that, in all these geographic groupings, rich voters are more Republican than poor voters. The lines are higher on the left side of the graph, which tells us that income polarization tends to be greater in local units.

During the past forty years, the South has shifted from the Democrats to the Republicans in congressional and presidential voting. The change began with higher-income suburban southerners, a group that remains strongly Republican. The power of the suburbs was given a boost in the mid-1960s by the Supreme Court's rulings in *Baker v. Carr* and *Reynolds v. Sims* that legislative districts must have equal populations—the so-called one man, one vote rule. Before then, rural areas were typically highly overrepresented in nearly all the states, tilting state legislatures and the U.S. Congress toward rural interests, as described by political scientists Stephen Ansolabehere and James Snyder in *The End of Inequality*. In the South in particular, residents of rural areas in the 1960s were more conservative than city dwellers on racial issues, while suburbanites had more conservative economic beliefs. The redistricting revolution shifted the region's racial policies toward the center and its economic policies to the right, and the voters in the new suburban congressional and state legislative districts had positions that were compatible with those of the national Republican Party. Meanwhile, the Democrats' social and economic policies were being viewed nationwide through a racial prism.

We found that income matters more in Mississippi (and other poor states) than in rich states such as Connecticut. Could the systematically varying income effects we have shown be merely a proxy for race? This is a plausible story. In Mississippi and elsewhere in the South, poor voters are mostly black and rich voters are mostly white. The racial division is much less stark in Connecticut, which has relatively few African Americans.

Perhaps the high slope in Mississippi reflects poor black Democrats and rich white Republicans, with Connecticut's flatter slope being the result of its more racially homogeneous population. To test this, we replicated our analysis, restricting our data to the approximately 80% of the survey respondents who are white. When we did this, we found similar patterns as before, but a bit weaker. About half of the difference in the income-voting pattern between Mississippi and Connecticut goes away when we consider only whites.

To see more systematically if the income patterns could be explained by other demographic variables, we looked at the data from 2000 and 2004 in more detail, considering race, sex, age, and education. After adjusting for all of these variables, the patterns for income remains: individual income is predictive of Republican vote within states, with steeper slopes in poorer states. The association of state income with state vote for the Democrats also persists. Differences in the racial or other demographic characteristics of states explain only some of the state differences by income.

EXPLAINING THE DIFFERENCES BETWEEN STATES

As summarized so far, we have found three striking patterns:

1. Voters in richer states support the Democrats even though within any given state, richer voters tend to support the Republicans.

2. The slope within a state—the pattern that richer voters support the Republicans—is strongest in poor, rural, Republican-leaning red states and weakest in rich, urban blue states.

3. The systematic differences between rich and poor states have largely arisen in the past twenty years.

The positive slopes within states are no surprise. Given both the history and the policies of the two parties, it makes sense that the Democrats would prevail among the poor and the Republicans among the rich, a pattern that has persisted for decades. At the same time, votes are far from being determined economically— even in Mississippi, which is the state with the strongest correlation between income and voting, over 30% of voters in the lowest income category support the Republicans. Income is only one of the many factors contributing to voters' ideological and partisan worldviews, and one could, for example, use detailed survey data to try to understand the positive correlation of income and Republican vote choice as coming from differential attitudes toward redistribution. Finally, about half of the pattern is explained by race: African Americans disproportionately live in poorer states and themselves tend to be poorer and vote for Democrats.

An alternative perspective is to consider state average income as a proxy for secularism or some kind of cosmopolitanism. In other words, the cultural or social conservatism of states may be increasingly becoming negatively correlated with average income. At the same time, if these social issues are increasingly important to voters (perhaps made more relevant to voters by Clinton's scandals), this would induce changes in the relationship between state income and individual vote.

To put it another way, economic issues might well be more salient in poorer states such as Mississippi, and so one would expect voting there to be more income-based. Conversely, in richer states, such as Connecticut, voters might be more likely to follow noneconomic cues. In any case, a challenge for explanations of this sort is to understand why they became more relevant in the 1990s, given that the relative rankings of states by income have changed little in the past century. As we discuss in chapter 8, diverging ideological positions of the parties can lead to diverging attitudes about the parties among voters, even if the voters themselves remain largely centrist and do not show strong patterns of consistency in issue attitudes.

We've found that living in a rich or poor state predicts not only the vote but also the difference between how rich and poor vote. This suggests another puzzle. The current red–blue voting patterns are only twenty years old, and the current differences between how rich and poor vote by state are only twenty years old. But the rankings of state incomes have been stable for a century. There must be some other factor explaining things. It's not just the South because we still see the red–blue income patterns when we exclude the South. It's not just race because we see it among whites (but race does explain some of the patterns). Income inequality would be a tempting explanation—especially because income inequality, both among and within states, has changed in recent decades— but that doesn't work either. We next turn to cultural explanations and political ideology.

Social issues don't explain all of the patterns—higher-income Americans are, on average, slightly more culturally liberal (as measured by survey questions)—but there nonetheless remains a clear pattern of rich people voting for the Republicans and poor people voting for the Democrats. When we try to unpack the income-and-voting pattern (in particular, that the difference between voting patterns in rich and poor states is greater for high-income voters than for low-income voters), we need to go beyond a simple comparison of rich and poor states. We move into the next chapters with the goal of explaining the red-state, blue-state division and understanding why it occurs among the rich but not the poor.

Religious Reds and Secular Blues

> I don't know that atheists should be considered citizens, nor
> should they be considered patriots. This is one nation under
> God.
> —*George H. W. Bush, 1987*

> There is a public perception and a press perception, fueled by
> the religious right, that if you're a person of faith, you're a
> conservative.... That is in dire need of correction, if you want
> progressive social change in this country.
> —*John Podesta, former chief of staff to Bill Clinton, 2004*

CHRISTIANITY has been central to American culture since before
the founding of the United States, from the Spanish missions and
the Massachusetts Bay Colony in the 1600s, the Great Awakenings
of the early 1700s and 1800s and the abolition, temperance, and
civil rights movements, up through the Moral Majority and modern
megachurches. At the same time, American religious life is end-
lessly diverse, with rich and socially prominent mainline Protestant
denominations, the immigrant-fueled Roman Catholic Church,
proselytizing evangelical movements, and various smaller but still
notable groups such as Mormons, Jews, and Muslims. Churches
have also been in conflict with the government, most notably over
issues such as secular public schools, abortion, and changes in
traditional sex roles.

As noted by Ronald Inglehart, director of the World Values Survey, people in richer countries tend to be less religious, but the
United States is an exception, as a rich country with a high rate
of religious observance and belief; see figure 6.1. Various causes

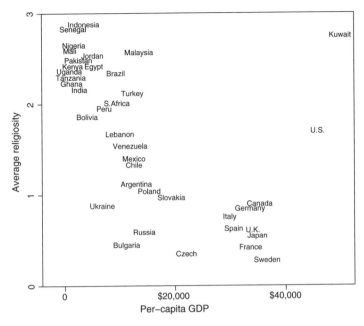

Figure 6.1: Wealth and religiosity (frequency of church attendance, belief in God, and stated importance of religious belief) as measured by a survey conducted in countries around the world. People in richer countries tend to be less religious, with the United States standing out as more religious than other wealthy developed nations.

have been suggested for America's distinctiveness, including: immigration from poorer, more religious societies; vigorous competition from a variety of active denominations (as compared to European countries, with their established national churches); and the relatively high level of economic inequality, which, in that respect, makes the United States more like a poor country. For our purposes, what is important here is that Americans' strong religiosity has long been part of its politics, from "In God We Trust" on the dollar bill to debates over Barack Obama's pastor.

What is new is the link between religion and the Republican Party (see figure 6.2), which shows voting patterns given religious attendance for several different religious groupings.

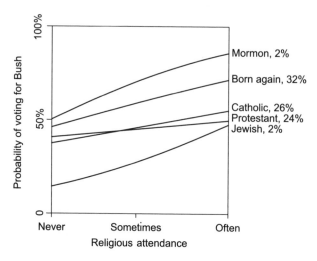

Figure 6.2: Probability of Republican vote given religious attendance for different denominations, based on a model fit to survey data from 2004. The percent of the population in each group is given next to the name of the denomination. Born-again Protestants are counted as a separate category, and various small religious groupings are not shown. Except for non-evangelical Protestants, frequent attenders of each religious group were much more likely than nonattenders to vote Republican. In addition, the 10% of respondents with no religious affiliation gave Bush 30% of their votes.

The correlation between church attendance and Republican voting is weakest among mainline Protestants and strongest among Mormons, evangelical Christians, and Jews.

The association between voting and religion can be explained partly by religious people choosing the Republicans and seculars moving to the Democrats, and partly by changes in religious behavior. From surveys in which individuals are followed for several years, we have learned that it is common for people to switch denominations. And in recent years, social conservatives have tended to go to church more often, while liberals have reduced their church attendance.

The relationship between religious values and behavior is not obvious or simple, though. Married couples in Massachusetts get divorced at less than half the rate of those in Arkansas, and a survey in 2001 found the divorce rate among born-again Christians to be the same as among married Americans in general. These sorts of findings are not mysterious—poorer, less-educated, and more religious people tend to marry younger and get divorced more often—but it is good to be reminded of the difficulty of generalizing about properties of states. In the words of sociologist Alan Wolfe, "If you want to go to a place in the United States where people live postmodern lives, constantly transforming their lifestyles to keep up with the latest cultural trends, go to the red states, not the blue states."

Religious America and Secular America

> Decidedly, joggers are the true Latter-Day Saints and the protagonists of an easy-does-it Apocalypse.
> —*Jean Baudrillard, 1986*

Religion is inextricably tied to social and political geography. Different religions and denominations are concentrated in different parts of the country, from Mormons in Utah and Jews in New York to larger groups such as evangelical Protestants in the South and Roman Catholics in the metropolitan areas of the Northeast and Midwest.

One clear connection between religion and geography is income. Figure 6.3 plots the states by average religious attendance (as estimated from survey responses) and average income. The most religious states are relatively poor—a microcosm of the international graph shown in figure 6.1—and in the South. The less religious states are in the West and Northeast and represent a range of incomes. Robert Putnam quips that the best predictor of the religiosity of a state is its distance from the Mississippi River.

The religion gap in voting, and the increased presence of religion in politics, coincides with a gradual and consistent *decrease* in religious participation over the past several decades; see figure 6.4. The country has become more secular and pluralistic in the past half century, leading to changes ranging from the decline

79

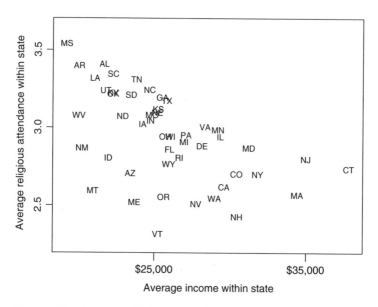

Figure 6.3: Average religious attendance (as measured on a 1–5 scale from "never" to "more than once per week") in each state, plotted with state average income. Religious attendance is generally higher in the South and Midwest and lower in the West and Northeast, and overall the residents of rich states are less religious.

of school prayer to openly gay ministers, which have provoked a reaction among conservative churchgoers. In addition, as regular church attendance has decreased, the political cohesion of those who have remained has increased and new religious organizations have sprung up, most notably the comprehensive suburban megachurches. As Alan Wolfe puts it, "while Americans may be 'bowling alone,' they certainly are not praying alone." In addition, lifestyle choices and political causes can take on a religious flavor in modern-day America, as indicated in the Baudrillard quote above.

Election surveys ask about religious attendance more often than they ask about denomination, so we focus on attendance here. Studies have estimated that Americans vastly overreport their churchgoing (presumably because it is socially desirable behavior),

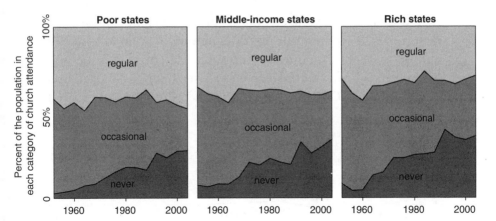

Figure 6.4: Percentage of survey respondents who go to church regularly, occasionally, or never, over time, separately among poor, middle-income, and rich states. In each group of states, the proportion of people who attend weekly has stayed steady, but there are fewer occasional church attenders and more people who never attend religious services. (The jump in reported nonattendance from 1968 to 1972 is explained by a change in the wording of the question.)

but our assumption is that people who report going to church once a week are more religious than those who report not going to church, regardless of their true religious attendance.

THE GEOGRAPHY OF RELIGION AND INCOME

> [President Bush] reads a devotional every day. And he is a very
> serious Methodist. . . . I think there is something about—you
> know, Methodism—you know, the Wesley brothers were
> Episcopalians who didn't like martinis. I mean, you know, they
> wanted to preach the gospel to the lower middle class, the
> lower classes in Britain and the United States, sort of a working
> man's Episcopalianism, and I think this egalitarianism of
> Methodism, the belief that every individual is worthy of respect
> is something that speaks to something that's deep inside him.
> —*Karl Rove, former deputy chief of staff to George W. Bush, 2007*

81

Red America is, on average, more religious than blue America. Our next step is to see how this plays out among rich, middle-income, and poor voters. Nationwide, the statistical correlation between income and church attendance is weak; see figure 6.5. If religiosity is measured in other ways, however, we see stronger patterns. The

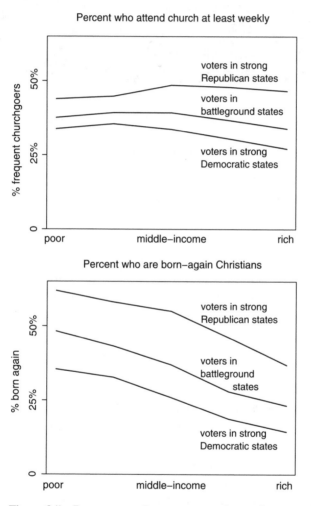

Percent who attend church at least weekly

voters in strong Republican states

voters in battleground states

voters in strong Democratic states

Percent who are born–again Christians

voters in strong Republican states

voters in battleground states

voters in strong Democratic states

Figure 6.5: Percentage of survey respondents who go to church at least once per week and percent who say they are born-again Christians, as a function of income. There is little correlation between income and church attendance, but in Republican, Democratic, and battleground states alike, lower-income people are much more likely to report being born again.

percent of people who say they are born-again Christians is much higher among the poor than the rich, especially outside the South. Similarly, lower-income people are much more likely to pray daily and to consider religion to be very important to their lives; see figure 6.6.

In figure 6.7 we compare the religious attendance of rich and poor *within* states. The relationship between income and church attendance is not strong in any state, but there is a consistent pattern that the correlation between income and churchgoing is positive in poor states and negative in rich states. Higher income would tend to make rich voters support the Republicans, but in rich states higher income is associated with being less religious and more socially liberal. This pattern goes some of the way toward explaining the relative unimportance of income in predicting voting in rich states: where the correlation of income and religious attendance is negative, higher-income voters are pulled toward the Democrats on social issues, away from what might be considered their natural economic interests.

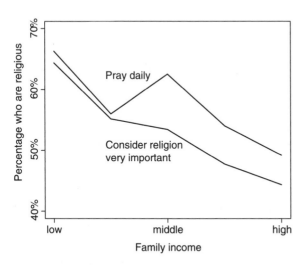

Figure 6.6: Adaptation of Pippa Norris and Ronald Inglehart's graph showing the percentage of Americans who pray regularly and consider religion to be very important, as a function of income. Richer Americans tend to be less religious by these measures.

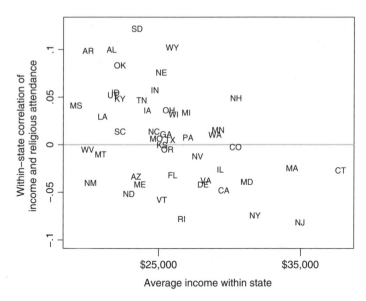

Figure 6.7: Correlation between religious attendance and income within each state, plotted with state average income. In most of the poor states, rich people tend to be slightly more religious than poor people, but in the rich states, the pattern goes the other way.

How Do Religious People Vote?

> The paradox of the Religious Right is that it becomes an important factor in American politics primarily because of liberal victories.
> —*E. J. Dionne, 1991*

The connection between religious attendance and Republican voting is recent. Until 1988 there was generally little difference in the voting patterns of church attenders and nonattenders. In 1992, things changed, with George H. W. Bush receiving 20% more support in his reelection campaign among regular churchgoers than among nonattenders. The difference remained high in the 1990s but dropped a bit in 2004. Figure 6.8 shows the pattern over the past half century.

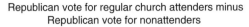

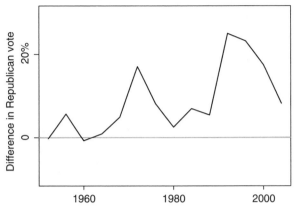

Figure 6.8: Difference in probability of voting for the Republican candidate for president, comparing people who went to church at least once per week to nonattenders. Not much happened between 1972 and 1992, and then suddenly Bill Clinton received 20% less of the vote among the religious than among the nonreligious. When the line goes above zero, this corresponds to church attenders being more likely to vote Republican.

We were surprised to find that the trend of churchgoers voting Republican took so long to develop. Candidates have made ethnic and religious appeals since the dawn of the Republic, but the recent rise of the Religious Right is associated with battles over abortion and gay rights, reaction to the Supreme Court's 7–2 decision in *Roe v. Wade* in 1973 upholding abortion rights, and reaction to laws such as Miami's antidiscrimination ordinance in 1977 (made famous by the anti-gay crusade of Anita Bryant, the orange juice spokeswoman). Congress sent the Equal Rights Amendment to the states in 1972 (on overwhelming votes of 354–24 in the House of Representatives and 84–8 in the Senate), setting up battles between feminists and social conservatives throughout the country as state legislatures deliberated over ratification. The most liberal states ratified the amendment almost immediately, and the most prolonged struggles occurred on turf more favorable to conservative mobilization efforts. Jerry Falwell founded the

85

Moral Majority in 1979 and played a prominent role in the 1980 election, using direct mail to raise money and grassroots support for Ronald Reagan and other Republican candidates.

Nonetheless, survey data from the National Election Study (displayed in figure 6.8) reveal that the gap between the religious and nonreligious in voting was actually less for Ronald Reagan in both 1980 and 1984 than for Gerald Ford in 1976. Breaking this up by denomination in figure 6.9, we see a steady trend of mainline Protestants moving from the Republican column to the center, Catholics going to the center from the other direction, and evangelicals moving strongly toward the Republican Party.

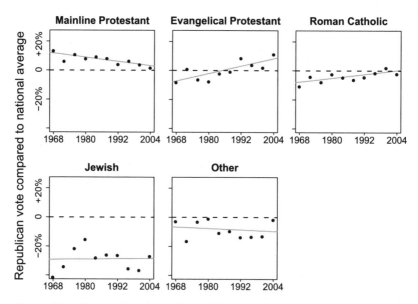

Figure 6.9: Time series plots of Republican vote for various religious denominations. In each year, we have subtracted the national vote so that the graph shows each denomination compared to the national average. Over the past several decades, mainline Protestants have become less Republican, evangelical Protestants have moved from the Democrats to the Republicans, and Catholics have lost their Democratic affiliation. Points that are above the zero line correspond to groups that are more Republican than the country as a whole.

We can look at how religious attendance is associated with voting in the same way we compared rich and poor. Plate 7 shows the winner of each state in 2004 among people who reported attending church frequently, occasionally, or never. We were not surprised to see that Bush did much better among the religious than the secular. Among the people who go to church at least once per week, Bush is estimated to have won almost every state. The map for occasional churchgoers is similar to the red–blue map of the country as a whole, and the nonattenders went strongly for Kerry.

Looking at the numbers in more detail, we see that each state voted pretty much the same way among the three categories of religious attendance, with just a general shift from the Republicans to the Democrats as we go down the charts in plate 7. This contrasts with the graphs in plate 3, where the orderings of the states changed dramatically when separately considering voters of high, middle, and low incomes. For example, Mississippi is one of the most Republican states among the rich but strongly Democratic among the poor. In contrast, the state is strongly Republican among all three categories of religious attendance.

The religion gap opened up in the 1990s during the same period that poor and rich states became red and blue. As we shall see, this is not a coincidence. Religion is a key step in our understanding of political differences between rich and poor.

How, then, do we understand the rise of religious voting in 1992? Part of the story is Bill Clinton, who repelled many religious conservatives who saw a connection between his adulterous lifestyle and his support for liberal social causes. (Reagan had been divorced, but that was long in the past, and he sided with the Religious Right on many issues.) There was also the growing strength of the evangelical movement as followers of Pat Robertson and others gained influence in state Republican parties, eventually moving the national party to the right on various social issues. On the other side, Democrats became more committed to liberal positions on abortion and gay rights, backed by groups such as People for the American Way and the National Organization for Women. With the closer alignment of moral issues to the political parties,

87

voters have sorted themselves on these attitudes, as we discuss in Chapter 8.

INCOME, RELIGION, AND POLITICAL ATTITUDES

We see some striking patterns when we display income, religion, and voting together in figure 6.10. Churchgoers are much more Republican than nonchurchgoers—as expected—but what surprised us is that this difference is much larger for richer voters. If anything, we were expecting the opposite pattern: that richer Americans would vote based on their economic interests and poorer voters would be more likely to be swayed by social and religious issues.

Understanding the interaction between income and religious attendance—the unequal slopes of the lines in figure 6.10—is tricky. A quick explanation that does not quite work is that a rich, religious person will naturally vote Republican, whereas a poor, religious voter feels cross-pressure and could go either way (as

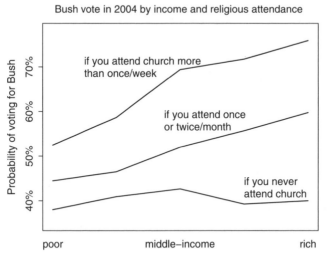

Figure 6.10: Support for George W. Bush as a function of income, plotted separately for frequent church attenders, moderate attenders, and nonattenders. The difference between rich and poor is large for religious people but disappears among the nonreligious.

indeed we see on the graph). This also explains why rich seculars are not far from evenly divided, but the explanation fails when it comes to poor seculars, 40% of whom still supported George W. Bush for president in 2004.

Rich churchgoers are much more Republican than poor churchgoers. But among the nonattenders (who represent about a quarter of Americans), rich and poor alike are solid Democrats. Looked at this way, the Democrats' base is low-income churchgoers and secular Americans, while Republicans win the votes of middle-class and upper-income churchgoers. This is consistent with the story of red and blue America and, again, it's not simply explained by race. Analyzing whites alone yields a similar graph.

We next return to historical polls to look at how religion and income together predicted voting in previous elections. The current pattern—of religious attenders being more Republican, especially among high-income voters—has been happening since Bill Clinton's election in 1992, with no consistent patterns before then.

Since then, religious voting patterns have become more partisan and more tied to income. As E. J. Dionne wrote after analyzing exit polls from 2004, "the religion gap exists—but it varies by region and by state. Republican strength in the South is enhanced by that region's religious commitment. Democratic strength in the West, particularly on the Pacific Coast, is enhanced by the region's relatively low levels of formal religious participation."

How closely do income and church attendance map to attitudes on economic and social issues? We constructed economic- and social-issue scales from several questions asked in a 2000 pre-election poll and used a statistical model to get estimates for all the states. The results are displayed in figure 6.11. As expected, income is more strongly related to economic issues (the correlation is above zero in every state), and religious attendance with social issues, but the pattern varies by state. Higher-income voters are more conservative, both economically and socially, in poor states, and frequent church attenders are more socially conservative in less religious states.

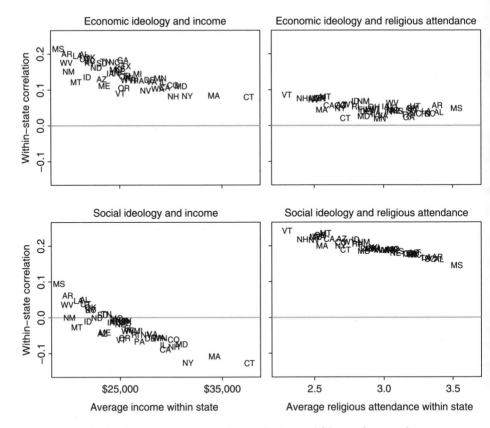

Figure 6.11: Top row: estimated correlations within each state between income and economic and social attitudes, plotted versus state income.

Bottom row: correlations with religious attendance, plotted versus state average religious attendance.

The correlations are low—people of all income groups and all levels of church attendance are diverse in their economic and social attitudes—but there is a consistent pattern that correlations with income are higher in poor states and correlations with religious attendance are higher in less religious states.

States vary more on correlations of income and religion with social attitudes than with economic attitudes. Once again we are finding that a key difference between red states (which tend to be poorer and more religious) and blue states (which tend to be richer and less religious) is in the people within each state who have liberal and conservative attitudes. On social issues, rich people tend to be more conservative than poor people in red states, but, in blue states, the opposite is true: the rich tend to be more socially liberal than the poor. When looking at church attenders and nonattenders, the comparison of states goes the other way: in blue states, religious attendance is more strongly associated with conservative social views.

Beyond this, when we predict presidential voting from social and economic attitudes, we find that both of these components of ideology are more important for high-income than for low-income voters. Within each income group, there is some evidence that economic issues are more important in Democratic-leaning states and social issues more important in Republican-leaning states, but these geographic differences are much smaller than the differences in income categories. Party identification is more closely tied to issue attitudes and ideologies for the rich than for the poor, a topic to which we return in the next chapter.

Religion Matters More in Rich States and among Rich Voters

Now let's put it all together. Karl Marx is often quoted to the effect that religion is the opiate of the masses; in modern times, people point to religious and cultural issues as reasons why many middle- and lower-income Americans support the Republicans. These critiques tie the current culture war to earlier battles on immigration and racial issues, dating back to the Know-Nothing movement against Irish immigrants in the 1850s.

A different perspective is taken by Ronald Inglehart and other scholars of postmaterialism, who find that voters consider cultural issues to be more important as they become more financially secure. From this perspective, it makes perfect sense that politics is more about economics in poor states and more about culture in rich states. And it also makes sense that, among low-income voters, political attitudes are not much different in red or blue states, whereas the cultural divide of the two Americas looms larger at high incomes. For predicting your vote, we suspect that it's not so important whether you buy life's necessities at Wal-Mart or the corner grocery, but that it might be more telling if you spend your extra income on auto-racing tickets or on a daily gourmet coffee.

We can understand differences between red and blue America in terms of cultural values of upper-middle-class and rich voters. Figure 6.12 shows that religious attendance is associated with Republican vote most strongly among high-income residents of all states. This does not mean that lower-income Americans all vote the same way—far from it—but the differences in how they vote appear to depend less on religious values.

A theme throughout this book is that the *cultural* differences between states—the things that make red and blue America feel like different places—boil down to differences among richer people in these states. In many ways, it's poorer people who are more

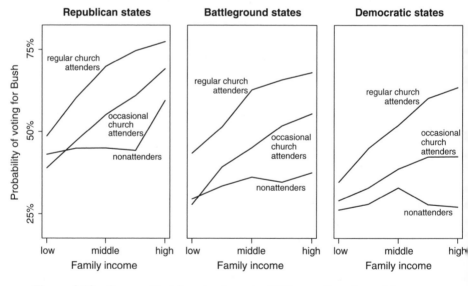

Figure 6.12: George Bush's vote share in 2004 as a function of income, plotted separately for people who attend church regularly, occasionally, or never (separately showing Republican, battleground, and Democratic states). Income predicts voting strongly among church attenders in all three groups of states. Conversely, nonattenders in Democratic states show no consistent relation between income and voting.

localized: lower-income people generally travel less, are more likely to have local accents, and are less likely to know people in other parts of the country. But in other ways that are relevant to the red–blue divide, differences are greater among people of higher incomes. Throughout the country, lower-income Americans are shopping at discount stores, eating at McDonald's, and taking the bus. It's disposable income that allows you to choose between SUVs and hybrids, NASCAR and the opera, and so forth.

The other piece of the puzzle is that the differences between religious and nonreligious Americans jumped dramatically in the 1990s. In the relatively poor states in the South, richer voters are more religious, resulting in a larger correlation between income and Republican voting. In contrast, in the rich northeastern states, richer voters are less religious, which contributes to flat pattern of voting across income groups in those states. We attribute the increasing importance of church attendance in voting to the stronger alignment of parties with social issues in recent years, which we discuss in chapter 8. But first, in chapter 7, we place the United States in an international perspective, analyzing regional voting patterns of rich and poor in Mexico, and comparing differences between rich and poor, and religious and secular voters, in countries around the world.

The United States in Comparative Perspective

ARE THE PATTERNS we have seen unique to the American polit-ical system, or are they a more general result of the interaction between geography and income? To get some international per-spective, we analyze the recent presidential elections in Mexico, in which there was a profound regional divide between high- and low-income states and controversy over the votes of rich and poor. We then compare voting patterns of rich and poor using survey data from a range of European, Asian, and Latin American countries.

NORTH AND SOUTH, RICH AND POOR, IN MEXICO

> The electorate is genuinely divided and the close election underlines it. Many are opting for a change while many are opting for continuity.
> —*Denise Dresser, in the Mexican newspaper* Reforma, *2006*

> The new map depicts an industrialized north, where business ties to the United States have played an enormous role in the rise of the right-leaning, conservative party, and a more agricultural south that is a hotbed of leftist discontent and anti-globalization sentiment.
> —*James McKinley,* New York Times, *2006*

After a half century of one-party rule, Mexico has entered a period of closely fought national elections featuring clearly defined parties of the left and right and with some regional divisions—much like the United States, although with a differ-ent history. The party of the left in Mexico, the Party of the

94

Democratic Revolution (PRD), split off almost twenty years ago from the then-ruling Institutional Revolutionary Party (PRI) and was founded by the amalgamation of the fleeing PRI members with a number of small left-wing parties such as the Mexican Communist Party, the Mexican Socialist Unified Party, and the Mexican Worker's Party. The party of the right, the National Action Party (PAN), rose to national prominence after decades as a pro-Catholic values party contesting state elections in the conservative northern region of the country. Unlike in the United States, where the Democrats and Republicans have represented distinct economic interests for over a century, the Mexican parties have only recently competed over national economic platforms.

The most recent Mexican election reached the national news in the United States after a nightmare version of the Bush–Gore deadlock: Felipe Calderón, the conservative candidate, won by a disputed 0.6% of the vote, but the opposition candidate, Andrés Manuel López Obrador, from the leftist PRD, did not take his defeat lying down. Instead, he organized protests that shut down the center of Mexico City (where he had previously been mayor) for six months before eventually dissipating.

One thing was evident from election day: the presidential vote was geographically divided, with the wealthier north and center-west supporting the PAN and the mostly poorer states of the center and the south supporting the PRD. In other words, the electoral result was characterized by a divide between rich and poor states. Figure 7.1 shows the states and regions of Mexico, and plate 9 shows the state-by-state winners in the three most recent presidential elections.

When we look at vote choice in purely economic terms, the positive link between income and support for the conservative party is clear, both at the state and individual levels, and both these patterns are consistent with the parties' historical constituencies. Nonetheless, Mexico's blue–yellow map is not a simple aggregation of rich voters voting for the conservative candidate and poor voters supporting the left-wing candidate. The key question for us to answer is this: to what extent do richer voters within states

95

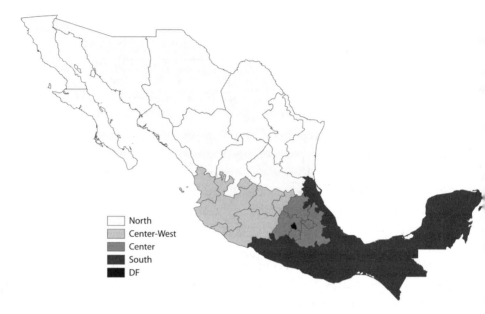

Figure 7.1: The states of Mexico, divided into the north, center-west, center, south, and Mexico City (Distrito Federal, or D.F.) Analysts typically study election results by region, but we also find large state-to-state differences within regions.

support the conservative PAN candidate and poorer voters support the leftist PRD and PRI?

So what happened in 2006 and in previous presidential elections? How much does living in a rich or poor state predict individual voting preferences? At the regional level, the pattern of income and voting is not so clear. For instance, the average Gross Domestic Product (GDP) per capita in the regions won by the PAN in 2000 was around $9,100 in U.S. dollars, while the GDP per capita in those regions where they lost was nearly the same at $8,800. At the state level, however, a different picture emerges. The average GDP per capita in the states won by the PAN was $10,000 for 2000, compared to $4,800 where the party lost. This simple comparison illustrates that collapsing multiple states into large regions discards information that might otherwise uncover sharper differences among states.

Figure 7.2 shows that state GDP per capita is correlated with support for the PAN—especially when we exclude the capital—but there are no definite regional partisan strongholds. This pattern differs from the one we have outlined in previous chapters. With three major parties, elections are competitive in many of Mexico's states, with different parties playing the role of principal challenger in different areas. In 2006, the PRI, the party that governed Mexico for the final seventy-one years of the twentieth century, did not win any states at all (see plate 9) but was competitive in a mix of rich and poor states, obstructing, to some extent, the creation of absolute partisan fortresses by the PAN and PRD.

So far, we have seen that, unlike in the United States, the conservative party in Mexico does better in richer states, with the only exceptions being Mexico City (which is richer than any state but with a voting pattern typical of lower-income parts of the country)

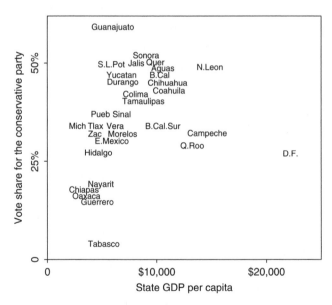

Figure 7.2: Vote share received by the conservative PAN party for each state in the 2006 Mexican presidential election, plotted versus average GDP per capita in the state (scaled to 2000 purchasing power parity U.S. dollars). The PAN generally did better in most of the richer states, with the exception of two oil-rich southern states (Quintana Roo and Campeche) and the capital (México, D.F.).

and two southern states that have oil wealth but much of whose populations are in poverty. The general voting patterns of rich and poor states have become increasingly distinct since the presidential election of 1994. Now we need to investigate whether living in a rich or poor state is predictive of voting preferences, after adjusting for individual income.

RICH AND POOR VOTERS IN MEXICAN STATES

> The only thing that the election shows is that social polarization is not a children's story and less an invention. This polarization is a reality. . . . It is or it seems to be the legitimization of the fight between the rich and the poor.
> —*Ricardo Alemán, in the Mexican newspaper* El Universal, *2006*

Like its northern neighbor, Mexico is a country full of striking geographical variety, with economic and political development and individual political preferences varying from one state to another. In contrast to the United States, where the Republicans have in recent years performed better in poor states, the PAN tends to do better in the wealthier parts of the country (north and center-west) and underperform in the mostly poorer states of the south.

Each of the past three Mexican presidential elections illustrates a transition in Mexico's political history. The 1994 presidential election was an election of fear, occurring around events such as the Zapatista uprising, the assassination of PRI presidential candidate Luis Donaldo Colosio, and the North American Free Trade Agreement. The PRI capitalized on these events in a huge marketing campaign suggesting that the country needed experience and continuity and not a new political party with no governing experience.

The 2000 presidential election, which we label the election of change, can be considered the apogee of Mexico's democratic transition that started in the late 1970s with the first comprehensive electoral reform. Most recently, the 2006 election pitted the conservatives against the neopopulists, with the PAN representing the right (fiscally and culturally), the PRD representing a pop-ulist left, and the PRI somewhere in the middle and swinging left and right contingent on local conditions. Other researchers saw the 2006 presidential race as an election where voters' percep-tions of the risks associated with the two frontrunners and their personalities were determinants in shaping peoples' vote choice.

Given each party's history, one could anticipate that the PAN would capture the votes of the rich, the winners of the economic model set forth in the late 1980s, while, given the backlash of neoliberal policies in other Latin American countries, it seemed plausible that the PRD would garner the vote of the less affluent voters. Given Mexico's socioeconomic conditions and the numeri-cal superiority of lower-income voters, many believed that the PRD would overwhelmingly win the national presidential election in 2006; however, this did not happen.

In Mexico, at the individual level, many observers have noted that higher-income voters have been, on average, more likely to back the conservative party, as compared to lower-income voters, who tend to support the PRI and the PRD. The question that arises here is whether this pattern holds when we take into account the interaction between individual and state-level incomes. Using exit-poll data from the 1994, 2000, and 2006 presidential elections, we explore this graphically. First we look at the proportion of voters who voted for the PAN given their income, and then we analyze the impact of individual income on the probability of voting for the conservative candidate within richer, middle-income, and poorer states.

Figure 7.3 shows voting by income for the two leading parties— the PAN versus the PRI (in 1994 and 2000) and versus the PRD (in 2006). In the 1994 election, the difference in voting patterns between rich and poor was most dramatic in the poorest parts of the country. The rich voters in the ten poorest states (Chiapas, Oax-aca, Tlaxcala, Zacatecas, Michoacán, Guerrero, Veracruz, Puebla, Hidalgo, and Nayarit) were more likely to vote for the conserva-tive PAN candidate than similar voters residing in the rest of the country. This echoes our finding in the United States of income being more important in poor states.

99

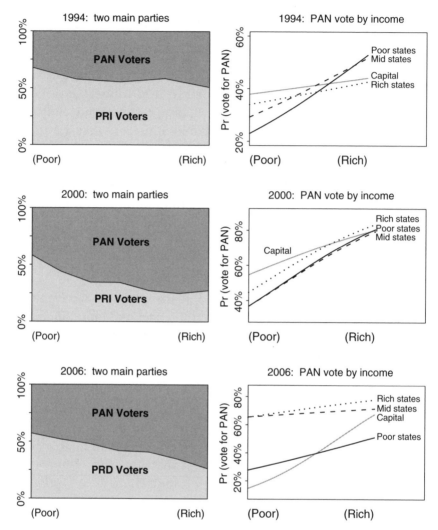

Figure 7.3: Left column: percentage of Mexicans at different income levels who voted for the conservative PAN and its main opposition on the left (the PRI or PRD) in the past three presidential elections. The conservative party consistently does better among richer voters.

Right column: estimated probability of voting for the conservative candidate, as a function of income, in poor, middle-income, and rich states, with the capital (México, D.F.) shown separately. Steeper lines correspond to a stronger relation of income and conservative voting. As in the United States, the difference in voting between high and low incomes tends to be less in richer states.

In 2000—the year when the PRI was ousted from "Los Pinos," the Mexican White House—the rich–poor voting gap was again large in the poor states but was also strong in the capital city. Most recently, in 2006, poor voters residing in the ten poorest states were more likely to vote for the PAN than poor voters residing in the capital. This pattern is reversed, however, at higher levels of income, where rich voters in poor states were less likely to vote for the PAN than their counterparts in the capital.

So what is the impact of income in shaping people's voting predispositions for the conservative party? As in the United States, richer voters are more likely to vote for the conservative party within nearly every state. Economics and geography interacted differently in the different elections. In 1994 and 2000 there was no strong regional divide in the votes for the two leading parties—in 1994 the PRI won all the states, and in 2000 the PRI and the PAN shared an assortment of states all over the country—and income mattered most in the poorer states in these elections. In contrast, the 2006 election showed a strong regional divide (see the bottom map in plate 9), with income mattering more in the poor states and especially the capital but less so in middle-income and rich states. As in the United States, the blue–yellow map and the differences between rich and poor states are not simple aggregates of differences in individual incomes.

INCOME AND VOTING AROUND THE WORLD

> The future has arrived; it's just not evenly distributed.
> —*William Gibson, 2001*

Our next step is to look into income and vote choice in other democracies. Why do poor people regularly vote for conservative parties whose economic and social policies do not seem to directly benefit them? Wouldn't the less affluent be better off by voting for a party that taxes the wealthy and redistributes money to the poor? We begin with an analysis by political scientists John Huber and Piero Stanig of polls from European countries, following their lead and complementing their analysis by including some countries from Asia and Latin America. In each country, we look at the rich–poor difference in the percentage of vote that goes to the conservative party or grouping of parties. As noted by Huber and Stanig, the differences are much higher when comparing rich and poor than when comparing either group to the middle class.

Figure 7.4 shows the rich–poor voting gap in recent elections from thirty-six countries around the world. The pattern between income and vote choice depends on national politics, with larger voting gaps in countries where the left and right parties are more distinct on issues of income redistribution. The difference between rich and poor voters varies greatly from country to country, with electoral support for conservative parties usually but not always positively associated with income. In this sample, conservative parties actually do about as well or better among the poor than the rich in several European countries and in Brazil, Israel, Japan, Hong Kong, and New Zealand. At the other extreme, the rich are most conservative in their voting patterns compared to the poor in Korea, the Czech Republic, Finland, and Peru. The United States is actually one of the more income-polarized countries, with a rich–poor voting difference that is greater than in most of the countries in our database.

The impact of income on voting patterns also can vary by time. For example, in the 1997 Mexican midterm election, the conservative party did better among lower-income voters, but the 2000 election reverted to a more traditional pattern of the poor voting for the party of the left, although with substantial partisan crossover voting in order to oust the PRI from the presidency.

RELIGIOUS ATTENDANCE AND CONSERVATIVE VOTING

Many of the international surveys we have been analyzing ask about religious attendance as well, and so we can mimic the U.S. analyses by studying the pattern of voting by income and religiosity within each country. Figure 7.5 shows the estimated vote for

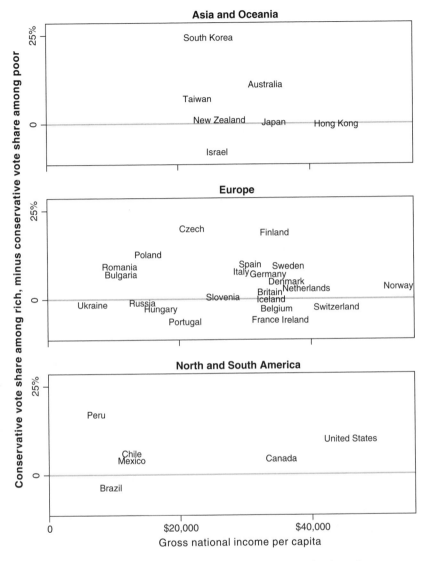

Figure 7.4: Rich–poor gap in vote for conservative parties based on survey data from countries around the world. Income matters in voting more in the United States than in most of the other countries in this dataset. When a country has a high position on one of these graphs, it means that rich people in that country are much more likely than poor people to vote conservative.

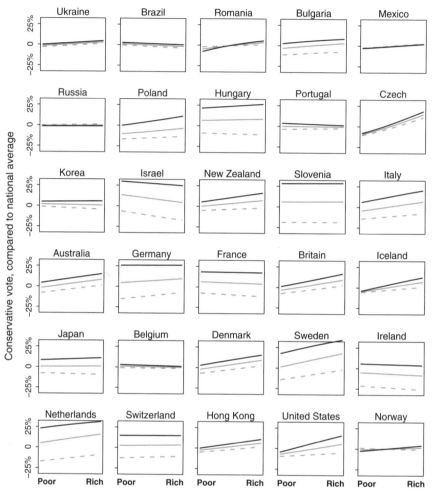

Figure 7.5: For each of thirty countries (gross national income per capita), vote for conservative parties by income and religious attendance. Each plot shows estimates for frequent religious attenders (solid line), occasional attenders (light line), and nonattenders (dotted line). With only a few exceptions, religious and richer people are more likely to vote for conservative parties.

Where the three lines are close to each other (as with Ukraine), there is no difference between how religious and nonreligious people vote. Where the lines are far apart (as in Germany), the religious are much more likely than the secular to vote for conservative parties. The slopes of the lines show the importance of income in voting. Where the three lines fan out (as in the United States), religion matters more for rich than for poor voters.

conservative parties among voters of different levels of income and religious attendance. People who regularly participate in religious services generally vote more conservatively than nonattenders, with some of the strongest religious voting patterns occurring in Slovenia, Israel, Germany, Hungary, Sweden, and the Netherlands. In Mexico, Brazil, Norway, Russia, and several other countries, there is essentially no difference between how the religious and nonreligious vote.

We continue our exploration by studying how income and religiosity together predict voting. On average, the God gap—the difference in conservative voting between religious attenders and nonattenders—is greater among the rich than the poor. This is a pattern we also saw in the United States (see figure 6.10 on page 88).

The prevalence of this pattern suggests that the American experience of religion and voting might be explainable in more general terms. In their article analyzing these data, Huber and Stanig argue that organized religion mediates the relationship between income and vote choice by highlighting a social policy dimension that trumps poor voters' preferences for supporting parties on the left based on concerns of economic redistribution. In other words, poor voters may not vote for the parties on the left, even if they would benefit in the short term from redistributive tax and spending policies, because they may care more about social issues. Huber and Stanig point out that, after accounting for ideological polarization on economic policy between left and right parties, the rich–poor gap in voting in the United States is comparable to that in other advanced democracies.

Religious predispositions play a substantial role not only in shaping people's lives but also in shaping their political orientations and political behavior. Religiosity is not only a good proxy of individuals' ideological orientations but also constitutes an important component of social division in many countries. Religiosity in Roman Catholic nations, for instance, may indicate the degree of voters' integration into the Catholic culture; in contrast, in societies where there is a mixed denominational system, this dimension may represent a secular–religious cleavage. For example, in recent U.S. presidential elections, the Republican Party has appealed to the religious conservative vote by highlighting particular policy issues, such as abortion, that divide religious and secular voters deeply.

The challenge of a comparative analysis is to explain the variation across countries. For example, religious attendance in Britain is only weakly related to voting for the conservatives, but in other northern European democracies such as Norway and Sweden the correlation is stronger, reflecting a stronger link between political parties and controversies over moral and lifestyle issues. In Israel, the strong association between religiosity and voting was consistent with the religious community's support of Benjamin Netanyahu's Likud Party electoral bid.

In Eastern Europe, the impact of religiosity on the probability of voting for the conservative candidate varies considerably, with large differences between high-income religious and secular voters in both Hungary and Poland. In the 1997 Polish election, the right-of-center Solidarity Election Action won a sweeping victory on an anticommunist platform that stressed Catholic values and social doctrine. In contrast, religiosity in the Russian Federation was not associated, positively or negatively, with voting for the economically conservative Union of Right Forces.

THE NORTHEAST IS LIKE EUROPE, THE SOUTH IS LIKE MEXICO

The rich Northeast and West of the United States, along with much of Europe, seem to have moved toward what might be called a postindustrial politics in which supporters of liberal and conservative parties differ more on religion than on income, and politics feels more like a culture war than a class war. Meanwhile, poorer states in the South and middle of the country look more like Mexico, with a more traditional pattern of votes of the rich and poor.

Our international analysis has revealed, first, that Mexico shows regional voting patterns similar to the United States (although with some important geographical differences, some of which are associated with the largest city, Mexico City, being in a middle-income rather than a rich part of the country). Second, we have found that income predicts voting more strongly in America than in many other places. Third, we saw that the United States is far from unique in the importance of religion in voting, consistent with general notions of postmaterialist politics.

Regions are important everywhere. In the United States, the richer states of the Northeast and industrial Midwest have in recent years supported the socially and economically liberal Democratic Party. Regions differ economically and also culturally, thus driving long-lasting political differences. Similarly, in Mexico, cultural and ethnic divides between the north, center, and south of the country coexist with large differences in economic development. Much work remains to study individual, state, and regional voting patterns within other countries to see, for example, if income generally predicts voting in areas within countries that are more exposed to international trade and cosmopolitan influences.

In an increasingly nationalized and globalized world, geography remains important in national voting. The United States is hardly unique in this regard, but in our current politics, we are a country where income matters as much as in many other places around the world. We next consider the ideological dimension—the ways in which Democrats and Republicans differ, not just demographically, but also on their attitudes and positions on issues.

PART III

WHAT IT MEANS

Polarized Parties

> Sometimes I think this country would be better off if we could
> just saw off the Eastern Seaboard and let it float out to sea.
> —*Barry Goldwater, 1961*

> People, I just want to say, you know, can we all get along?
> —*Rodney King, 1992*

THE DISCUSSION of red and blue states is not just about political
strategy—figuring out which states are needed for an electoral college majority—it's also motivated by an active debate, in the press
and in academia, on whether the division on the maps indicates
a fundamental political divide. In a famous poll in 2004, half the
people surveyed thought George W. Bush was a "uniter" and half
thought he was a "divider." Similarly, pundits seem divided as to
whether the United States is polarized. The pattern of income and
voting is important because of what it implies about what the two
parties represent.

Red and blue states come up in political discussion as a symbol
of partisan divisions that strike at America's unity and make the
country harder to govern. Conservatives' jokes about partitioning
the country, and liberals' dreams of joining the blue states with
Canada (see figure 8.1), reflect real frustration about sharing a
country with people who have not only different opinions but also
what seems like an entirely different outlook on life. This in turn
leads to a worry that polarized, negative politics is contributing to
divisive attitudes.

At the same time, polarization serves a useful function insofar as
it makes party brand names meaningful, ultimately making elected
officials more accountable to relatively uninformed voters. Parties
really mean something these days, much more so than they used

Figure 8.1: A map widely circulated on the Internet immediately after the 2004 election emphasizing the geographic contiguity of the states that went for Bush and Kerry.

to. Our goal is not to label polarization as good or bad, but to assess whether it truly has been increasing.

One way to measure partisan polarization is by using so-called feeling thermometer survey questions in which people are asked how they view each of the major political parties on a 0–100 scale. As figure 8.2 shows, since the 1970s, attitudes have diverged: Republican voters have taken an increasingly negative view of the Democratic Party, and Democrats likewise think less of Republicans.

Our next steps are to see how Democratic and Republican voters differ on specific issues and to see how well represented their views are in Congress. Is it the voters who are polarized, the politicians, or both? But first we step back and consider what people mean when they talk about polarization. How can we measure the political divisions in our society?

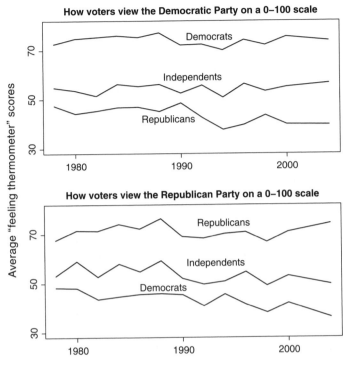

Figure 8.2: Feelings (on a 0–100 scale) about the Democratic and Republican parties over the past thirty years from the perspective of the average self-declared Democrat, independent, and Republican. Unsurprisingly, Democrats prefer Democrats and Republicans prefer Republicans (with independents in the middle). What is interesting is that the gap between partisans has widened, with Americans on each side having an increasingly negative view of the other party.

DIFFERENT FLAVORS OF POLARIZATION

Social scientists who study American political elites have generally concluded that politicians have become substantially more ideologically polarized over time. But what does this polarization consist of? The term conflates three complementary, but conceptually distinct, notions.

First, there is *partisan polarization*. This refers to a sorting by which ideologues find a political home in one of the two major parties in the United States. In the past, conservative southern Democrats and liberal northeastern Republicans were commonplace, but nowadays, conservatives typically call themselves Republicans and liberals Democrats. One consequence is that partisans have increasingly negative views about the opposition party, as can be seen in figure 8.2.

A second form of polarization is *opinion radicalization*, in which people gravitate away from the political center toward more extreme positions on issues. That is, on any given issue, people could come to hold more diverse opinions.

A third form of polarization is *issue alignment*. To what degree are issue positions correlated with each other, or, equivalently, what constraints exist on the freedom with which people come to a set of beliefs about controversial issues? The more that issue positions correlate with each other, the more we can say that liberals and conservatives are in opposite camps. In contrast, if issue positions are uncorrelated, a set of cross-cutting cleavages exist, and divisions are less clear.

These three aspects of polarization can, at least in theory, combine in different ways. People could be highly polarized on individual issues or correlated on groups of issues, but with meaningless partisan labels. Conversely, partisans can be in strong disagreement in total without having extreme positions on particular issues, so that if we could aggregate each person's ideological position into a single measure, people would be further apart than ever before.

INCREASING PARTISAN DISAGREEMENT

Democratic and Republican voters differ sharply on particular issues as well, most dramatically in foreign policy, an area where the two parties have always differed but not like they do today. By 2006, the Iraq War was supported by 80% of Republicans and only 20% of Democrats, a widening of a partisan gap that had already been large when the war began in 2003; see figure 8.3.

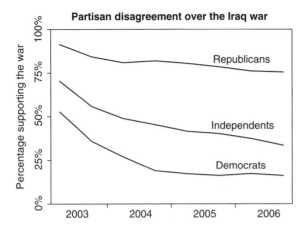

Figure 8.3: Trends in support for the Iraq War by party. Republicans have consistently supported the war much more than Democrats.

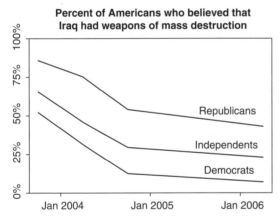

Figure 8.4: Belief that Iraq had weapons of mass destruction. Differences between partisans remained large; by 2006, nearly half of Republicans but nearly no Democrats answered "Yes" to the survey question.

Some of this discrepancy can be tracked down to disagreement over the underlying facts, with nearly half of Republicans but almost no Democrats thinking that Iraq had weapons of mass destruction; see figure 8.4. Asking the question in different ways gives similar results. For example, in March 2006, nearly 40% of

Republicans agreed with the statement, "most experts agree that Iraq had weapons of mass destruction," over 30% believed there was "clear evidence" that Iraq had weapons of mass destruction, and nearly 30% believed that the United States had found such weapons, with very few Democrats assenting.

Thirty to sixty years ago, Americans were divided on many issues, but the divisions cut across, rather than along, partisan lines. For example, the Vietnam War was controversial as early as 1965, when only about 60% of Americans supported the war, and before long, this level fell to less than a third; see figure 8.5. But what is most striking from a modern perspective is how little difference there was between partisans. True, Democrats supported the war more when Lyndon Johnson was in power and Republicans supported the war more when Richard Nixon was in power, but overall the differences between parties were small. Partisan disagreements over the Korean war were larger, especially by the end of Truman's term in office, but still much less than with Iraq.

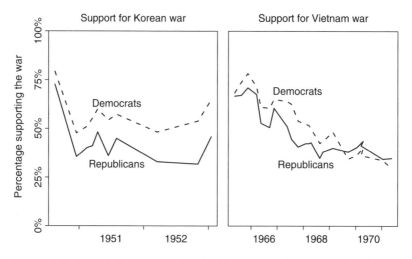

Figure 8.5: Trends in support for the Korean and Vietnam Wars, by party. There is a clear pattern of more support for the war among the president's party (the Democrats in Korea, and Vietnam through 1968; the Republicans in Vietnam starting in 1969), but partisan differences are much smaller than for Iraq (compare to figure 8.3).

Even objective features of the economy are viewed through partisan filters. For example, a survey was conducted in 1988, at the end of Ronald Reagan's second term, asking various questions about the government and economic conditions, including, "Would you say that compared to 1980, inflation has gotten better, stayed about the same, or gotten worse?" Amazingly, over half of the self-identified strong Democrats in the survey said that inflation had gotten worse and only 8% thought it had gotten much better, even though the actual inflation rate dropped from 13% to 4% during Reagan's eight years in office.

The concern—and it is a real one—is that ideology has become so strong that it is currently impossible for opposing sides to have a reasoned discussion or even agree on a common set of underlying facts about the world, leading ultimately to policies supported by 50%-plus-one of the voters and considered illegitimate by the other half.

POLARIZATION ON SOCIAL ISSUES

> In every society, the definition of marriage has not ever to my knowledge included homosexuality. That's not to pick on homosexuality. It's not, you know, man on child, man on dog, or whatever the case may be.
> —Rick Santorum, U.S. Senator from Pennsylvania, 2003

Some of the most striking examples of partisan alignment are on moral issues, as have been found by political scientists Joseph Bafumi and Robert Shapiro. Figure 8.6 shows how attitudes on abortion have diverged between liberals and conservatives and especially between Democrats and Republicans. But we can't tell the extent to which people have been switching parties or changing their opinions on abortion, or both.

Polarization as a perceptual screen on reality appears ubiquitous. We can see an example of this in a recent survey on 9/11 conspiracy theories. One prominent conspiracy theory about the attacks centers around the claim that President Bush knew about

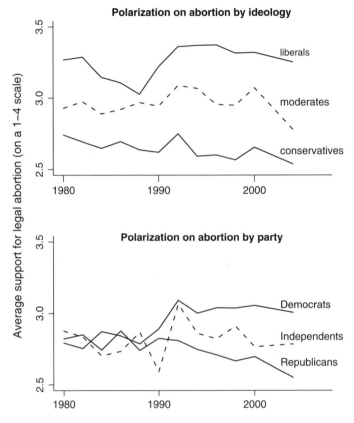

Figure 8.6: Attitudes on abortion for the past twenty-five years among self-identified liberals, moderates, and conservatives and Democrats, independents, and Republicans. The partisans separated in 1992 and have been moving further apart ever since.

the attacks in advance. This conspiracy comes in the form that Bush either planned the attacks himself or was too incompetent to do anything about them despite his knowledge of their imminence. Respected commentators of all political stripes have categorically rejected this theory. But what about the public? Republicans in the survey rejected the idea that President Bush knew about the attacks in advance by a 7-1 margin. On the other hand, Democrats were close to evenly split on the question.

The country is divided geographically as well as by party. For example, Edward Glaeser and Bryce Ward note that in 2004, "twenty-three percent of respondents in Oregon, Washington and California thought that Saddam Hussein was personally involved in the September 11, 2001, attacks. Forty-seven percent of respondents in Texas, Oklahoma and Arkansas had that view." Glaeser and Ward also report that "56 percent of Mississippi residents think that AIDS is God's punishment for immoral sexual behavior. Only 16 percent of Rhode Island residents share that view."

Looking back a few years, racial integration and specific policies such as school busing and affirmative action have been wedge issues splitting the Democratic Party. Racial issues became increasingly central in twentieth-century American partisan politics after it was clear that the Democratic Party, minus its old southern wing, had become the civil rights party. Disputes in this area have generally shifted to concerns such as welfare and immigration policy, which, like race, have both social and economic dimensions in American politics. On racial issues specifically, survey data show increasing divergence over the past twenty years between conservatives and liberals and between Republicans and Democrats on questions such as whether government intervention is the most appropriate way to ensure equal treatment between blacks and whites.

THE STUBBORN AMERICAN VOTER

> Excess partisanship literally inhibits Americans from processing information that challenges their biases.
> —*Carl Cannon, White House correspondent for the* National Journal, *2006*

The Democratic and Republican parties in Congress have moved apart in their voting patterns, and so it is perhaps not surprising that voters have diverged in their perceptions of the parties. Views about Iraq are strikingly partisan—especially compared to foreign-policy attitudes during the Korean and Vietnam Wars—but one might attribute these differences to particular characteristics of the wars. Large numbers of troops were first sent into Korea by Truman and to Vietnam by Kennedy and Johnson, whereas Iraq has so far been solely a Republican affair, without the high American death toll of the previous wars. Beyond this, the Iraq War revolved around specific, hard-to-verify claims about Saddam Hussein's threat to the world, whereas Korea and Vietnam fit more smoothly into existing Cold War ideology. Divergence on social issues is also interesting but perhaps merely reflects a shift of attention rather than any fundamental change in the meaning of partisanship.

It makes sense to explore the idea of polarization further by looking at attitudes about the economy, which is generally agreed to be the area most important to people when evaluating politicians and when voting. Here we have found no historical trends in the basic questions on taxes, government spending, and economic welfare: self-declared liberal and conservative voters (or Democrats and Republicans) differ strongly on these issues and have remained in disagreement for decades.

Where we do see changes is in perceptions, of both the national economy and personal finances. Voters are less willing to vote based on past performance but more willing to offer evaluations that, even if inaccurate, fit their partisan predispositions and voting choices. The evidence we present shows that Americans tend to rationalize the state of their personal financial situation over the previous year. They seek to bring their voting preferences and their view of their personal financial situation in sync.

Bafumi finds that two sources of survey data support the claim that voters are influenced by their political attitudes when assessing the economy. First, look at the National Election Study from 1956 to 2004, for each year predicting individuals' views of the economy from partisanship and the party of the incumbent president. Indeed, voters of the administration's party tend to view the economy more positively, with this pattern increasing in recent decades.

Supporters of the opposition party were most likely to say that their personal financial situation stayed the same. This response serves as a way station for respondents whose situation may have improved but who are unwilling to admit to it given their dislike for the incumbent administration. Slightly more respondents were likely to say that their financial situation had improved rather than worsened, but with a difference of only about 5%. In contrast, members of the president's party were much more upbeat about their personal finances, being more likely to say that things had improved and much less likely to say that they had worsened.

Through 1980, people who supported the president's party were nearly 10% more likely to say their situation had improved as compared to those in the opposition party. Since 1984, partisan differences in economic perceptions have been much larger. This could represent an increasing level of bias and misperception (as indicated by the confusion about economic conditions during the 1980s, as noted on page 117) and also perhaps an increasing ability of administrations to deliver economic rewards to their partisan supporters.

To assess more directly the distinction between perception and reality, Bafumi turned to two sets of National Election Studies, 1972–1974–1976 and 1992–1994–1996, in which people were followed up and surveyed three times about their political attitudes and financial situation.

In 1972, Richard Nixon was running for reelection. In that year, the survey found income growth to be associated with a higher propensity to say one's financial situation had improved. Respondents were relying on real, objective retrospection to inform their responses. Closeness to the president's party had no significant impact: there was no evidence that people's responses were distorted by their political positions. In 1992, another Republican incumbent president was seeking reelection, but the story was the reverse. Members of the president's party were more likely to say their financial situation had improved as compared to partisans at the opposite end of the scale, but actual income growth was not strongly associated with reported financial situation. There is no evidence for retrospective thinking in 1992 but strong evidence for rationalization.

The waves of interviewing in 1976 and 1996 tell much the same story. Party was not a significant predictor of one's personal financial situation in 1976, while income growth neared statistical significance at traditional levels. In 1996, party affiliation was a strong predictor: the incumbent president was a Democrat, and as respondents became more Republican in 1996, they were less likely to say their financial situation had improved. In addition, respondents' income growth did not predict their views of their personal financial situations in 1996.

Rather than voting on their objective retrospective evaluation of the economy, voters now seem to be deciding how to vote first and then generating a biased retrospective evaluation second, one that accords with their predetermined partisan allegiance. This in turn may be a product of the relatively mild economic conditions of the past twenty years. A sharp recession could at some point push people back toward more objective perceptions of the economy.

POLARIZATION IN CONGRESS AND AMONG VOTERS

> I didn't leave the Democratic Party. The party left me.
> —*Ronald Reagan, 1962*

> Each political party has marginalized the political center,
> because they feel that all they have to do is energize their base.
> It's a political strategy. Before, you know, when I was in politics,
> it was a matter of both parties competing for the center,
> competing for the independents. That is gone now.
> —*John Danforth, former U.S. senator from Missouri, 2006*

Parties are indeed more polarized, at least when measured by the way Democrats and Republicans vote in Congress. This is evident using the left–right voting scores developed by political scientists Keith Poole, Howard Rosenthal, and Nolan McCarty based on congressional roll-call votes. These scores are similar to the ratings of interest groups such as the Americans for Democratic Action and the American Conservative Union but have the advantage of being based on all the votes in each congressional session (rather than

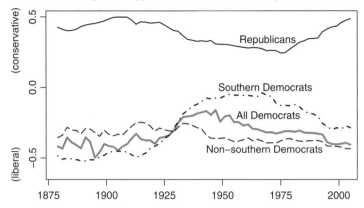

Figure 8.7: Graph from Nolan McCarty, Keith Poole, and Howard Rosenthal of the average positions of Republican and Democratic congressmembers, on a liberal–conservative scale, for each session of Congress since the end of Reconstruction. Democrats are further divided into those from the South and the rest of the country. The parties gradually moved closer together from 1900 to 1950, stayed at a constant distance apart until 1975, and have diverged sharply during the past thirty years. Trends for the U.S. Senate are similar.

just a select few) and can easily be extended backward in time to make historical comparisons.

When Poole, Rosenthal, and McCarty examined congressmembers' ideological scores over the past century and a half, they found that the Republican Party has consistently been more conservative and the Democrats more liberal on the main left–right dimension of legislative voting, but with major changes over time. Figure 8.7 displays the results for the House of Representatives; the Senate shows similar trends. In the first half of the twentieth century, the two parties moved closer, reaching a minimum distance in the period of economic expansion from the end of World War II to the recession of the mid-1970s. This is the thirty-year period that economists Claudia Goldin and Robert Margo have called the Great Compression, when the country was near full employment and the income gap between rich and poor declined. In his recent book, Paul Krugman associated the Great

Compression with bipartisan consensus on economic policy. (As Richard Nixon said when implementing wage and price controls, "We are all Keynesians now.")

Starting in the 1970s, however, there has been a change, with congressional Democrats moving in the liberal direction and Republicans becoming much more conservative. This has occurred not so much from individual congressmembers changing their ideologies as by replacement due to political and geographic realignment. Moderate Democrats, especially in the South, have retired or were defeated and replaced with conservative Republicans, and, to a lesser extent, moderate Republicans have been replaced by more liberal Democrats. (And a few politicians, such as Texas Congressman, then Senator, Phil Gramm, kept their ideologies but switched parties.) The result is that the two parties overlapped less in their voting patterns. From the 1950s period of domestic consensus on an enlarged American welfare state (compared to the pre–New Deal era) and a Cold War consensus on foreign policy, we have moved to today's more ideologically coherent political parties at the elite and activist level.

How does the American public fit into this? We present here some of the results of a research project in collaboration with political scientist Michael Herron, placing voters and their representatives on a common ideological scale. Just as legislators' positions can be identified using their votes on controversial issues, we can estimate the ideologies of individual voters by surveying them and asking how they would themselves vote on these same issues. We used responses on about forty different topics, including tax cuts, the minimum wage, abortion, stem cell research, immigration, trade, gun control, the environment, and foreign policy, to get a sense of people's ideological leanings relative to their representatives.

When we put voters and congressmembers on the same scale, as shown in figure 8.8, we find that the median American voter was well represented by Senate and House medians after the 2006 midterm elections. Looking at the distributions as a whole, we find that congressmembers tend to be more extreme than voters. Voters are fairly represented on average, but centrists are

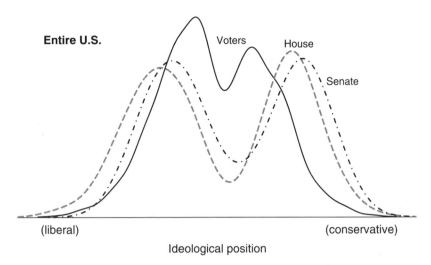

Entire U.S. Voters House

Senate

(liberal) (conservative)

Ideological position

Figure 8.8: Michael Herron's estimate of ideological positions of voters (solid line) and congressmembers (dashed lines) after the 2006 midterm elections, on a common left–right scale. The median position of the voters is not far from the medians of the House of Representatives and the Senate, but the distributions are clearly different, with voters in general being closer to the center and congressmembers being more extreme (Democrats on the left and Republicans on the right).

few in the House and the Senate. The polarization on issues that has occurred in the electorate is not as strong as the divergence between the two parties in Congress. The relatively extreme ideologies of congressmembers—to be more precise, their consistency in issue positions—should not be a surprise because elected representatives are constrained by their political parties, interest groups, and funders in a way that voters are not. In between voters and politicians are political activists, who tend to have ideological positions that are more extreme (that is, internally consistent) positions than the general population but less coherent than those of officeholders.

Evidence for trends in polarization can be seen in political behavior. As shown in figure 8.9, split-ticket voting was rare in the 1950s and 1960s, with only about 15% of voters pulling the lever for a Republican for president and a Democrat for Congress,

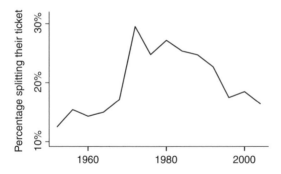

Figure 8.9: Split-ticket voting: for each election year, the percentage of voters who voted for a Republican for president and a Democrat for Congress, or vice versa. Ticket-splitting increased during the era of party disaffiliation in the 1970s and 1980s but has recently been returning to lower levels as voters have become more polarized.

or vice versa. Candidates ranging from the broadly popular Eisenhower to the polarizing Goldwater did not induce many voters to split their tickets. Then, in the less partisan era of the 1970s and 1980s, ticket-splitting jumped to over 25% of all ballots. More recently, party identification has become stronger and split-ticket voting more rare, nearly returning to its low point fifty years earlier. This trend is not in itself conclusive evidence of polarization—split-ticket voting can be motivated by views of the roles of Congress and the president—but it is consistent with the other signs we have discussed of partisan divergence on individual attitudes and in perceptions of the parties.

Similar trends have occurred with self-reported political ideology and party identification: the number of voters describing themselves as purely independent (not even leaning toward the Democrats or Republicans) was below 10% in the 1950s, peaked near 15% in the 1970s, and since then has declined to less than 10%. Also during these past thirty years, political ideology has become much more strongly associated with partisanship, with self-described liberal voters leaving the Republican Party and conservatives leaving the Democratic Party.

Another way to see the importance of party cues is to break out the data for each election year, analyzing individual vote choice from party identification and several demographic variables (sex, race, age, education, religion, and income). When we do this, we find that the effect of party identification was fairly high in the 1950s, declined in the 1970s and 1980s, and then has increased dramatically since the 1990s, tracking other measures of the return of partisanship.

ISSUE ATTITUDES, IDEOLOGY, AND PARTISANSHIP

> The pundits like to slice-and-dice our country into red states and blue states: red states for Republicans, blue states for Democrats. But I've got news for them, too. We worship an awesome God in the blue states, and we don't like federal agents poking around in our libraries in the red states. We coach little league in the blue states and, yes, we've got some gay friends in the red states. There are patriots who opposed the war in Iraq, and patriots who supported the war in Iraq.
> —*Barack Obama, Democratic National Convention, 2004*

Although Americans have become increasingly polarized in their impressions of the Democratic and Republican parties (see, for example, figure 8.2), each person maintains a mix of attitudes within himself or herself. For instance, 40% of Americans in a 2004 survey were self-declared Republicans, but only 23% identified themselves as both Republican and conservative. Almost half of Republicans do not describe themselves as being ideologically conservative. If we also consider issue preferences, the constraint of people's political preferences looks even weaker. Only 6% of respondents are Republicans who think of themselves as conservatives, oppose abortion, and have conservative views on affirmative action and health policy. Fully 85% of self-declared Republicans are nonconservative or take a nonconservative stand on at least one of these three traditional issues.

A similar picture emerges if we look at Democrats. In this case, of the 49% self-declared Democrats in the sample, only 36% call themselves liberals. Overall, almost 90% of Democrats are non-liberal or have nonliberal views on abortion, affirmative action, or health policy. These numbers should not be surprising, given that in general, the correlation between party identification or ideology and opinion on political issues is low. Knowing somebody's political identification increases our chances of guessing his or her issue preferences, but not by much. This supports David Brooks's notion of red and blue America as cultural constructs rather than bundles of issue positions.

The preceding analyses consider five positions (party, ideology, and three issues): if each were determined by a simple coin flip, there would be about 3% of the population (more precisely, 1 in 32), in each of the pure categories; instead, we see about 6% for each: more than would be expected by pure randomness, but far less than if attitudes on the different positions were perfectly correlated.

The picture does not change if we look at correlations among issue preferences alone. For example, consider opinions on health insurance and abortion. Overall, 46% of respondents favored government support for health insurance. Among the people who supported abortion, 51% supported government health insurance. Similarly, 55% of respondents support abortion. Among those supporting health insurance, 62% were also in favor of abortion.

Political polarization is commonly measured using the variation of responses on individual issues. By this measure, research has shown that—despite many commentators' concerns about increased polarization—Americans' attitudes have become no more variable in recent decades. What has changed in the electorate is its level of partisanship.

At the elite level, American political history shows that all three kinds of polarization—partisan polarization, opinion radicalization, and issue alignment—have been happening. Officeholders at both the federal and state levels are better sorted in terms of partisan polarization. They are also more distant from each other along the dominant left–right ideological dimension. Finally, political scientists have found that one, or at most two, dimensions explain most of the ideological differences in Congress.

So far, so good, for elites. What about the public at large? Are voters more polarized than ever before? We find a more complex story here. The public has, over the past few decades, definitely become more sorted into partisan labels. Still, the absolute level of this partisan polarization of the electorate is relatively small compared to that of professional politicians. This makes sense, given that most people like to spend their time thinking about things other than political philosophy.

On the other hand, we find that Americans as a whole have not become substantially more polarized on the issues. First, they have not typically moved away from each other on any given issue. Morris Fiorina, in his book *Culture War?*, provides plenty of evidence for this. Second, thanks to our own research, we know that the correlation of issue positions is still low, and thus the implicit complexity high, among the general population.

However, this pattern is different among one important subgroup of the American population. Americans who are wealthier look more like politicians in terms of the ideological consistency of their beliefs, matching what we would expect to see among political activists. The same is not true for those with college degrees as opposed to those without. Nor is it true for southerners versus non-southerners, or religiously observant people versus nonobservant people.

Among ordinary Americans, it is true that ideologues are better sorted into Democratic or Republican camps. But those camps are big and not very constraining. The electorate is made up of all sorts of people—liberals, moderates, conservatives, and those difficult to classify with well-known labels—and they don't seem to be narrowing into extremely coherent ideologies. Hard-core partisans and the wealthy, however, are beginning to look more like the political elites that control the levers of government, rather than regular Americans. And the polarization that pundits decry has definitely occurred among those elites.

RED AMERICA AND BLUE AMERICA

> While most Americans are moderate in their political views,
> there are sharp divisions between supporters of the two major
> parties that extend far beyond a narrow sliver of elected officials
> and activists. Red state voters and blue state voters differ fairly
> dramatically in their social characteristics and political beliefs.
> —*Alan Abramowitz and Kyle Saunders, 2005*

The partisan divisions implied by the red–blue map are real. Figure 8.10 shows the distribution of political ideologies of voters and congressmembers in Republican, battleground, and Democratic states, as estimated from a combination of roll-call and opinion-poll data. Voters in Republican and Democratic states are slightly more conservative and liberal, respectively, on the issues. Elected representatives are more geographically polarized: winner-take-all elections generally magnify differences that are already there. In a strongly Democratic-leaning state, it is likely that both senators will be Democrats and will be on the left side of the political spectrum. Such a state will also typically have many strongly Democratic congressional districts. The reverse pattern holds in Republican states.

Voters are polarized in different ways within different states. One way to see this is to compare states in terms of average level of religious observance. As discussed at the beginning of chapter 6, Americans as a whole are strikingly observant (especially compared to people in other industrialized countries), but states vary widely in this respect, with much higher church attendance in Mississippi and elsewhere in the deep South compared to states such as New Hampshire, Vermont, and Nevada.

We use survey data to study polarization—comparing the differences in voting patterns between Democratic and Republican identifiers, rich and poor, and religious and secular—within each state. Plate 8 summarizes what we found. In less religious states, which tend to be richer as well, voters are strongly divided along party lines. But in more religious states, party differences are weaker: Democrats are still more liberal than Republicans, but not by so much.

2004 election

Plate 1. States won by George Bush (in red) and John Kerry (in blue) in 2004.

1976 election

Plate 2. States won by Gerald Ford (in red) and Jimmy Carter (in blue) in 1976.

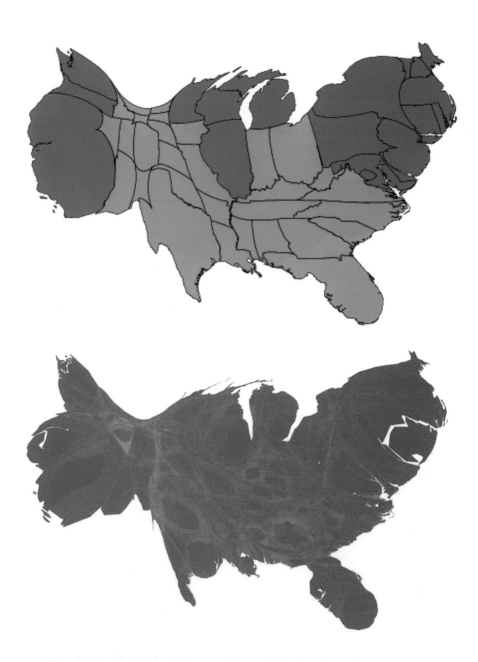

Plate 6. Maps by Michael Gastner, Cosma Shalizi, and Mark Newman, distorted so that areas are proportional to population. Top map colors states red (for Bush) or blue (for Kerry); bottom map colors counties using different shades of purple.

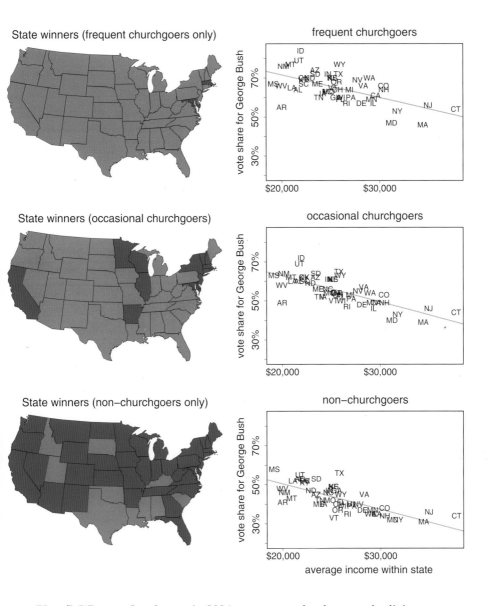

Plate 7. Winner of each state in 2004 among people who attend religious services at least once per week, occasionally, and never, as estimated by a model fit to exit polls. The maps show the basic picture (red for Bush, blue for Kerry); the scatterplots show more detail. The ranking of states' votes is about the same within each religious category (which is not true when breaking down vote by income; compare to the maps of high-income, middle-income, and poor voters in plate 3).

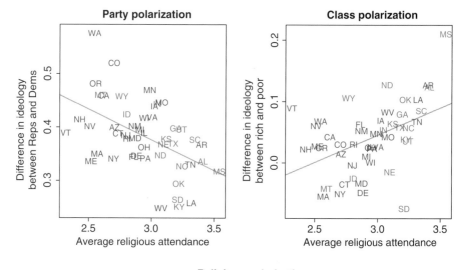

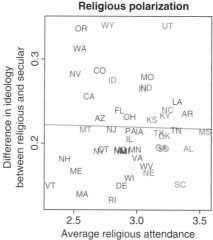

Plate 8. Three different state-level measures of ideological polarization plotted versus state-level religiosity. The left graph shows the difference in self-reported liberal–conservative ideology, comparing the average Republican to the average Democrat in the state. The center graph shows the difference in ideology, comparing the average high- and low-income voters in the state. The right graph displays the difference in average ideology, comparing weekly religious service attenders to nonattenders.

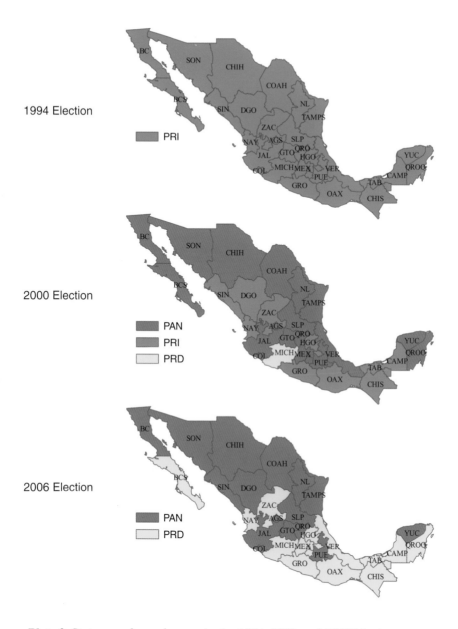

Plate 9. States won by each party in the 1994, 2000, and 2006 Mexican presidential elections. Green represents the former ruling party, the PRI; yellow indicates the leftist PRD party; and blue represents the rightist PAN party. The PAN is strongest in the rich northern part of the country, while the PRD does best in Mexico City and the poorer states in the center and south.

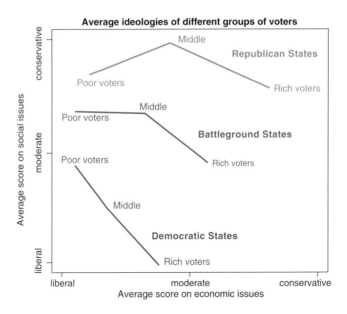

Plate 10. Average attitude scores on social and economic issues among high-, middle-, and low-income Americans, looking separately at solid Republican (red), battleground (purple), and solid Democratic (blue) states. Rich people tend to be more conservative on economic issues (especially in Republican states) and more liberal on social issues (especially in Democratic states).

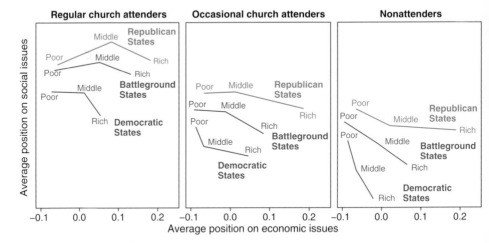

Plate 11. Average attitude scores on social and economic issues among high-, middle-, and low-income Americans, looking separately at regular church attenders, occasional attenders, and nonattenders, in solid Republican (red), battleground (purple), and solid Democratic (blue) states. These graphs show the data from plate 10, broken down by religious attendance. The difference between red and blue states is consistently largest among high-income voters.

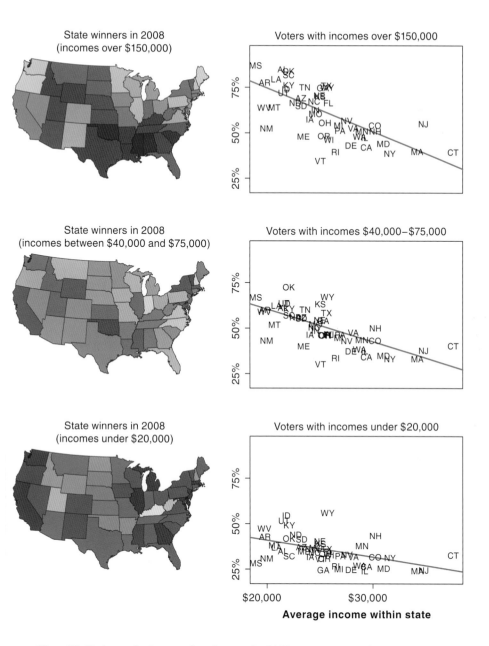

Plate 12. Estimated winner of each state in 2008 among upper-income, middle-income, or lower-income voters. Lighter shadings of red or blue represent states where the split was closer to 50–50. There were big differences in the voting patterns in rich and poor states among rich voters but not among poor voters.

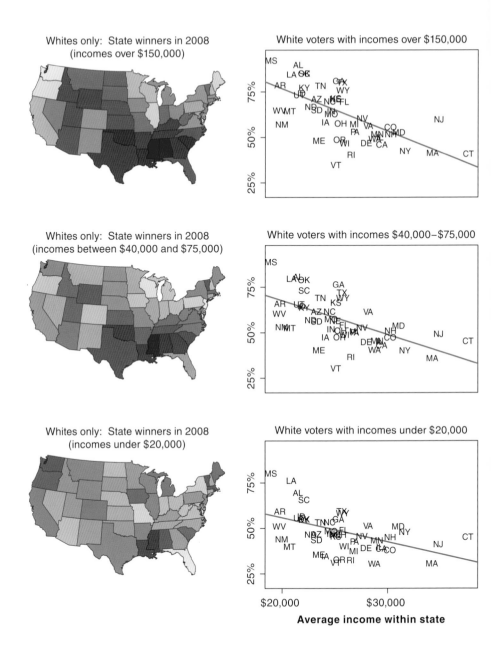

Plate 13. Estimated winner of each state in 2008 among white voters only. Lighter shadings of red or blue represent states where the split was closer to 50–50.

Obama's vote share among nonblacks varied by region

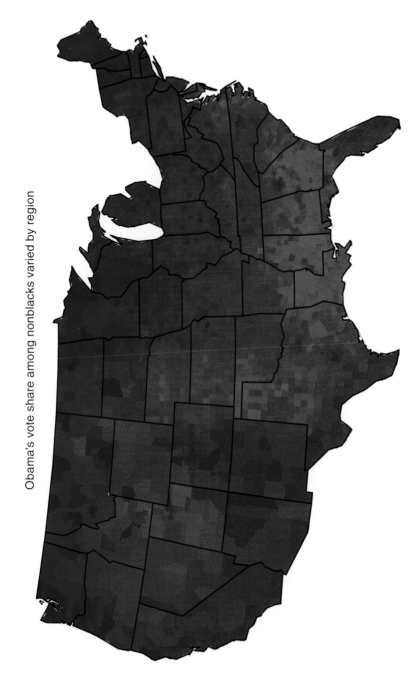

Plate 14. Obama's estimated vote share among nonblacks, by county. Map created by Ben Lauderdale.

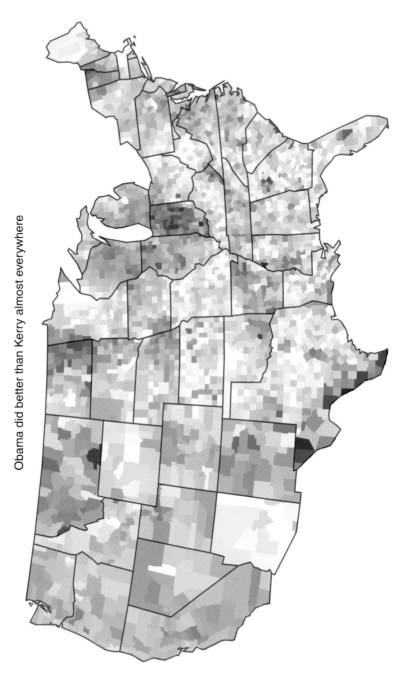

Obama did better than Kerry almost everywhere

Plate 15. County-level map of the difference between Obama's vote share in 2008 and Kerry's share in 2004. Blue and red colors indicate counties where Obama did better and worse, respectively, than Kerry. Obama outperformed Kerry everywhere except in a strip of counties in the South. Map created by Ben Lauderdale.

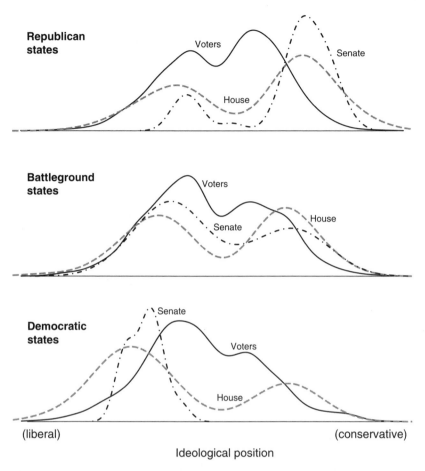

Figure 8.10: Estimated distributions of ideologies of voters (solid lines) and the House of Representatives and Senate (dashed lines) within strongly Republican, battleground, and strongly Democratic states. Voters are slightly more conservative in Republican states and liberal in Democratic states, but the differences in the House and, especially, the Senate, are much larger. Taking national averages, Congress represents the voters reasonably well, but the division between red and blue states is much more dramatic in the legislature than among the voters.

Conversely, class divisions are larger in religious states. There, lower-income voters are more liberal than upper-income voters (although still not as different as Democrats and Republicans). In contrast, rich and poor voters in less religious states do not differ much in their overall ideological orientations. Higher-income voters in blue states tend to be more conservative on economic issues but more liberal on social issues, compared to poor voters in these states. Finally, states vary in their amount of religious polarization—the extent to which regular churchgoers are more likely to be conservative—but this pattern is not consistently stronger in religious or nonreligious states.

Much of the difference between red and blue America can be explained by the two parties finding coherent positions across many issues. In turn, this helps to explain how the national political map can change, with traditionally conservative voters in Connecticut, for example, switching to the Democrats because of cultural issues and voters in working-class strongholds such as West Virginia going in the opposite direction.

Figure 8.11 shows trends in correlations of issue attitudes with partisanship and ideology and with each other over the past thirty-five years, tracking changes separately in rich and poor states and separately considering issues in the economic, civil rights, moral, and foreign-policy domains.

Issues have become more strongly tied to political party, with the strongest trends being economic issues in poor states—they have long been correlated with party identification in rich states—and civil rights and moral issues in both rich and poor states. Moral issues have also become increasingly correlated with liberal–conservative ideology and with each other, now reaching a coherence comparable to that of economic and civil rights issues. Americans' views are least predictable on general foreign policy.

Democrats and Republicans have moved apart on individual issues, and we attribute this to a divergence between the positions of the elected officeholders of the parties, followed by a sorting of voters. The result of this sorting is some increased ideological consistency of voters—polarization in Congress has affected voters' positions. Nonetheless, Americans—especially those at the low end of income, education, and interest and participation in politics—remain complex in their opinions, often showing incompatibility with clear left–right opinion clusters. Divisions between red and blue America are increasingly ideological. But, distinctions between parties are more important in rich states, and class differences are more important in poor states. We are still far from having consistent national political divisions.

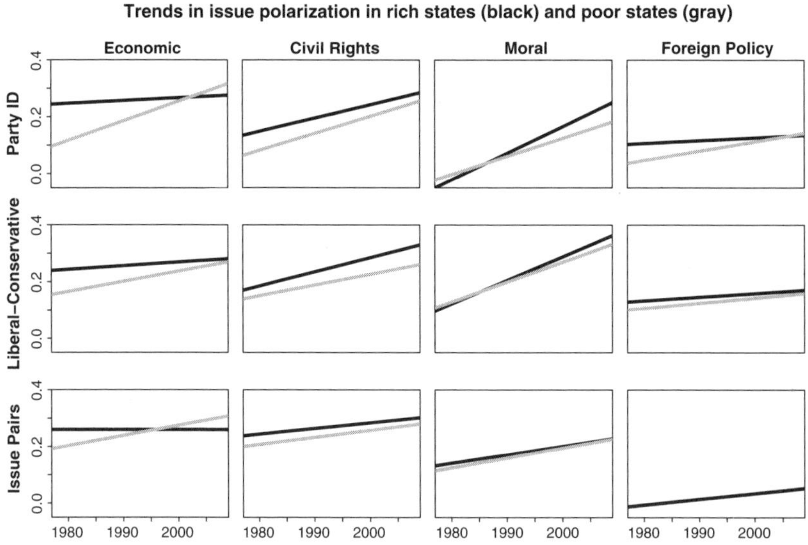

Trends in issue polarization in rich states (black) and poor states (gray)

Figure 8.11: Trends in issue partisanship and alignment, comparing rich and poor states in each year. Each box compares the correlation trends in an issue domain for two mutually exclusive subgroups. In each column, the first row reports the model issues interacted with party identification, the second issues interacted with liberal–conservative ideology, and the third is the model for issue pairs. x-axis=time (1972–2004); y-axis=correlation (−5% to 40%). Black and gray lines show the estimates in high- and low-income states, respectively.

The increasing slopes of the lines in the top row of graphs indicate that party identification has become increasingly associated with specific attitudes, most notably with economic issues in poor states and civil rights and moral issues everywhere. The increasing slopes in the second row reveal similar trends in correlation with liberal–conservative self-positioning. Finally, the increasing but gently sloping lines in the third row reveal that attitudes on individual issues have become only slightly more tied together.

YOUR FRIENDS AND NEIGHBORS

> The divisions are so great that we have two parallel universes,
> the red and blue states, in which people speak to those who are
> like-minded, thus reinforcing their divisions.
> —*John Kenneth White, Catholic University of America, 2005*

Social networks are indeed politically segregated—surveys find
Democrats are more likely to know more Democrats and Republicans more likely to know more Republicans—but it is difficult to
know how much is from geography (red or blue states, regions,
neighborhoods, and workplaces) and the extent to which polarized social networks cause, or are the product of, polarization in
attitudes.

One source of information on polarization in political networks
is the 2000 National Election Study, which asked each respondent
to give details on up to four people with whom he or she discussed
important political matters. On average, people named 1.9 others,
of whom about one-quarter were family members. Democrats and
people living in Democratic states named more Democrats, and
similarly for Republicans. The respondent's personal party identification was a stronger predictor than the party composition of his
or her state; see figure 8.12.

More recently, we put questions on another national study, the
2006 General Social Survey, asking people how many Democrats
and Republicans they know, how many they trust, and whether
most of the people they trust are Democrats, Republicans, or
roughly equal amounts of each. Again, people tend to know and
trust more people of their party, and this is especially true of people
who live in states where they are in the majority.

These results are hardly shocking, and it is difficult to use them
to assess time trends, but they are consistent with the partisan
polarization that we have seen in attitudes and with studies of the
atomization of American society such as Robert Putnam's *Bowling Alone,* in that case focusing on the political implications of
people socializing across a narrower range of society, with less
direct exposure to diverse points of view.

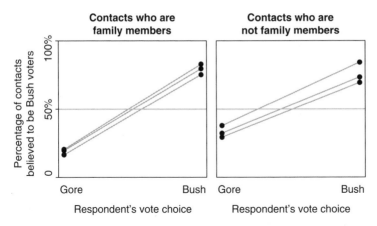

Figure 8.12: From a survey of voters in the 2000 election, the estimated percentage of people they talk politics with who supported Bush for president. Each respondent was asked to name up to four contacts. On average, each respondent discussed politics with 0.5 family members and 1.4 others. The two plots show separate estimates for the two groups. The top, middle, and bottom lines on each plot show the results for Gore and Bush voters in strongly Republican, battleground, and strongly Democratic states, respectively.

Unsurprisingly, Gore voters were much more likely to know Gore voters and the reverse for Bush voters. The differences between red, blue, and purple states are tiny among family members (about three-quarters of whom share the political affiliation of the survey respondent) but are larger for friends. On average, Bush voters perceived their nonfamily conversation partners to be more similar to themselves compared to the perceptions of Gore voters.

Moderate Voters in a Polarized World

> Most Americans are ideological moderates on both economic and moral issues ... Over the course of the twentieth century—a period of impressive economic and cultural convergence—we have not seen a great political chasm opening between the states, but rather a noteworthy political convergence.
> —*Stephen Ansolabehere, Jonathan Rodden, and James Snyder, 2006*

Can the differences between red and blue states be explained by income levels and attitudes on social issues?

135

The superficially intuitive story of political polarization is that voters are moving apart, maybe not on economic issues but in cultural values. As we noted in the previous chapter, the percentage of Americans who don't go to church keeps going up, but regular church attenders are more Republican than ever. If the country is divided into secular liberals who are becoming disgusted with George W. Bush and the Republicans, and religious conservatives who were unhappy with Bill Clinton and remain distressed about gay rights, immigration, and other changes in American society, and if these liberals and conservatives are living in different parts of the country, get their news from different sources, and don't talk with each other, then this is a recipe for even more polarization.

Reality is different, however. Looking at one issue after another, pollsters have found that most Americans' positions are *not* diverging over time but remain relatively stable. There certainly have been some changes—consider general views on government revenues and spending in the wake of the tax revolts of the late 1970s, or the increasing demand for organized health care, or attitudes about the roles of gays in society. But there is not much evidence for polarization in the sense of half the people moving to one extreme and half to the other.

Scholars generally agree that Americans are mostly near the center in their attitudes on most issues. At the same time, voters are concerned about polarization and are often unsatisfied with the Democratic and Republican parties. A resolution of this puzzle, as articulated by political scientist Morris Fiorina and others, is that the two parties have diverged ideologically, leaving many voters stranded in the center and disillusioned about politics. The partisan polarization that has occurred at the elite level of elected officials has become increasingly evident, to a lesser extent, in the mass electorate.

Competing to Build a Majority Coalition

Tuesday's exit polls added to the sense that the red–blue schism might be more intractable than we would have liked to believe. That's because it is defined less by issues of the day than by battling cultures.
—Los Angeles Times *editorial, 2004*

The common lament over the recent rise in political partisanship is often nothing more than a veiled complaint instead about the recent rise of political conservatism.
—*former House Majority Leader Tom DeLay, 2006*

As WE HAVE DISCUSSED, the red-state, blue-state political divide occurs among the rich, not the poor. Because of this, it makes sense that the cultural differences between the parties are often framed in terms of how people spend their disposable income.

But it helps to put concerns about polarization in recent historical context. In the late 1960s and early 1970s, political scientists and journalists such as David Broder started writing books with titles such as *The Party's Over*, worrying about the diminished importance of political organizations in American life, and expressing concern with a more shallow mass-media presentation of politics in books such as Joe McGinness's *The Selling of the President*, written about Richard Nixon's 1968 presidential campaign.

Why were the increased importance of the media and decreased importance of political parties viewed as such a bad thing? For one thing, political scientists and journalists were more likely to be Democrats than Republicans—as was true of the country as a whole at that time. But Americans continued to vote Republican in presidential elections. Theories of divided government and balancing aside, this would be disturbing to someone who saw the

Democrats as the natural majority party, hence the concern about the decline of party influence.

Fast forward to the late 1990s and beyond. Political scientists and journalists are now bemoaning the increase in political polarization. Why is polarization such a bad thing? Again, political scientists and journalists are more likely to be Democrats. They have noticed that many Americans agree with the Democrats more than Republicans on specific issues but nonetheless vote for Republicans. What is going on? Political polarization is a possible culprit: with more Americans identifying with the conservative than the liberal label, perhaps they are voting Republican out of an ideological consistency that is not actually in accordance with their issue positions.

Similarly, after the 2000 and 2004 elections, discussions of the electoral map had a partisan tinge. Republicans, focusing on stabilizing and expanding their base in the red states, emphasized the all-American nature of these relatively low-income states compared to the residents of the blue states, who were perhaps too rich to fully appreciate the concerns felt by ordinary Americans. President George W. Bush's plan for individual Social Security accounts and other efforts to develop an ownership society were, among other things, an attempt to turn his party's narrow lead into more of a permanent majority.

On the other side, Democrats debated how to chip away at the Republicans' strongholds: perhaps by moderating their positions on social issues and reaching out to religious voters in the South, perhaps by reeling in low- and middle-income voters through a more populist economic platform, or perhaps by forgetting about the solid Republican South and picking off mountain West states with more libertarian social and economic policies.

In any case, the road toward a political majority typically leads to the political center, so it is in many ways surprising that in a period of near fifty-fifty division, the parties should remain so polarized. But it is perhaps less surprising now that we have seen that ideological partisanship, and the red-state, blue-state divide, have developed steadily over the past twenty or thirty years. In this chapter, we discuss some of the issues that the political parties have had to consider when trying to build their electoral coalitions.

THE MAP AS PARADOX, OR THE PUZZLING PERSISTENCE OF ECONOMIC CONSERVATISM

> The Republicans always looked bad three years out of four. But the year they look good is election year. A voter don't expect much. If you give him one good year he is satisfied.
> —*Will Rogers*

> [The Democratic Party's] leaders are always troubadours of trouble; crooners of catastrophe.
> —*Clare Boothe Luce, 1956*

One of the big questions in politics, in the United States and elsewhere, is why lower-income people vote for economically conservative parties. Or, to put it another way, why don't the 51% of the people on the lower end of the income scale raise taxes on the upper 49% at will? These and related concerns of the so-called tyranny of the majority motivated James Madison, Alexander Hamilton, and the other founders of our Constitution in setting up federalism and the separation of powers in the 1780s. The strategy of tax and spend seems to work some of the time (as the quote on page 15, attributed to Franklin Roosevelt's adviser Harry Hopkins, illustrates), but in recent decades, taxes have generally not been popular, even when framed as a redistribution from the rich minority to the lower-income majority.

There are lots of reasons why poorer voters might not support redistributive policies, including, in no particular order, aspiration ("I may be poor now but I would like a chance of getting rich"), fairness ("high-income people got there through hard work, and it's not right to take their money away"), skepticism ("I don't trust the government to spend any more of my money, or anyone else's, than is absolutely necessary"), the two-party system ("neither party proposes dramatic changes in economic policies, and what

139

redistribution is offered by the Democrats is tied to liberal views on social and military issues that I might not like"), and history ("redistribution does not work well—recall the Soviet Union—so I might prefer a capitalist system even if it does not immediately benefit me personally").

A partisan on the other side could characterize these attitudes more negatively as combinations of delusion, resentment, apathy, false consciousness, and complacency. In any case, although these are all strong reasons, it is interesting to see that Republicans are actually doing better in the poorer states. But there are different flavors of distribution: spending on military bases and prisons or Medicaid and welfare.

Overall, lower-income Americans have tended to vote for Democrats. The logic is clear—redistribution and lower taxes for the poor with the bill paid by the rich—and can also be supported by economic data. Figure 9.1 reproduces a graph created by political scientist Larry Bartels showing that incomes since World War II have grown faster under Democratic presidents, especially for people on the low end of the scale. Income has grown much more for the rich than for the middle class or poor under Republican presidents, whereas growth has been more even under the Democrats. These are just averages and do not occur every year (recall the stagflation that sank Jimmy Carter's presidency), but they show a consistent pattern.

This pattern is correlation, not causation, but it is still relevant to how people view political parties and the economy. Bartels sliced the data in a number of ways, and the evidence seemed convincing that, at least in the short term, economic growth was better under the Democrats. (By comparing first-term to second-term presidents, Bartels found that the result couldn't simply be explained as a rebound or alternation pattern.)

But then, why have the Republicans won so many elections? Why aren't the Democrats consistently dominating? Noneconomic issues are part of the story, but lots of evidence shows that the economy is a key concern for voters, so it's still hard to see how, with the pattern shown in figure 9.1, the Republicans could keep winning.

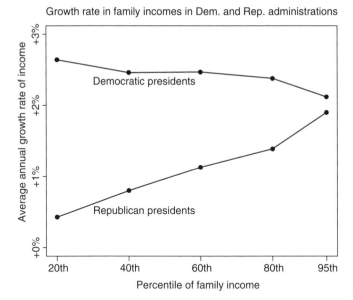

Growth rate in family incomes in Dem. and Rep. administrations

Figure 9.1: Larry Bartels's graph of average income growth under Democratic and Republican presidents since World War II, broken down by income category. Americans, especially low-income Americans, have consistently done better in Democratic administrations, although there is room for debate as to why this is.

The Republicans have been doing well in presidential elections for decades. During the forty-year period from 1950 to 1990, the Republicans only decisively lost one presidential election (in 1964, when Barry Goldwater lost to Lyndon Johnson). Other than that, they had six victories and three elections that were essentially ties. This is a pretty good record for a minority party. Economic conservatism might not have worked so well in Herbert Hoover's reelection campaign, but it has had an enduring appeal over the decades.

One purely economic explanation is that, although the economy does better under Democrats on average, the Republicans have tended to outperform the Democrats during the fourth year of each presidential term (even if 2008 may be an exception). Why this happens isn't completely clear—there is a large amount of economics and political science literature on "political business cycle" models (see the Notes for some references). One way to view it is as a natural consequence of the different goals of the

141

two parties, and the general belief that a president has the most ability to do what he wants during the first two years after his election. The Democrats generally have unemployment-reduction and economic-expansion goals, which expand the economy in the first two years of a term, but then some combination of budgetary constraints and a desire to move toward the political center lead to contraction in the second part of the term. Conversely, Republicans are more likely to pursue deflationary policies when they can (at the beginning of the four-year term), and then they move to the center later on, which has the electoral benefit of expanding the economy.

Figure 9.2 is a quick graph that tells the story of elections and the economy. It's based on the "bread and peace" model created by political scientist Douglas Hibbs to forecast elections based solely

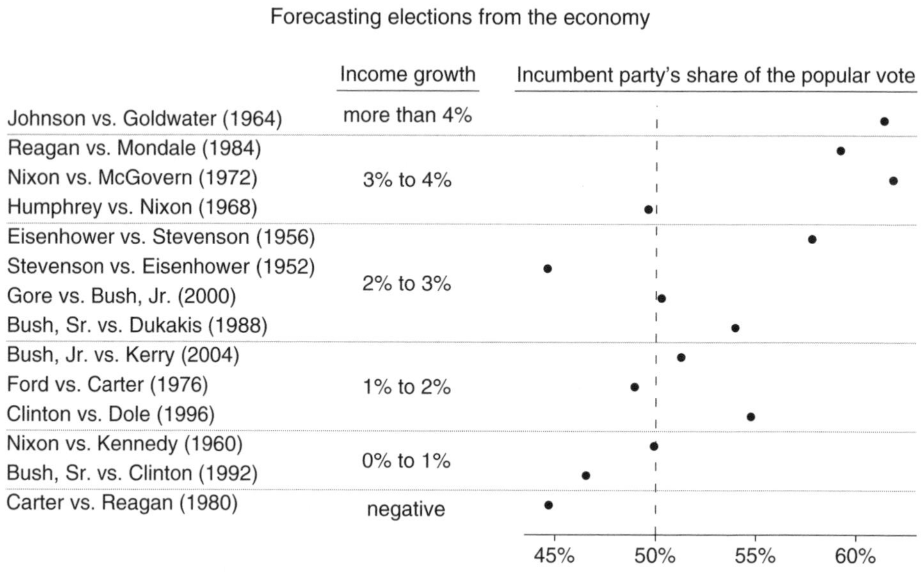

Forecasting elections from the economy

	Income growth	Incumbent party's share of the popular vote
Johnson vs. Goldwater (1964)	more than 4%	
Reagan vs. Mondale (1984)		
Nixon vs. McGovern (1972)	3% to 4%	
Humphrey vs. Nixon (1968)		
Eisenhower vs. Stevenson (1956)		
Stevenson vs. Eisenhower (1952)	2% to 3%	
Gore vs. Bush, Jr. (2000)		
Bush, Sr. vs. Dukakis (1988)		
Bush, Jr. vs. Kerry (2004)		
Ford vs. Carter (1976)	1% to 2%	
Clinton vs. Dole (1996)		
Nixon vs. Kennedy (1960)		
Bush, Sr. vs. Clinton (1992)	0% to 1%	
Carter vs. Reagan (1980)	negative	

45%   50%   55%   60%

Figure 9.2: Douglas Hibbs's "bread and peace" model of voting and the economy. Presidential elections since 1952 are listed in order of the economic performance at the end of the preceding administration (as measured by inflation-adjusted growth in average personal income). Matchups are listed as incumbent party's candidate versus other party's candidate. The better the economy, the better the incumbent party's candidate does, with the biggest exceptions being 1952 (Korean War) and 1968 (Vietnam War).

on economic growth (with corrections for wartime, notably Adlai Stevenson's exceptionally poor performance in 1952 and Hubert Humphrey's loss in 1968, years when the Democrats were presiding over unpopular wars). Better forecasts are possible using additional information (most notably, incumbency and opinion polls), but what is impressive here is that this simple model does pretty well.

Who Cares How Rich People Vote?

> This is an impressive crowd—the haves and the have-mores. Some people call you the elites; I call you my base.
> —*George W. Bush (in jest), 2000*

> I believe my pardon decision [of fugitive financier Marc Rich] was in the best interests of justice.
> —*Bill Clinton, 2001*

> We have had upper-class conservatives since the dawn of the Republic; by themselves they can't win elections to any office other than treasurer of the country club.
> —*Thomas Frank, 2005*

Debates about income, social class, and voting have two sides: why do large segments of the poor and middle class vote against income redistribution, and why are many of the rich sympathetic to economically liberal policies? But why should people care about this second question? Rich people are not a numerically large voting bloc, so why does it matter how they vote? One reason is voter turnout: approximately 75% of the richest Americans vote for president, compared to about 50% of the voting-age population. The voters in the top 10% of income account for nearly 15% of the total vote. Still, this is a small proportion of the total—especially if voters on the lower end of the income scale can be motivated to vote against, or in the opposite direction of, the rich.

One clue to the interest in how rich people vote is their importance to politics in general, a factor that does not relate to the

143

regional patterns of support for the two parties (the red–blue map) but motivates the goal of understanding the political attitudes of people on the higher end of the income scale. Federal officeholders have high salaries ($165,000 and up for members of Congress, $149,000 and up for judges, and similar salaries for various appointed officials) and commonly are well-off before entering government, so it makes sense to assume that they share many tastes and attitudes with upper-income Americans.

It is hard to say much for certain about the political leanings of the rich beyond what we can lean from polls about the upper 5% or so. Probably the best evidence comes from studies of political contributions. Political scientist Thomas Ferguson has tracked political donations of top corporate executives and the Forbes 400 richest Americans (or their equivalents in earlier periods). The data presented in his 1995 book, *Golden Rule*, indicate that America's superrich have generally leaned Republican, but with some notable exceptions that have changed over time. Certain industries have persistently higher rates of contributions to the Democrats. In the New Deal, these included industries with a strong interest in free trade. Since the Reagan years, finance, and high technology firms have been much friendlier to Democratic presidential candidates than most of the rest of American business.

For 2004, Ferguson consolidated the lists of top executives and richest families into a lot of 674 firms and investors. Out of this list, 53% contributed to George W. Bush's reelection campaign and 16% donated to Kerry, with Bush doing better among the aerospace, oil, and pharmaceutical industries and Kerry getting more from investment banks and hedge funds.

Richer people are more likely to participate in politics beyond voting, as donors and party activists. For example, even going beyond campaign contributions, upper-income Americans are more than twice as likely as those with low income to work on a campaign, contact a public official, or participate in a protest. Raising money should be easier for a party that is supported by the rich, and, indeed, both parties have been criticized for being too dependent on corporations, high-income donors, and elite opinion makers. Political activist Carrie McLaren voices a common attitude: "Both parties are too enslaved to the dollar, the whole system is just totally corrupt. It's all about who's paying your bills."

For the Democratic Party in particular, being tagged with the support of affluent professionals in upscale areas can discredit that party's traditional populist appeal: no matter how the poor vote, if Democrats are doing something to woo the votes of urban professionals in the rich cosmopolitan states, it might be seen as not to be the best thing for the rest of the country. Conversely, identifying Republicans' strength in wealthy enclaves or Sunbelt suburbs rhetorically marginalizes that party by associating it with a small sample of well-to-do voters.

The Republican Party's long-standing pro-business philosophy has a natural enduring appeal to higher-income voters. In contrast, it is a surprise when rich people vote for Democrats, suggesting that the party may have departed from its traditional populism. Conservative pundits hit the Democratic Party for losing relevance and authenticity, while liberals slam the Democrats for selling out. For example, Thomas Edsall quoted labor leader Andy Stern, president of the Service Employees International Union, saying that the perception of Democrats as "Volvo-driving, latte-drinking, Chardonnay-sipping, Northeast, Harvard- and Yale-educated liberals is the reality. That is who people see as leading the Democratic Party. There's no authenticity; they don't look like them. People are not voting against their interests; they're looking for someone to represent their interests." If Republicans are led by Benz-driving, golf-playing, Texas, Harvard- and Yale-educated conservatives, this is not such a problem because, in some sense, the Republicans never really claim to be in favor of complete equality.

Just as politicians would like the endorsement of Oprah Winfrey or Bruce Springsteen, it also seems desirable in our democracy to have the support of the so-called waitress moms and NASCAR dads—not just for the direct benefits of their votes but also because they signal a party's broad appeal. In recent years, prestige votes for Democrats have included teachers and nurses; Republicans have won the prestige votes of farmers and many in the armed services.

145

Rich people are an anti-prestige vote: just as politicians generally don't seek out the endorsement of, for example, Barbra Streisand or Ted Nugent (except in venues where these names are respected), they also don't want to be associated with obnoxious yuppies or smug suburbanites in gated communities. The parties want the money of these people—in fact, in their leadership, both parties to some extent *are* these people—and they'll take their votes, but they don't necessarily want to make a big deal about it.

SHOULD THE DEMOCRATS MOVE TO THE LEFT ON ECONOMIC POLICY?

> Run to the right in the primary, run to the center for the general election.
> —*attributed to Richard Nixon*
> Read my lips—no new taxes.
> —*George H. W. Bush, 1988*
> I actually did vote for the [war funding bill] before I voted against it.
> —*John Kerry, 2004*

Could John Kerry have gained votes in the recent presidential election by more clearly distinguishing himself from George W. Bush on economic policy? At first thought, the logic of political preferences would suggest not: the Republicans are to the right of most Americans on economic policy, and so in a one-dimensional space in which voters know exactly where the parties stand, the optimal strategy for the Democrats would be to stand infinitesimally to the left of the Republicans. Political scientists speak of the "median voter theorem" that each party would do best by keeping its policy positions just barely distinguishable from the opposition.

With multiple issue dimensions, however, or when voters vary in their perceptions of the parties' positions, a party can benefit from keeping some daylight between itself and the other party on an issue where it has a public-opinion advantage (such as economic policy for the Democrats).

In the 2004 presidential election campaign, it has been suggested that voters saw little difference between the parties on economics but large differences on other issues. The Democrats are traditionally closer than the Republicans to the average voter's view on the economy. Should the Democrats have moved to the left on economic issues? Could such a strategy win them votes?

We are not addressing whether it is appropriate for a party to make such a shift, or how any particular politician should balance the desire to win and the goal of standing fast to positions about what would be best for the country.

In a two-party system, the median voter theorem states that it is in each party's best interest to move toward the median of the distribution of voters—the position to which half the voters are to the left and half are to the right. The basic idea is shown in figure 9.3. If either party is not at the median, the other party has a winning strategy. For example, in the graph on the left, the Republicans have a position to the right of the average voter and the Democrats sit at the median attracting more than half the voters. But the Democrats will do even better by moving to be just infinitesimally to the left of the Republicans (see the graph

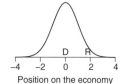

Position on the economy   Position on the economy

Figure 9.3: Two possibilities in a one-dimensional spatial model: the curve indicates the opinions of voters on economic issues, and D and R show the positions of the Democratic and Republican parties, respectively. In both pictures, the Republicans are right of center. In the left graph, the Democrats are at the median voter; in the right graph, the Democrats are just barely to the left of the Republicans, thus optimizing their vote share if the Republicans are not free to move. (We are assuming here that the Republican position is fixed, perhaps because they are the incumbent party or perhaps because of strong policy preferences.)

147

on the right) and getting the votes of everyone to the left. If the Republicans are also free to move to optimize their votes, the two parties will converge to an equilibrium where they are both at the median.

As political scientists have long realized, simplistic interpretations of the median voter theorem are regularly falsified by actual data. Politicians regularly depart from the median despite the clear evidence of an electoral benefit for having moderate positions. Legislators' distances from the median have been found to be correlated with district characteristics. There are many practical reasons for politicians to move away from the center. Ideological positioning is only one of the factors influencing election outcomes, and a candidate might well sacrifice a few percent of the vote in order to be better positioned to implement desired policies in the event of an election victory. There are also other constituencies to satisfy, including campaign contributors, party activists, and primary election voters.

Models of uncertainty about candidate positions in multidimensional spaces are interesting, counterintuitive, and potentially appealing if you would prefer the two parties to be further apart to present a clearer choice to voters. We set up an empirical test using voters' placements of themselves and the candidates on economic and social issues in the 2004 National Election Study.

We take three questions for each set of issues, using all of the relevant survey questions in which respondents were asked to judge the positions of Bush, Kerry, and themselves. We then sum the responses in each dimension, yielding a -9 to $+9$ scale on economic issues and a -8 to $+8$ scale on social issues. We then have six data points for each respondent, representing economic and social positions as judged for Bush, Kerry, and self. Our display of these data in figure 9.4 reveals not only correlation across issue dimensions but also a lot of variation. It is perhaps surprising that voters differed so much in their assessments of where Bush and Kerry stand on the issues. (We are using views on specific issues, so these results cannot simply be explained by different people assigning different meanings to liberalism or conservatism.)

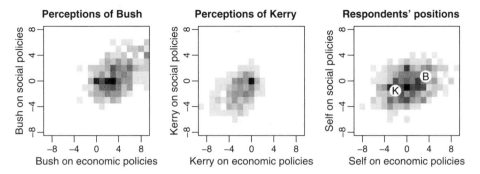

Figure 9.4: Distributions of respondents' views of Bush, Kerry, and themselves on a scale of −9 (extremely liberal) to +9 (extremely conservative) for economic policies and −8 (extremely liberal) to +8 (extremely conservative) for social policies. B and K in the third graph show the average perceived positions of Bush and Kerry. In each graph, darker shading represents a greater density of voters. For example, the most frequent view of Kerry was as a centrist, but many voters placed him to the left on both economic and social issues.

To estimate the effect of a change in party positions, we analyze the data on issue attitudes and voting preference in three steps. First, we analyze the extent to which views of Bush's and Kerry's policy stances match respondents' party identification and self-placements on the issues. Second, we estimate how likely voters are to support Bush (among those respondents who express a preference) given party identification and relative distance from each candidate on the issues. Third, we consider hypothetical scenarios in which the candidates' perceived issue positions change in order to see what would happen to aggregate voting preferences.

We skip the details here and opt to report two of our more interesting findings. First, people differ systematically in how they view the candidates' stances on the issues. In particular, the more liberal a Democrat is on economic issues, the more he or she views Bush as having conservative stances and Kerry as holding liberal positions. Conversely, Republicans with more conservative economic views were more likely to view Bush as more conservative and Kerry as more liberal. Apparently, there is a strong motivation to believe that your party's candidate is similar to you in his political views.

Second, we found that positions on economic issues are more important than positions on social issues in predicting how you will vote. This was consistent with other studies in this area. Furthermore, the importance of both economic and social issues was greater for Democrats than for Republicans.

Our next step is to consider hypothetical shifts in the candidates' positions on economic and social issues and see how these would translate into vote changes. Figure 9.5 shows the estimated effects, under this model, of shifting the positions of either Kerry or Bush on economic or social issues by as much as three points in either direction. (To get a sense of the scaling here, recall figure 9.4.) The answer to the question posed previously appears to be no, Kerry should not have moved to the left on economic policy. Conventional wisdom appears to be correct: Kerry would have benefited by moving to the right and Bush by moving to the left. The optimal shifts for Bush are greater than those for Kerry, which is consistent with the observation that voters are, on average, closer to the Democrats on issue attitudes.

According to our calculations, Kerry was close to an optimal issue position, with a small move to the right on economic and social issues having the potential to have gained him about 1% of the vote. Bush, on the other hand, could have gained more than twice as much by moving about twice as far to the left in both dimensions.

We could continue along these lines by allowing the two candidates to move simultaneously, but this is not our goal here. We do not consider our calculations to represent a realistic causal model of what would happen if candidates were to reposition themselves; rather, it is a way of exploring the multidimensional space of voters' perceptions of themselves and the candidates. Comparing these shifts to the candidates' average perceived positions (see the rightmost plot in figure 9.4), the optimal position for Kerry is to the right of his position at the time, but still far to the left of the perceived position of Bush. Given that the Republicans are far to the right of the median voter on economic issues—and given the

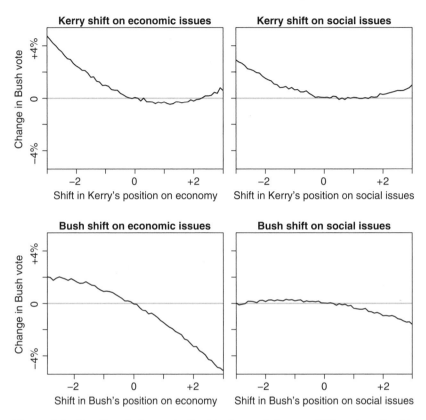

Figure 9.5: Predicted change in Bush's share of the vote if Kerry's or Bush's position on economic or social issues were to shift by a specified amount. The predictions are calculated based on how voters' choices could change if the candidates had moved left or right on economic or social issues. Positions on the economy and on social issues are measured on a −9 to +9 scale and a −8 to +8 scale, respectively. When the curve is above the zero line, the model says that Bush would have gained vote share; when below the line, Kerry would have done better. Based on our calculations, it would have been beneficial for Kerry to have shifted slightly to the right in both dimensions, for Bush to have shifted slightly to the left on social issues, and for Bush to have moved a great deal to the left on economic issues.

large variation in voters' perceptions of the candidates' positions— it appears to be best for the Democrats to stay in the center, quite a bit left of the Republicans, in order to make their relative location clear to the voters.

This is not to say that either candidate could have actually made such a move. Candidates' positions are constrained by many things, including their past statements—in fact, as the quotes at the start of this section remind us, John Kerry and George H. W. Bush were both slammed during election campaigns for expediently changing their positions.

Our analysis treats the two parties asymmetrically and also treats the issue dimensions differently. Is it reasonable to suppose that Kerry could move ideologically but Bush could not? And is it plausible that the Democrats are free to move to the left on economic policy but cannot move to the center on foreign policy and social issues?

We would answer yes to both of these questions. It is reasonable to suppose that, as the party in power in 2004, the Republicans were less inclined to make an ideological shift. As for the Democrats, we would expect that most of their stakeholders would prefer a move to the left on economic issues—if anything, it might be that their moderately conservative position was chosen partly from median-voter thinking as exemplified by figure 9.3. Moving to the left would not be costless for the Democrats, however, even beyond the anticipated direct cost in votes. One would expect them to lose some contributions from businesses and affluent individuals, and support of policies such as tariff barriers could be unpopular among elite opinion makers such as those who determine newspaper endorsements. In contrast, internal party pressures could make it more difficult for the Democrats to move toward the center in other dimensions.

A related question is how the parties can signal their position changes to the voters. Our models simply assume the ability to do so, but presumably the voters would need to be convinced that a move to the center is not just a pre-election ploy. Also, we are focusing on positions of existing nominees. Another way a party can move is by selecting a candidate on the left or right side of the party, such as Dwight Eisenhower in 1952 or Barry Goldwater in 1964.

Finally, a common counterargument to spatial voting models is that moving to the median might gain votes at the middle at the expense of the other party, but at the cost of diminishing turnout among one's core supporters. We have seen no particular evidence that this happened in 2004.

Moderation in the Pursuit of Moderation Is No Vice

A key part of the story of polarized America is that most voters are near the center, with their representatives in Congress taking more extreme positions (as in figures 8.8 and 8.10). How can these unrepresentative politicians stay in office? In a two-candidate election, it should be beneficial for candidates to claim the political center by holding moderate positions. This claim is supported by theory, along with empirical evidence of candidates moving to the center as elections approach, as well as anecdotal evidence such as the failures of the Goldwater and McGovern presidential campaigns.

However, there is evidence on the other side indicating that there must be some benefit to holding more extreme positions. The U.S. House and Senate have become polarized in recent years between Democrats and Republicans, with few congressmembers holding moderate positions, and some commentators have noticed more ideological polarization in recent political debate. The most successful vote-getters and longest-serving members of Congress are often at the extremes (liberal Democrats and conservative Republicans), and large national vote swings often knock out the moderates in the losing party (the congressmembers in swing seats) leaving stronger partisans standing. And, as we have discussed, polarization within Congress has led to voters having more extreme opinions about the two parties, even if voters themselves have become no more polarized in their own attitude positions.

In estimating the effects of candidate positions on vote-getting, we have to correct for the well-known pattern that more ideologically extreme congressmembers tend to be in districts that strongly favor one party or another. Figure 9.6 illustrates this with a graph of the ideologies of the members of the 1993–94 House of Representatives on the eve of Newt Gingrich's sweep plotted versus

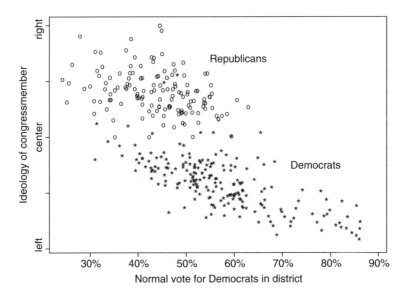

Figure 9.6: Political ideology of members of the 1993–94 House of Representatives versus district normal vote (adjusted Democratic vote for president in 1992). Democrats and Republicans are indicated by asterisks and circles, respectively. The moderates of both parties tend to sit in more marginal districts.

the Democratic share of the vote for president in their districts in 1992. The pattern, well known to political scientists, is that, in comparable districts, Democratic congressmembers are much more liberal than Republicans, with the more moderate officeholders for both parties tending to be in swing districts.

We estimate the effect of political moderation on the vote by analyzing votes received by a congressmember running for reelection, given their ideology scores and also the historical pattern of votes for the parties in each district. We then estimate the expected difference in vote share, comparing districts that have the same general partisanship but with incumbents who are ideologically moderate or extreme. We define the range of moderate to extreme based on the ideological scores of Poole and Rosenthal for that year—the same measures we used in chapter 8 to summarize congressional polarization.

We were not surprised to find that moderation benefits incumbents when they are running for reelection. The effect has averaged around three percentage points; see figure 9.7. To put it another way, suppose we compare two congressmembers running for reelection in similar districts: one who is at the moderate end of his or her party's spectrum and one who is at the liberal (if a Democrat) or conservative (if a Republican) extreme. The more moderate candidate would be expected to get about 3% more of the vote in a contested election.

Voters prefer the median, but moderate congressmembers are more vulnerable. This is possible because more moderate congressmembers tend to serve in districts that are more closely divided between Democrats and Republicans and can thus be dislodged by national political swings. The appropriate way to study the electoral success of moderate or extreme incumbents is after adjusting for party strength in their districts in previous elections.

As would be expected from standard political theory (and common knowledge), moderation is associated with higher votes in congressional elections, after controlling for the partisan predisposition of districts. This finding also sheds light on some recent political battles. Contrary to some press reports, there is no evidence supporting the claim that favoring Nixon's impeachment in 1974, or opposing Clinton's impeachment in 1994, was politically harmful to Republican congressmembers.

Given the various forces *against* moderation (party discipline, fund-raising, primary elections, personal convictions, and so forth), we would expect the pressure to move toward the center to be easily resisted by legislators who are not in swing districts. But election outcomes can be highly uncertain, and so a push toward moderation may be important even for not-so-close elections. (For example, whether or not Clinton's famed "triangulation" before the 1996 election was necessary, he did not know a year ahead of time that he would beat the Republican candidate so handily.)

The decline of competitive districts in Congress is consistent with current ideological polarization. This is consistent with our

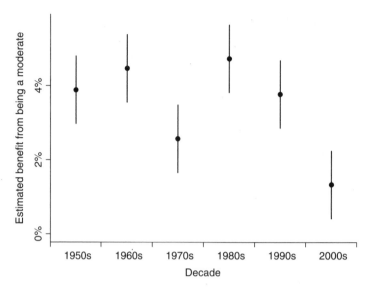

Figure 9.7: Estimated benefits to congressmembers of moderation, in terms of the percentage of the vote they could expect to gain by having a moderate record in congressional voting, compared to being at the liberal end (for Democrats) or the conservative end (for Republicans). On average, moderation helps, but only by a few percentage points. The vertical lines are error bars that indicate the range of uncertainty in the estimate for each decade.

results. As figure 9.7 shows, the benefits of moderation, in vote terms, have been in the 3% range for the past half century; however, a 3% effect is less important in recent years, now that there are fewer closely fought seats. For congressmembers in most districts, these few percentage points of the vote are unlikely to be necessary. In comparison, the effect of incumbency has been estimated to be close to 10% of the vote for individual House members in recent years. In this environment, moderation appears to give a real but small benefit.

To return to our theme of polarization in red and blue America, we have discussed how the growing partisan divisions in Congress contribute to the polarization of voters. The relatively small benefits of moderation show why most congressmembers can accept being more extreme than the median voters in their districts.

The Demise of the New Deal Coalition?

> To those who say that we are rushing this issue of civil rights,
> I say to them we are 172 years late. To those who say that this
> civil-rights program is an infringement on states' rights, I say
> this: The time has arrived in America for the Democratic Party
> to get out of the shadow of states' rights and to walk forthrightly
> into the bright sunshine of human rights.
> —*Hubert Humphrey, 1948*

In the usual narrative of how the United States came to its currently divided state, journalists and scholars go back to the late 1960s and the decline of the liberal consensus, triggered partly by the Vietnam War and partly by the decline of Democratic dominance in the South. In this scenario, racial issues helped conservatives in two ways, first by removing a big chunk of the Democrats' electoral college coalition, and second by cracking open the liberal monolith in the Midwest and Northeast.

Skepticism about government's good intentions on issues such as welfare and school busing went along with more conservative positions on taxes and business regulation. For example, David Broder reported in his book *The Party's Over* that "a Gallup Poll in October, 1969, found almost 78 percent of the people saying Federal taxes are too high."

It was in this period, from the late 1960s to the early 1970s, when journalists such as Broder and political operatives such as Kevin Phillips (*The Emerging Republican Majority*) argued that the stable postwar two-party system was disappearing. These trends can be traced back further to the 1950s, when Eisenhower made gains in the South (following President Truman's desegregation of the military and the national Democratic Party's move toward civil rights) and 1964, when Goldwater won several southern states with his opposition to the Civil Rights Act.

How does this story—of the gradual decline of the New Deal coalition and the replacement of party and economic voting by racial and, more generally, social issues—fit with the increasing importance of income in voting from the 1960s through the 1980s (as in the lower panel of figure 4.3)? The key link is party positioning: responding to the Democrats' dominance in the 1930s and 1940s, the Republicans moved to a more centrist position on the economy and a less isolationist stance in the Cold War, as exemplified by President Eisenhower on both counts. Since the mid-1960s, however, the parties have moved apart on economic as well as social issues.

Another political factor, as discussed by Stephen Ansolabehere and James Snyder, was the switch in the 1960s to one-person, one-vote districting for the House of Representatives and state legislatures. The resulting redistricting weakened the power of rural voters and suddenly moved the center of gravity in the South to more conservative economic positions while making it more difficult for the Democratic Party to maintain its traditional conservative stance on racial issues.

From Attitudes of Voters to Votes in Congress

> Can we defend the rational public against charges of fiscal profligacy? Yes ... Majorities of the public [in 1990] were, in fact, willing to cut certain programs (foreign aid, overwhelmingly; military spending, by more than a two to one margin) and to raise some taxes (on beer and liquor, and on incomes over $200,000, both by overwhelming margins), which could have reduced or eliminated the deficit—but not the way the elites apparently had in mind.
> —*Benjamin Page and Robert Shapiro, 1992*

After reporting on trends on a number of tax and spending issues, Page and Shapiro write, "People oppose general tax rises that would be spent on things they don't want.... [But surveys] report that vast majorities of Americans say they are willing to pay more taxes for specific purposes like medical care and research, Social Security, education, and the environment.... It is not inconsistent for Americans to want to limit taxation to what is needed."

The responsiveness of the government to voters' economic positions has long been a concern of activists on both the left and right. More generally, politicians' positions relate directly to our discussion of red and blue America. As discussed in chapter 8, much of the divergence of Democratic and Republican voters can be attributed to the positions taken by their political leaders. It is helpful to understand how politicians can "defy gravity" and continue to get reelected with attitudes more extreme than those held by most voters (again, recall Figure 8.8). As we have seen, congressmembers have incentives to follow the voters' desires, but these incentives are small and need not come into play except in close elections.

On the other hand, some elections are close, as we recall from the presidential contests of 2000 and 2004. In fact, the increasing polarization of voters in the two parties could imply a greater probability of close elections in the future, in that it will take more to swing voters away from their usual attachments. (Recall the decline in split-ticket voting, as shown in figure 8.9.) In these elections, positions that appear far from electorally optimal—most strikingly, some of George W. Bush's stances on economic issues—can be identified with strong policy preferences on the part of the political leadership.

This discussion is not meant to imply that politicians should simply mirror voters' existing preferences. As Lawrence Jacobs and Robert Shapiro describe in their 2002 book *Politicians Don't Pander*, political leaders typically see public opinion as a tool they can manipulate to reach their policy preferences rather than an external constraint that forces their hand. This is particularly true where public opinion is fluid, which includes issues as diverse as the estate tax, attitudes toward gays, and health care policy (the subject of Jacobs' and Shapiro's book). Presidents don't always succeed in their attempts to ride the wave of public opinion—consider Bill Clinton's abortive health care plan and George W. Bush's failed attempt to change Social Security—but their occasional successes, such as Bush's tax cuts, remain a motivation.

THE POLITICS OF RICH AND POOR STATES

> In the aftermath of this civil war that our nation has just fought, one result is clear: the Democratic Party's first priority should be to reconnect with the American heartland.
> —*Nicholas Kristof, 2004*

In our office is a map from 1924 titled "Good Roads Everywhere" that shows a proposed system of highways spanning the country, "to be built and forever maintained by the United States Government." The map, made by the National Highways Association, also includes the following explanation for the proposed funding system: "Such a system of National Highways will be paid for out of general taxation. The 9 rich densely populated northeastern States will pay over 50 per cent of the cost. They can afford to, as they will gain the most. Over 40 per cent will be paid for by the great wealthy cities of the Nation.... The farming regions of the West, Mississippi Valley, Southwest and South will pay less than 10 per cent of the cost and get 90 per cent of the mileage." Beyond its quaint slogans ("A paved United States in our day") and ideas that time has passed by ("Highway airports"), the map gives a sense of the potential for federal taxing and spending to transfer money between states and regions.

Both parties compete for swing voters in swing states, and in addition they are motivated to reward their supporters. Republicans win the votes of middle- and upper-income people in poor states, and Democrats tend to get the support of people of all incomes in rich states. Government programs that target these groups include military contracts in the South (if you're a Republican) and mass transit in the Northeast (if you're a Democrat).

Now consider that income predicts voting in poor states more than rich states. In states such as Mississippi, the connection between income and partisanship implies that there's not much motivation for Republicans to support measures that help poor people in poor states. But in states such as New York, Democrats get the support of rich as well as poor voters, so there is a motivation for the party to help out local industries such as finance (even

160

if this means opposing taxes on high earners) and to support programs such as Amtrak that benefit upper-middle-class voters in the
Northeast.

To put it another way, recall that the red-state, blue-state divide
occurs among the rich, not among the poor. So you might expect
each of the parties to have pretty consistent national policies on
targeted benefits to the poor but to be much more localized
when considering benefits to their upper-income constituents,
with, for example, the Democrats favoring the financial and
high-tech industries and Republicans favoring agribusiness and
small-business owners.

RICH AND POOR VOTERS IN RICH AND POOR STATES

As a thought experiment, let's imagine some alternative scenarios
in which voting patterns are different and see how the Democrats
and Republicans might react. We sketch the scenarios in figure
9.8. In each case, the Republicans win the poor states and the
Democrats win the rich states, but the scenarios differ in the
pattern of income and voting *within* states.

- In *Statesworld*, voting varies by state income but not at all by individual
  income within a state. In this world, states that vote more Republican
  do so uniformly at all income levels.
- In *Reverseworld*, rich people everywhere favor the Democrats. This
  is the scenario that people may assume after seeing the red-state,
  blue-state map: a world in which the Democrats win the rich vote,
  and the Republicans the poor vote, in every state.
- In *Votesworld*, rich people tend to vote Republican, with income predicting vote choice in the same way across all states. This is how
  we had imagined the nation to be after checking out the patterns
  of income and voting at the state and national levels but before
  analyzing income patterns within states.
- Finally, in the *real world*, richer people within any state are more
  likely to vote Republican, but the relation between income and vote
  choice is much stronger in poor states than in rich states.

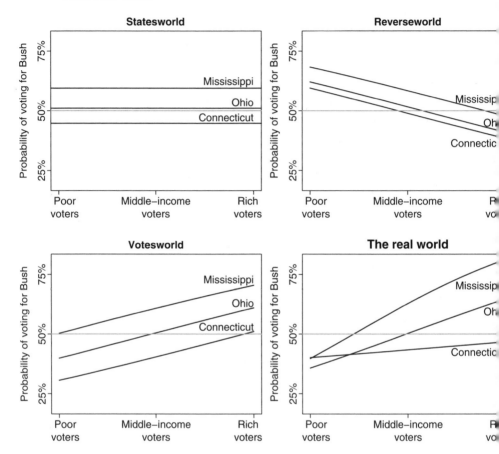

Figure 9.8: Alternative scenarios of income and voting. In each world, the Republicans win the poor states (such as Mississippi), the Democrats win in rich states (such as Connecticut), and the parties split the middle-income states (such as Ohio). The scenarios differ in how rich and poor vote within each state: in Statesworld, income does not predict vote at all within states; in Reverseworld, rich people favor the Democrats in every state; in Votesworld, rich people are more Republican (as in reality) but with equal slopes in all states; in the real world (the 2004 election), income was associated with Republican voting more strongly in poor than in rich states.

How would politics play out in each of these worlds? In States-world, we would expect politicians to have strong geographic loy-alties: Republican officeholders would fight for Mississippians of all income groups and Democrats would lobby for richer states.

There would be no particular reason for the parties to disagree on rich–poor issues, except to the extent that these intersected with states. For example, Republicans might favor higher federal transfers to the poor (who are more likely to live in low-income states), and Democrats might favor reducing the top rate of income tax (which disproportionately hits the residents of rich states).

In Reverseworld, the connection between party and income is even clearer, with Republicans dominating among low-income voters in Mississippi and other poor states and Democrats relying on richer voters in rich states. In this world, it would make sense for the yuppie Democrats to strongly resist the graduated income tax (which takes money from high-income people in rich states) and for the middle-American Republicans to support higher taxes and income transfers.

How would this work? Politicians are motivated to give benefits to their voters. Part of this is simply the overlap between voters, political activists, and politicians themselves. Beyond this, candidates generally get into Congress from primary elections, at which point they need to appeal to the voters of their party in their state or congressional district. We have already discussed in chapter 8 how the two parties in Congress are ideologically divided; here we are relating this to divisions between high- and low-income voters.

Continuing with our hypotheticals, neither the Statesworld nor Reverseworld stories are plausible; it is the Democrats who favor higher transfers to the poor and the Republicans who prefer lower tax rates. This makes sense in Votesworld, a scenario in which the Democrats consistently get the votes of poorer voters and Republicans win richer voters throughout the country. In Votesworld, the Republicans rely on rich votes in Mississippi and the Democrats, symmetrically, dominate among the poor in Connecticut.

Votesworld is not far from the truth, but in the real world there is a much steeper income–voting divide in poor states than in rich states. What might this imply about politics? In Mississippi, the Republicans win with a coalition of middle- and upper-income voters, and as such we would expect them to support policies that directly benefit these groups. On the other hand, in richer states such as Connecticut, the Democrats are the leading party but with the support of all income groups. Thus, unlike in Votesworld, it would not make sense for the Democrats in Connecticut to simply dismiss the concerns of high-income voters.

Add this up at the national level and there is a net benefit for the rich and middle class: they are represented in the winning coalitions in both rich and poor states, whereas lower-income voters are only supporting the winning party in the rich states. This oversimplifies—a graph of all fifty states looks much messier than the picture of Mississippi, Ohio, and Connecticut—but it captures an essential asymmetry between the patterns of support for the Democrats and the Republicans.

Putting It All Together

RICH STATES vote Democratic, poor states vote Republican, and this pattern has become stronger over time. This sets up the red–blue paradox.

The simplest explanation would be that Democrats now get the support of rich voters, with lower-income people voting for the Republicans. But we know from the polls that this is not what is happening: income predicts Republican voting, and the pattern is actually stronger in the United States than in most other countries we've looked at.

Then maybe it's social issues. People are more socially liberal in rich states and conservative in poor states, and that drives their voting. There's some truth to this, but it still doesn't explain how individual people vote. Rich Americans are, if anything, socially more liberal than poor Americans, but the rich are more likely to vote Republican and more likely to define themselves as conservative. Social attitudes don't explain why the rich vote differently from the poor.

Voting patterns at the individual and state levels seem contradictory. So let's consider what's happening within each state. In any state, the higher your income, the more likely you are to vote Republican. But the difference in how the rich and poor vote varies by state. In the states that strongly favored George W. Bush, voters in the upper third of income were 24% more likely than voters in the lower third to pull the Republican lever. In the richer, deep blue states on the map, higher-income voters were also more likely to vote for Bush, but by only half as much.

This has left us with two puzzles to explain—rich states supporting Democrats, and income mattering more in poor states than in rich states—to which we'll add a third puzzle, which is that both of these patterns are relatively recent, showing up only since the

1980s. Figure 10.1 shows how the rich-state, poor-state gap in voting has diverged among voters of different income levels.

We can explain some of the differences between states with demographics. For example, South Carolina is a conservative state. But as we were reminded when Barack Obama won the primary election there, many of the Democrats in South Carolina are African American, with Republicans in the state being mostly white and having higher incomes, on average. In contrast, the rich–poor divide in Connecticut is mostly among whites.

As we discussed in chapter 5 and show in a new way in figure 10.2, about half of the differences between rich and poor states can be attributed to race, but even among whites alone, the voting gap between rich and poor states increases as you go up the income scale.

Another key difference between red and blue states is religion. Residents of poor states attend church more often and belong

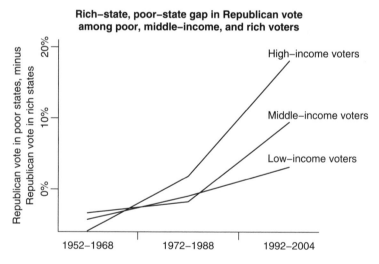

Figure 10.1: Difference in how people in rich and poor states vote, looking separately at high-, middle-, and low-income Americans. The association of Democrats with rich states has occurred since 1990 and is strongest among high-income voters, with little difference among low-income voters. Where lines are higher on the graph, residents of poor states are more Republican than people in rich states.

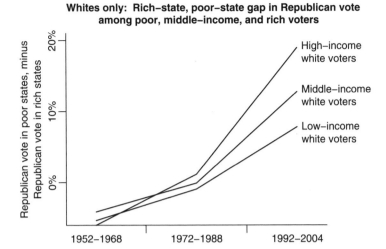

Figure 10.2: Difference in how people in rich and poor states vote, looking separately at high-, middle-, and low-income voters, restricting to *whites only*. Compared to figure 10.1, about half the differences between income categories is explained by race (that is, in many of the poor states, the income gap is also to some degree a racial gap).

to more conservative denominations than people in rich states. Religiosity is correlated with conservative attitudes on social issues and with Republican voting, especially among the rich.

High-income voters in Republican states such as Texas and Mississippi are much more conservative than poor voters, especially on economics. But in strongly Democratic states such as New York and California, the rich are only slightly more economically conservative than the poor, and they are actually more liberal than the poor on social issues. The patterns are summarized in plate 10. It makes sense that income strongly predicts Republican voting in red America but not in blue America, where rich people are conflicted in their economic and social views.

At this point, it helps to restate the second part of the paradox: income matters more in poorer than richer states. In other words, the difference in voting between rich and poor states—the red-state, blue-state pattern—occurs among rich voters, and somewhat among the middle class, but less at the lower end of the income scale.

By making the problem more complex—by looking at incomes within as well as among states—we have actually reduced what we need to explain. The key question is, what has happened in the past twenty years to explain the red–blue pattern among upper-income voters?

Our answer: with growing political polarization, parties have started to take ownership of social and religious issues, such as abortion, that used to straddle the political divide. Party identification is more ideological now than it has ever been (at least since such things have been measured in surveys). The states that are rich now, in the Northeast, upper Midwest, and West Coast, are mostly those that were also the richest states a century ago, and we have no reason to believe that voters in these states haven't been more liberal on social issues for many years. But only recently has this translated into *voting* for the Democrats.

Plate 11 shows that low-income voters in red and blue states are pretty similar in their political attitudes, but high-income voters show much more geographic variation, with rich red-staters being clearly more conservative on both economic and social issues than rich blue-staters. As Ansolabehere, Rodden, and Snyder recently wrote, "Those who sense a growing culture war in American elections have tapped at least one important trend: Moral issues have become increasingly important over the past 30 years. Such issues have grown from insignificance to a clear second dimension in American elections." We have found that differences in voting patterns between red and blue states can be explained by differences in both economic and social issues, comparing upper-income voters in rich states to those in poor states.

MOVING OR STAYING PUT

Americans in the upper end of the income distribution have the means to move to places more congenial to their lifestyles—or to stay put, if that is what they prefer. As Richard Florida wrote in *The Rise of the Creative Class*, Americans have not simply been moving from the rust belt to the Sunbelt but also have been choosing the cities and neighborhoods that fit a new range of careers and lifestyles. This could be one explanation as to why the red-state, blue-state culture war shows up among the voting patterns of the rich but not the poor, who have less flexibility to move by choice. The red and blue states are defined by social attitudes among high-income voters, even while rich and poor are still divided on economic issues.

In an analysis of National Election Study data, political scientists James Gimpel and Jason Schuknecht found that Republicans have been more likely to change residences and Democrats more likely to stay put, and that this difference persists after adjusting for income, age, and race. As they point out, voters who move among states can affect the politics in their new locations and also, by subtraction, change the political leanings of the areas they leave behind. We do not have the individual-level data needed to test this hypothesis, but it is interesting that these changes in voting patterns have coincided with a major shift in population to warm-weather states. The broad availability of cheap air conditioning has made these areas more desirable at the same time that the decline of manufacturing industries has reduced some of the economic motivation for staying in the Northeast and Midwest. The upper-income people who moved to the low-tax Sunbelt states may likely be Republicans.

To get a sense of recent patterns of internal migration, we looked at Census data from 1995 to 2000 and found that about 48% of Americans moved during this period. There was some variation by income: 28% of people in the top tenth of income moved within-state in the five-year period, compared to 35% in the bottom tenth. About 10% in all income groups moved between states.

We then broke the data down by the partisanship of states. We define the red states as those where George W. Bush won the two-party vote by at least a 10% margin in both 2000 and 2004 (these

169

eighteen states had a total of thirty million voters and 148 electoral votes in the 2004 election), blue states as those where Bush lost in both years by at least 10% (these eight states and the District of Columbia include thirty-six million voters and 146 electoral votes), and the battleground states in between (the remaining twenty-four states, with fifty-five million voters and 244 electoral votes).

Looking at people who moved from red (strongly Republican) states: those who move to other red states are poorer, those who move to purple states are slightly richer (on average), and those who move to blue states are richest. Among those who moved from purple (battleground) states, we see the same pattern: the poorer go to red states, the richer go to blue states. Looking at those who moved from blue (strongly Democratic) states, we again see that the poorest went to red states and the richest went to other blue states. In fact, people who moved from one blue state to another are in the richest category, on average. This does not demonstrate that people move to states or regions that are more culturally compatible to them, but the data are consistent with that possibility. A related idea is that higher earners are moving to richer states because of the economic opportunities available for educated professionals in these places.

One link between economics, voting, and social attitudes has been noticed by journalist Steve Sailer, who hypothesizes that rich, coastal states now favor the Democrats because of increasing house prices, which reduces affordable family formation (marriage and childbearing), in turn limiting the electoral appeal of Republican candidates running on family values. Sailer attributes some of this home price difference to what he calls the Dirt Gap—coastal and Great Lakes cities such as New York, Chicago, and San Francisco are bounded by water, which limits their potential for growth, as compared to inland cities such as Dallas or Atlanta: "The supply of suburban land available for development is larger in Red State cities, so the price is lower." The Republicans do better among married voters, who are more likely to end up in more affordable states that also happen to be more culturally conservative.

The geographic argument—fewer families in coastal metropolitan areas because there is less room for affordable suburbs—makes sense, even if it doesn't really explain why the people without children want to vote for Democrats and people with children want to vote for Republicans. It makes sense that more culturally conservative people are voting Republican, and these people are more likely to marry and have children at younger ages, but in that sense the key driving variable is the conservatism, not the family formation.

Income strongly predicts Republican vote individually and within counties and states. But richer people are less likely to be religious believers and are able to pay more for housing; as a result, a state full of higher-income people is likely to be less religious and have more expensive housing, two features that make it less hospitable to potential migrants with conservative attitudes and lifestyles as defined in modern American politics. Economists Edward Glaeser and Bruce Sacerdote conjecture that a more religious environment will make all the voters in a state more conservative because of socially learned beliefs. In other words, individual Mississippians will have more conservative attitudes than would be expected from their incomes alone.

This theory does not in itself explain why the difference in voting patterns between red and blue America occurs among the rich but not the poor: if anything, we might expect lower-income voters to be more susceptible to social context. The missing piece is that religion and social issues are directly, at the individual level, more predictive of vote choice among richer Americans; see figure 6.10. We would like to understand what has happened in the past twenty years to create this pattern.

POSTMATERIALIST POLITICS

> There are now 7 million households in America with incomes over $100,000 a year, and their influence on the marketplace, the culture, the media, and the categories of thought is enormous. This mass upper class—even its many liberals—

does not think in terms of class conflict. Its members think in
bohemian-versus-bourgeois terms. . . . Maybe you could build a
class movement when the Democratic Party was staffed by
proletarian ethnics organized into urban machines. But now
the Democratic Party is staffed by lawyers and media
consultants.
—*David Brooks, 1998*

Consistent with Ronald Inglehart's hypothesis of postmaterialism,
survey data show social issues to be more important to higher-
income voters. This can be viewed as a matter of psychology and
economics, with social policy as a luxury that can be afforded once
you have achieved some material comfort. Our results stand in
contradiction to the commonly held idea that social issues distract
lower-income voters from their natural economic concerns.

Another framework for understanding voting patterns is
through policies and party platforms. John Huber and Piero Stanig
have found that the countries with the strongest rich–poor voting divides are those in which the major parties are furthest apart
on issues of redistribution. It is possible that, in richer societies,
opposing parties can come to more of a tacit agreement on economic policy—roughly, a level of social support that is generally
popular within the constraints of acceptable tax rates—leaving
less room for rich and poor to differ in how they vote. Realistically, both the psychological and institutional explanations have
some truth to them. Religious and secular Americans are increasingly different in their voting patterns higher up the income scale,
and this is reflected in their attitudes on economic and social
issues as well. Plate 11 shows how high-, middle-, and low-income
Americans differ in their economic and social attitudes, separately
displaying people who attend church frequently, occasionally, and
never.

The policy connection is there, too. In particular, the correlation between income and voting was large in the 1940s, in the
aftermath of the New Deal, but declined to nearly zero in the
1950s and early 1960s, a period where the two parties differed little
in their economic policies: the Republican Eisenhower accepted

Social Security, Kennedy was a tax-cutting Democrat, and both parties used the proceeds of economic growth to increase domestic and military spending. In 1964, Barry Goldwater put some distance between the parties on economic policy with a platform of cutting taxes and spending, and the gap in voting between rich and poor increased sharply. Since the 1970s, the two parties have diverged on policy, and the difference in voting between rich and poor has remained large. As discussed in chapter 5, income inequality has increased since then, with the largest increases in the richer, Democratic-leaning states. Perhaps surprisingly, these are the states where income matters least in voting, but that can be explained by the more liberal social attitudes of high-income voters in those areas, along with the increasingly ideological nature of party attachments.

It is richer Americans in richer parts of the country, more than the poor and rural, who are voting based on "God, guns, and gays." In the words of Ansolabehere, Rodden, and Snyder: "Moral issues have a slightly larger impact on the vote choices of blue-state residents than red-state voters, and a slightly smaller impact on the vote choices of rural residents than urban and suburban residents ... low-income Americans are significantly less inclined to vote based on moral values than are high-income groups." Political scientists Matthew Fellowes, Virginia Gray, and Davie Lowery have found that these attitudes affect government as well: "States with larger and wealthier economies and greater representation by Democrats in the legislature allocate more agenda space to postmaterialist policies."

Correlations between income and beliefs on economic issues are weak, and the many low-income Americans who vote Republican can do so in coherence with their economic attitudes. At the higher income brackets, we see the red-state, blue-state deadlock that has been so apparent since the Bush-Gore contest in 2000. Changes in the parties' positions on racial issues have certainly been part of this, but we see these divisions on many other issues as well, ranging from taxes to abortion. Americans remain more moderate than their representatives in Congress, but the separation between Democrats and Republicans has increased the ideological coherence of people's beliefs, especially for more educated and higher-income voters.

Red state versus blue state is a compelling theme because it speaks to the motivations of voters and has implications for who the parties represent, as well as inspiring fears of gridlock and other concerns about governing. The worries are real, especially given that the red–blue divide is sharpest among the richer, more politically influential Americans. (This may also be why it has been noticed by the national news media.) However, some of the quick and natural generalizations about voters are not supported by the data. In particular, it does *not* appear to be the case that rich people vote based on their economic interests, with lower-income voters being more likely to be swayed by emotional appeals. And, while choosing a more liberal economic policy would more clearly distinguish Democrats from Republicans on the key-issue dimension, we see no evidence that this would gain them votes.

Americans disagree about important issues. But the division is not simply between rich and poor voters, or religious and secular, or rich and poor states. Each of these factors is important, but the true differences lie in subsets of the population: rich versus poor voters in poor states, high-income religious versus high-income secular voters, red states versus blue states among rich voters, and so forth. As the trends in voting by occupation show, the rich–poor divide is a superposition of many changes.

These divisions have been around for a while but they have become more important in recent years with the increased ideological polarization of the political parties. We don't have a simple explanation for where the polarization comes from. Political scientists such as Nolan McCarty, Larry Bartels, and Morris Fiorina and economists including Paul Krugman and Edward Glaeser have identified increasing income inequality as a driving force behind the increase and continuation of political polarization: activists and officeholders of the Democratic and Republican parties have moved to the left and right, and voters have to some extent followed, as a result linking previously unrelated issues, as we discussed in chapter 8. Income inequality keeps the economic issues relevant and allows the polarization to continue.

At the same time, the national economy has been transformed. In 1973, Daniel Bell wrote in *The Coming of Post-Industrial Society* about the social effects of the shift from production to a service economy. In American politics it is impossible to separate economic and racial issues, and the shift of the parties apart on economic policy is tied to the movement of conservative southerners out of the Democratic Party from the 1950s onward. It also makes sense to look at other changes in politics during the past twenty-five years, during which the red-state, blue-state division and the importance of social issues arose among upper-income Americans.

Another theory revolves around the role of the media. Some research has found that the partisan perspective of newer media sources such as Fox News can reinforce the ideological tendencies of their viewers. Online organizations such as MoveOn.org and Daily Kos similarly provide opportunities for reinforcement of attitudes. This may be particularly true for richer people, who tend to consume political information at higher levels. Ideological competition among media sources is far from new in American history, but its recent revival has come at the same time as the return of partisan polarization. Even if it is not a cause of the red–blue split, partisan media could be keeping the divisions alive.

Rich and Poor Voters in Red and Blue States

By analyzing poll data not as national aggregates but as votes within states, we found that the red–blue division is greatest among the rich. Especially among upper-income Americans (who, of course, include most of the opinion makers), voting and political attitudes are correlated with location and lifestyle, making it that much more difficult for individual voters to understand or sympathize with the other side on key issues. Rich people in red America are much more conservative—on both economic and social issues—than their counterparts in the blue states.

Upper-income voters have also seen greater increases in polarization in recent years, with their attitudes on a range of issues

175

being tied more closely to political affiliation and self-described liberalism or conservatism. Conflict is certainly not new in recent American politics: consider the struggles in the 1960s and 1970s over civil rights and neighborhood schools, the tax revolts of the late 1970s, and the foreign policy debates of the 1980s. But partisan divisions are in some ways even deeper now, as can be seen in the differing views of Democrats and Republicans on George W. Bush (partisan divergences that are greater than have been measured for any previous president) and the increasing impact of partisanship on views of the economy.

How do people—journalists, scholars, and citizens—try to understand political trends? If you look only at maps, just seeing who won each state, you end up with misleading stereotypes of rich East Coast Democrats and low-income southern Republicans. This leads to confusion about how rich and poor actually vote. Meanwhile, academic analysts of polling data tend to ignore states entirely, thus working from an inaccurate model in which voters are simply a product of their demographics.

We wrote this book as a corrective to what we see as persistent confusion about the role of class in the American electoral process. On the one hand, it is natural to personify states—to see Democrats winning rich states and to then assume that this implies that rich people now vote Democratic. In fact, this is only true for a handful of rich states—ironically, precisely those states where national journalists are likely to live.

Suburban Montgomery County, Maryland, is a Democratic stronghold—but so is rural south Texas. Kansas has been a symbol of working-class Republicanism and, indeed, low-income Kansans gave George W. Bush half of their votes—but high-income Kansans gave him 70%. Some analysts have traced the rise of political polarization to increasing income inequality, but, in some of the most unequal states, there is little difference in how rich and poor people vote. Looking internationally, the countries with the biggest differences in voting between rich and poor are those where the left and right parties are furthest apart on economic issues. But we see huge variations among states in U.S. presidential elections, where the two parties have national platforms. Religious and moral concerns have been given as the explanation for why poor people don't vote consistently for Democrats. But there is little difference in voting patterns when comparing low-income religious and secular voters. It is among higher-income voters that religious attendance is strongly predictive of Republican voting.

Putting individual and geographic information together, we are reminded that voters in Texas are not like voters in New York and that the voting gap between rich and poor is larger in Republican than in Democratic states. Recognizing the importance of context allows us to learn that political polarization—the divide between red and blue America—looks different in different places and among different groups. We need to move beyond stereotypes of income and place in order to understand how Americans of different backgrounds, attitudes, and cultures express their views in the electoral process.

The 2008 Election

AN ELECTION takes a measure of public opinion and transforms it into the opportunity to change policy. A 53–47 divide—or even a 50–50 divide—is enough to change history. Following the pattern of Harry Truman, George W. Bush attained office indirectly but held—and was reelected with—strong partisan positions. In 2008, the Democrats' gain of a few percentage points of the vote was enough to give Barack Obama his mandate in turn.

What really happened in the 2008 election? We concern ourselves here not with campaign strategy but rather with explaining the ultimate outcome. How did Barack Obama and John McCain do in different places and among different groups of voters?

THE NATIONAL VOTE

With the economic recession and stock market crash, 2008 was a bad year to be a Republican at any level—as much political science research shows, voters assign responsibility for economic outcomes, good or bad, to the party of the incumbent president. People base their voting decisions not only on *their* pocketbook but also on their evaluation of the *nation's* pocketbook: the state of the economy. Obama won by about 6% of the vote, about as well as would be expected for a challenger in a weak economy. (Recall figure 9.2, which shows the historical pattern since the 1950s.) In periods of low economic growth, the incumbent party can lose. A 53–47 margin would be typical; you wouldn't expect the challenger to get a lot more than that, even after taking into account the slight increase in voter turnout from 2004; see figure A.1.

Another piece of evidence for economic voting comes from survey responses. In an NBC/*Wall Street Journal* survey in August—a

179

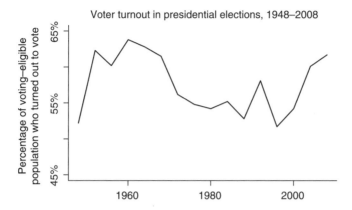

Figure A.1: Turnout increased slightly from 2004 to remain at about 60% of those eligible to vote.

month *before* the financial meltdown of 2008—when asked what should be the top priority for the federal government, 59% gave economic issues (job creation and economic growth, energy and gas prices, and the mortgage/housing crisis), with another 11% mentioning health care, which also manifests itself as an economic concern. Only 37% gave priority to noneconomic issues (Iraq, terrorism, immigration, and the environment). Another survey commissioned at about the same time by CBS News showed roughly the same results, illustrating, once again, the importance of economic considerations in voting decisions.

Rich and Poor Voters

As with previous Republican candidates, McCain did better among the rich than the poor, but, according to some polls, the pattern changed among the very highest income categories; see figure A.2. Obama did best among the lowest-income voters, and McCain did respectably but not overwhelmingly well at the high end—in fact, he did worse than George W. Bush in every income category.

Does the Democrats' improved performance among rich voters represent a new trend? Should we ask not "What's the matter with

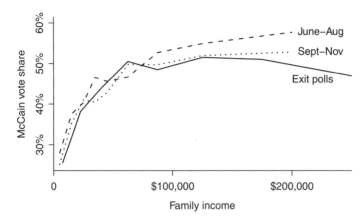

2008 exit polls and Pew surveys before and after Labor Day

Figure A.2: Income and voting based on exit polls and Pew Research pre-election surveys. In 2008 as before, the Republican candidate did much better among the rich than the poor. Unlike Bush in 2004, however (see figure 2.2), McCain did not do even particularly well among the highest-income group.

Connecticut?" but rather "What's the matter with rich people?" Are we in a new era in which, at a national level, the upper middle class and rich are divided evenly between the two parties? Or maybe this change is coming from the economic crisis, which in financial terms is hitting the wealth of higher-income voters harder. (After all, consider who has money in the stock market.)

As in previous elections, higher-income voters were more likely to vote Republican *within* almost every state. Figure A.3 shows the income and voting pattern in red, purple, and blue states and in our characteristic comparison of Mississippi, Ohio, and Connecticut. The patterns we identified in the first edition of our book have continued, and figure A.4 shows that this pattern is typical of all states. The latter graph illustrates how higher- and lower-income voters differ in each of the fifty states. We perform the exercise first for all voters and then looking only at whites to isolate income from race. Our analysis of the polls shows richer people voting more Republican—among all voters and considering whites alone—in forty-seven of the fifty states.

181

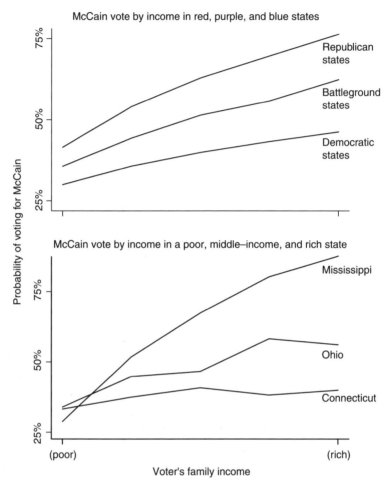

Probability of voting for McCain

Figure A.3: *Top graph*: As in previous years, Republican voting in 2008 increased with income, especially in Republican-leaning states. Data from Pew pre-election surveys. *Bottom graph*: In 2008, income predicted Republican voting strongly in the poorest state (Mississippi) and somewhat in a middle-income state (Ohio). But in the richest state (Connecticut), higher-income voters were actually less likely to support John McCain. Estimated from a multilevel model fit to Pew pre-election surveys.

We can also display our estimates as a series of maps. Plate 12 shows the states that Obama and McCain would have won, had only the votes of upper-, middle-, or lower-income voters been counted. Among higher-income voters, McCain won the poor states and

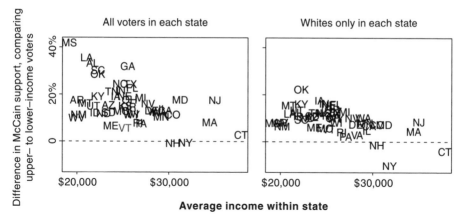

Figure A.4: Estimated rich–poor difference in the McCain vote share within each state; thus, states that are high on this graph are those where richer people were much more Republican than poorer people were. Looking at whites only, the rich–poor voting gap remains higher in poor than in rich states, but the pattern is much weaker when ethnic minorities are excluded from the analysis.

Obama the rich states. The difference in voting pattern between states was much less among lower-income voters.

RED STATES AND BLUE STATES

Obama won the presidency by winning several important states that George W. Bush had carried in the two previous elections. Did this represent a reshuffling of the red-state, blue-state pattern, or was it merely a manifestation of a national swing in the Democrats' favor?

To see how the vote swing varied across states, we show in figure A.5 a state-by-state graph of the Obama vote in 2008 versus the Kerry vote in 2004. The interquartile range (a measure of variability) of the state swings (excluding the District of Columbia and the unusual case of Hawaii) was 5%. That is, after accounting for the national swing in Obama's favor, most of the states were within 5 percentage points of where they were, compared to their relative positions, in 2004.

The swing from 2004 to 2008 was pretty uniform

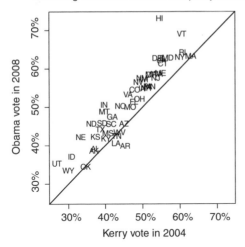

Figure A.5: The Obama vote in 2008 compared to the Kerry vote in 2004, by state. Except for the unusual case of Hawaii (where Obama grew up), there was close to a uniform swing of about 5 percentage points, with only a small variation from state to state. Most of the states sit above the 45-degree line, indicating that Obama did better than Kerry in nearly all states.

By comparison, the interquartile range of the state swings between the 2000 and 2004 elections was only 3%. This was even less variation: Bush–Kerry was basically a replay of Bush–Gore. Still, the relative state swings of 4% in 2008 were not large by historical standards. As figure A.6 shows, state-by-state election swings have generally been declining over the past few decades. The red–blue map is much more stable from election to election than it used to be.

The pattern of rich states voting Democratic and poor states voting Republican also continued in the 2008 election. For example, Connecticut, the richest state, gave Obama 61% of the vote, while McCain won 57% of the vote in Mississippi, the poorest state.

WHITES, BLACKS, LATINOS, AND ASIANS

Obama gained among almost all groups but did particularly well among ethnic minorities. The exit polls found that, compared to

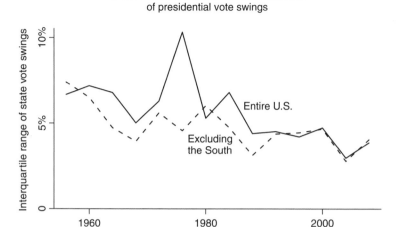

Figure A.6: Interquartile range (that is, the difference between the seventy-fifth and twenty-fifth percentiles) of vote swings in each pair of successive presidential election years since 1952. Volatility of the states relative to the national swing has generally declined. The two lines show interquartile ranges for all the states and for all excluding the South. (The spike in the graph represents 1976, when Jimmy Carter did very well in several southern states that Nixon carried in 1972.)

Kerry, Obama gained 3% among whites, 7% among blacks, 12% among Asians, and 13% among Latinos. Figure A.7 shows the trends, and plate 13 shows our estimates of the states won by Obama and McCain among whites of high, middle, and low incomes.

In the words of Stephen Ansolabehere and Charles Stewart, "Obama gained not only by bringing new minority voters into the electorate, but also by converting minority voters who had previously been in the GOP stable." The year 2008 was a Democratic one, Obama was a Democrat, and he won in one of the ways the Democrats could have won. With a different candidate there might have been different demographics but roughly the same national swing, and maybe a slightly different electoral map with a similar electoral vote total.

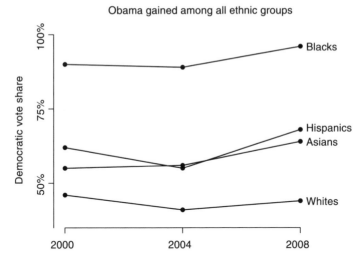

Figure A.7: Democratic vote share from 2000 to 2008, by ethnic group, as estimated from exit polls. Obama gained among all groups but did particuarly well among minorities.

Young and Old

Immediately after Barack Obama's historic election, there was speculation about the role of young voters in the winning coalition: was there something about the Obama campaign or the candidate's relative youth that motivated younger voters? Exit-poll data did in fact show that Obama performed particularly well among the young, but was this really newsworthy? For example, political consultant Mark Penn wrote on the *New York Times* Web site, "Sure, young people voted heavily for Mr. Obama, but they voted heavily for John Kerry." Was Penn right?

The clearest way to make a comparison is using a graph. Figure A.8 shows the Republican candidates' share of the two-party vote among each of four different age groups in several recent elections. The gap between young and old increased—a lot. Obama beat McCain 2–1 among voters under thirty, an unprecedented margin among any age group in recent years.

The 2008 election clearly was different, and Mark Penn was wrong—another case of a pundit looking at numbers and not

The youngest voters swung to the Democrats

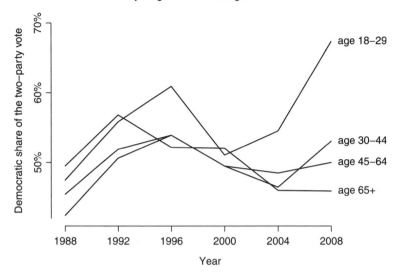

Figure A.8: Voting trends among different age groups, as estimated from exit polls in recent presidential elections. Obama's 2–1 margin among those under thirty in 2008 was far better than any other candidate's performance in any of these age groups in earlier years.

seeing the big picture. This is what graphics are all about: showing the details and the patterns all at once.

At the same time, there was no massive turnout among young voters. According to the exit polls, 18% of the voters this time were under thirty, as compared to 17% of voters in 2004. (By comparison, this age group represents 22% of voting-age Americans.)

Exit polls also show a relation between age and race: many more young voters were ethnic minorities. Among blacks and Hispanics, there were three times as many voters under thirty as over sixty-five, a natural demographic trend at least among Latino voters, many of whom are the offspring of migrants who arrived in the late 1980s and early 1990s. By comparison, among whites, there were more voters over sixty-five than under thirty.

People tend to vote like their parents—children of Republicans are, on average, more likely to vote Republican—but generational change is relevant too. And it's not just about Obama; as figure A.9

187

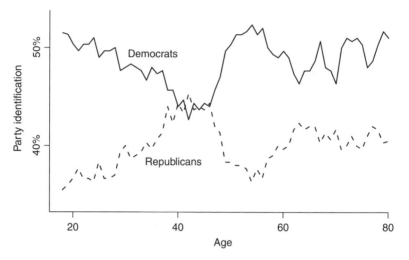

Democratic and Republican identification by age in 2006

Figure A.9: Percentage of Americans who identify as Democrats or Republicans, by age, from Pew Research surveys in 2006. Most likely to be Republican are people in their mid-forties, who came of political age during the era of Jimmy Carter and Ronald Reagan. The most recent cohort of voters, whose reference points are Bill Clinton and George W. Bush, are mostly Democrats.

shows, the young were already trending Democratic in the 2006 congressional elections.

RELIGIOUS AND SECULAR

As in all presidential elections since 1992, regular church attenders were more likely to vote Republican in 2008—John McCain's share of the two-party vote ranged from 35% for nonchurchgoers to 62% of those who attended religious services more than weekly.

Figure A.10 breaks this down by religion and denomination. As in 2004, churchgoing is more strongly associated with Republican voting among Catholics and born-again Protestants than among other Protestants. These three groups represent approximately equal proportions of the population. The patterns for Jews and Mormons are also interesting (and consistent with 2004). Finally,

188

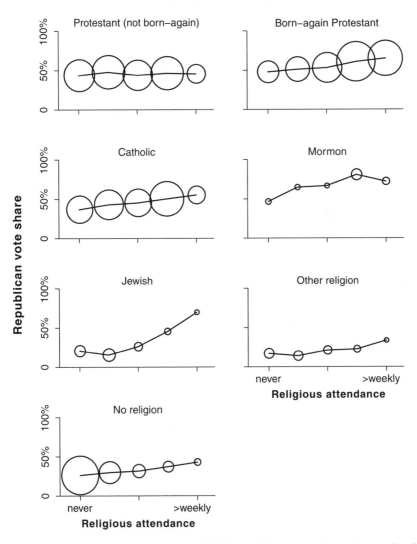

Figure A.10: The McCain vote in 2008 by religious attendance for each of several religious groups. The size of each circle is proportional to the number of people represented in the survey. In particular, most of the people who attend church more than weekly are born-again Protestants. Also, some non-religious people go to church; we assume this is typically for family reasons, but we haven't examined the question in detail.

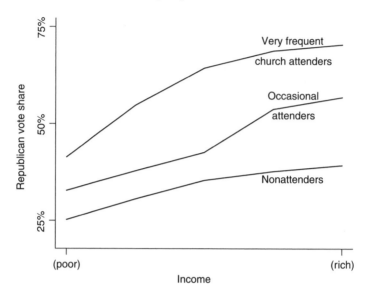

Figure A.11: Income was associated with the McCain vote more among religious attenders. Compare to figure 6.10, which shows a similar pattern for 2004.

the people who identify themselves as having no religion continue to be a strong Democratic bloc.

The pattern of income, religious attendance, and voting is also similar to what we saw in 2000 and 2004; see figure A.11. We also looked at the income and voting pattern within each religion. Among the nonreligious, income is associated very weakly with vote choice, whereas among born-again Protestants, higher-income voters are strongly Republican. Catholics and mainline Protestants fall in between. In other words, low-income religious and nonreligious voters aren't very different, whereas rich people vote very differently depending on whether they are religiously observant.

RED AND BLUE COUNTIES

When we slice up the vote swing by counties in different regions of the United States, we find a similar story to the one we have been telling about states. Obama did close to uniformly better than Kerry nearly everywhere, except for Republican-leaning poor counties in the South (where Obama pretty much stayed even with Kerry). The geographic patterns are striking. Plate 14 shows the counties where Obama did better or worse than Kerry. Allen Gathman has pointed out that this map is similar to that of cotton production in 1860, indicating the importance of longstanding geographic differences.

Given that Obama's only declines (compared to the Democrats' 2004 vote share) were in the South, it is natural to consider differences between whites and blacks. We don't have voting data by race, but from the Census we know the racial composition of each county. In figure A.12 we plot Obama's vote share as a function of the percentage of African Americans in each county. The percentage of blacks acts as a floor on Obama's vote share; beyond that, it predicts his vote better in some regions than others.

But really there are two things going on. First, Obama's getting nearly all the black vote; second, depending on the region, whites and others are voting differently in places with more or fewer African Americans. Obama got 96% of the black vote. If he got 96% in every county—which can't be far from the truth—then we can use algebra to figure out his share of the *nonblack* vote in every county.

This is only an approximation—for one thing, it assumes turnout rates are the same among blacks and others—but we doubt it's too far off. In figure A.13 we plot Obama's estimated vote share among nonblacks, by county, and plate 15 displays these estimates in a map. None of this is a huge surprise: outside the South, places with more African Americans tend to be liberal, urban areas where people of other ethnicities also vote for Democrats; in the South, many African Americans live in counties where the whites are very conservative.

What happened in poor, middle-income, and rich America? Obama gained in almost all the middle-income and rich counties but not so uniformly in poorer counties; see figure A.14. In the Midwest and West, Obama outperformed Kerry in all sorts of counties. In the Northeast, Obama did just a bit better than Kerry

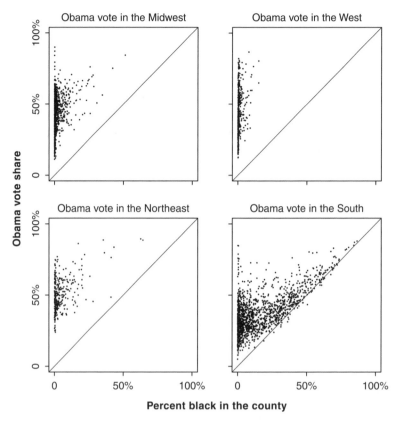

Figure A.12: Obama's vote share plotted vs. the percentage of African Americans, by county.

(who had that northeastern home-state advantage). In the South, Obama did almost uniformly better in rich counties, also did well in middle-income counties (although less so in Republican-leaning areas), and basically showed no improvement from Kerry in poor counties. Looking at the corresponding plots for earlier elections, we find that Gore performed about as well as Clinton in most of the middle-income and rich counties, but he got nuked in poor counties in all regions of the country. This is consistent with the David Brooks story about growing divisions between red and blue America.

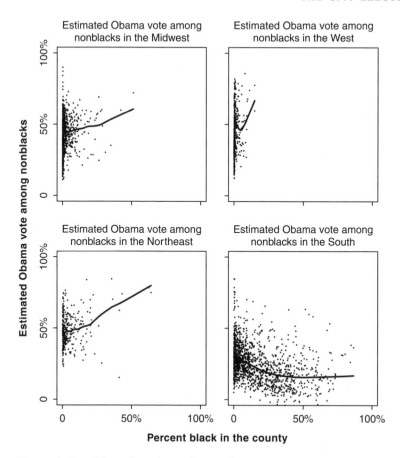

Figure A.13: Obama's estimated vote share among nonblacks, by county, with lowess regression lines superimposed. These graphs represent non-blacks, not whites. Some of the variation has to be explainable by the presence of other minority groups. For a few of the southern counties, our estimates are negative; that just means that Obama got less than 96% of the black vote there, or there was differential turnout, or some combination of these.

PRE-ELECTION POLLS

As in earlier years, polls taken a few days before the general election pretty much nailed the national vote, and they also did well at the state level. (There was much discussion of the problems of the polls during the primary election season. But the general election

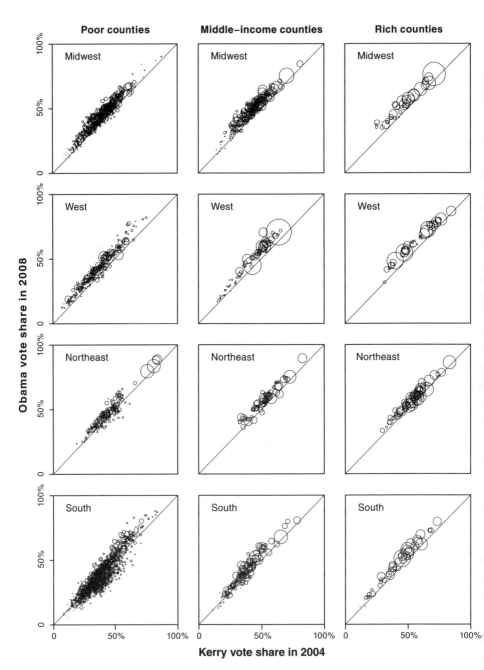

Figure A.14: Obama's vote share, compared to Kerry's, in counties in the lower, middle, and upper third of income, plotted separately for the four regions of the country. Circles are sized proportional to county population.

The 2008 vote closely matched the final pre–election polls

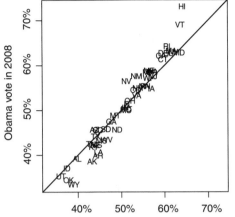

Obama's predicted vote (from Monday poll aggregation)

Figure A.15: State-by-state election returns from 2008, plotted against poll aggregates from the day before the election. The polls were close to perfect in all but a few states.

is different: with a long campaign and only two major candidates who are clearly ideologically differentiated, opinions are much more stable.) Figure A.15 shows the election outcome for each state, compared to an aggregation of polls put together on the day before the election.

The discrepancies between poll data and election results are small, but we do see some systematic patterns: Obama underperformed where the polls had him way down, and he outperformed where the polls had him up. The polls were highly informative but not infallible.

Two aspects of a presidential election are often used for prediction: the national popular vote and the relative positions of the states. The national vote can be forecasted months ahead of time, given the economy and other predictors, for example, by using Douglas Hibbs's model as discussed in chapter 9. And the relative positions of the states don't change much from election to election; see figures A.5 and A.6.

So all that's needed for a good forecast is (1) a prediction of the national swing, and (2) minor adjustments of individual states to

195

capture the differences from uniform swing. Macroeconomic conditions give us (1), and state polls give us (2). Actually, even the February polls turn out to be pretty good—when combined with previous election results—to pin down the relative positions of the states.

For example, in collaboration with statistician Kari Lock, we made state-by-state forecasts using a combination of Hibbs's national popular vote projection and state polls from Feburary 2008. At that time, the Democratic candidate was going to be either Hillary Clinton or Barack Obama, and so we were able to get state-by-state forecasts if either one were running against the Republican nominee, already known by that point to be John McCain. Clinton and Obama were forecast to do similarly well in the popular vote but with some differences in their strengths in individual states, with Clinton, for example, predicted to do better in Arkansas and Obama looking stronger in Virginia.

LOOKING FORWARD

Obama didn't redraw the map; he shifted the map over in his favor. Or, to put it more precisely, the economy shifted the map over in the Democrats' favor and Obama took advantage of this.

What will we see in 2012? Based on recent patterns such as shown in figure A.5, it is reasonable to expect that the relative positions of the states won't change much, and that the national election result will depend more on the economy than on other issues or on the particular appeal of the candidates in that year.

Notes and Sources

FOR further information on what we did, see our article "Rich state, poor state, red state, blue state: What's the matter with Connecticut?" published in the *Quarterly Journal of Political Science,* and the book *Data Analysis Using Regression and Multilevel/Hierarchical Models* by Andrew Gelman and Jennifer Hill. Other information is at our Web site, http://redbluerichpoor.com, and some related discussion is at http://www.stat.columbia.edu/~gelman/blog/.

Our statistical analyses are based on county, state, and national election results and on various opinion polls, most notably the National Annenberg Election Survey in 2000 and 2004, national and state exit polls from 1988 to 2004, the American National Election Study from 1948 to 2004, and the Cooperative Congressional Election Study from 2006. So many surveys are performed nowadays that we suspect our results could be replicated many times over by any researcher willing to put in the effort to put together data from commercial polls. When analyzing votes, we generally work with the Republican Party's share of the two-party vote, ignoring minor parties and nonvoters.

Our key methodological tools in this work have been graphics, repetition, and multilevel models. Graphics help us find unexpected patterns in data, summarizing results so we can understand seemingly contradictory patterns at once, most notably in figure 2.7, the Mississippi/Ohio/Connecticut "superplot." We display all our results graphically in order to bring you closer to our statistical reasoning, to make our conclusions less a matter of trust and more something we have worked through together.

Graphical displays also set us up for our strategy of repeating our analyses on multiple years of historical election results and National Election Study data. Although obvious, this sort of replication is not always done, and when it is done, the resulting pile of analyses can seem too overwhelming to display. Using time-series plots of data summaries and parameter estimates (as in many of the figures here) and repeated graphs (also called "small multiples" and used by graphical innovators such as Jacques Bertin in France and Edward Tufte in the United States), we were able to make these patterns clear in a way that would be difficult using tabular representations. (See Bertin's 1967 book *Semiology of Graphics* [translated by William Berg] and Tufte's *Envisioning Information* from 1990.) The method of repeated modeling, followed by time-series plots of estimates, is sometimes called the "secret weapon" because it is easy and powerful but yet is rarely used as a data-analytic tool. We suspect that one reason for its rarity of use is that, once one acknowledges the time-series structure of a dataset, it is natural to want to take the next step and model that directly. In practice, however, there is a broad range of problems for which a cross-sectional analysis is informative and for which a time-series display is appropriate to give a sense of trends. In our example, the secret weapon allows us to see how cross-sectional estimates for individual states and the entire United States vary over time.

Finally, the statistical method of multilevel regression allows us to estimate separate patterns within each of the fifty states, including state average income as a predictor, while also allowing unexplained state-level variation. In other cases, we batched states into rich, middle-income, and poor, or into Democratic, battleground, and Republican-leaning, to have reasonable sample sizes within each group.

We obtained state and county income numbers from the U.S. Census, the Current Population Survey, and the Bureau of Economic Analysis. We define upper-, middle-, and lower-income states in each election year by ranking states in order of per capita income and dividing so that about one-third of the national population is in each category of state. We similarly define rich, middle-income, and poor voters by approximate thirds of family income, except where otherwise noted. In 2004, the thirds correspond to incomes of under $35,000, between $35,000 and $70,000, and above $70,000.

For some of our 2000 and 2004 analyses, we compare Republican states (those where George W. Bush won at least 55% of the vote in both elections), Democratic states (where Bush received less than 45% both times), and battleground states. Except where otherwise noted, we define the South as Alabama, Arkansas, Florida, Georgia, Kentucky, Louisiana, Mississippi, North Carolina, Oklahoma, South Carolina, Tennessee, Texas, and Virginia.

We made all our graphs and performed most of our statistical analyses using the statistical package R, fitting multilevel models using the "lmer" function written by Doug Bates and also using our own "arm" package for applied regression and multilevel modeling. R (http://www.r-project.org) is an open-source language that was adapted from the statistical environment S, which was developed by John Chambers and others at Bell Labs in the 1970s and 1980s. We worked with much of our survey data using Stata (http://www.stata.com), a commercial statistics package that is widely used in political science and has an active user community. Finally, we performed some of our multilevel analyses in R using Bugs (http://www.mrc-bsu.cam.ac.uk/bugs), a public-use program for Bayesian inference originally developed in the 1990s by David Spiegelhalter and others at the Medical Research Council in England.

We have also benefited from the accumulated wisdom of decades of survey research. Political scientists have been interested in patterns of voting by income or social class for as long as there has been mass voting, and we do not attempt to review the literature here. A few references that are particularly relevant to our discussion are Robert Alford's "The role of social class in American voting behavior," from the *Western Political Quarterly* in 1963; V. O. Key's *The Responsible Electorate*, posthumously published in 1966; Gerald Wright's "Level-of-analysis effects on explanations of voting" in the *British Journal of Political Science* in 1989; John Filer, Lawrence Kenny, and Rebecca Morton's 1993 *American Journal of Political Science* article "Redistribution, income, and voting"; *Statehouse Democracy: Public Opinion and Policy in the American States*, by Robert Erikson, Gerald Wright, and John McIver (1993); Clem Brooks and David Brady's "Income, economic voting, and long-term political change in the U.S., 1952–1996," published in *Social Forces* in 1999; *Class and Party in American Politics*, by Jeffrey Stonecash (2000); Morris Fiorina, Samuel Abrams, and Jeremy Pope's 2005 book, *Culture War? The Myth of Polarized America*; Stephen Ansolabehere, Jonathan Rodden, and James Snyder's 2006 article, "Purple America," in the *Journal of Economic Perspectives*; and the 2006 book, *Polarized America: The Dance of Political Ideology and Unequal Riches*, by Nolan McCarty, Keith Poole, and Howard Rosenthal. In addition, the volume, *Red and Blue Nation? Characteristics and Causes of America's Polarized Politics*, edited by Pietro Nivola and David Brady in 2005, is a wide-ranging collection of articles by journalists and political scientists.

CHAPTER 1: INTRODUCTION

Page 3: Tucker Carlson made his statement about rich Democrats on his show *Tucker* on 16 October 2007.

CHAPTER 2: RICH STATE, POOR STATE

Page 8: In this initial scatterplot (but not most of the others in the book), we have adjusted the positions of some of the state abbreviations slightly so they don't overlap.

Page 9: Thomas Frank's invocation of the hardworking Americans and the liberal elite appeared in his article "What's the matter with liberals?" in the *New York Review of Books* on 12 May 2005.

Page 10: The 2004 exit poll data by income can be found at CNN.com, http://www.cnn.com/ELECTION/2004/pages/results/states/US/P/00/epolls.0.html. Additional exit poll data can be found at the Inter-university Consortium for Political and Social Research, http://www.icpsr.org, study number 4183.

Page 10: David Brooks's description of upscale areas supporting the Democrats comes from his article, "One nation, slightly divisible" in the *Atlantic Monthly* in December 2001. Sasha Issenberg responded a few months later with a dissenting take, "Boo-Boos in paradise," a few months later in *Philadelphia Magazine*. More recently, Mark Liberman discussed the "stir-fry/bbq index" at http://itre.cis.upenn.edu/~myl/languagelog/archives/005326.html.

Pages 12 and 13: We took the income data from Texas and Maryland counties from the U.S. Census. The county-level election results used here and elsewhere come from David Leip's Atlas of U.S. Presidential Elections, http://uselectionatlas.org.

Page 13: The poll asking about which party looks out for the economic interest of the average American was conducted by CNN from 10–22 October 2006.

Page 14: We have discussed *What's the Matter with Kansas?* in the context of divisions between Democrats and Republicans, but Frank's book focuses more on the fight between moderates and conservatives within the Republican Party and the presence of class-based, anti-elitist language in conservative thought and writing. Income is not the same as wealth, which in turn does not completely align with social class; for a recent analysis of these differences, see Ruy Teixeira and Alan Abramowitz's 2008 article "The decline of the white working class and the rise of a mass upper middle class," to appear in *The Future of Red, Blue, and Purple America.*

For another take on Frank's arguments, see Larry Bartels's "What's the matter with *What's the Matter with Kansas?*" which appeared in the *Quarterly Journal of Political Science.* Bartels confirms that white voters without college degrees have become significantly less Democratic; however, the trend is entirely limited to the South. Bartels also finds culture does not outweigh economics among working-class white voters. In his response, "Class dismissed," published in that same journal, Thomas Frank countered that Bartels incorrectly conflates "people with family incomes in the bottom third of the income distribution" with "working-class." Jeffrey Stonecash wrote "Scaring the Democrats: What's the matter with Thomas Frank's argument?" in *The Forum*, where he wrote that the "last 40 years shows a growing class division in American politics, with less affluent whites more supportive of Democrats now than 20–30 years ago. Indeed, even in Kansas less affluent legislative districts are much more supportive of Democrats than affluent districts."

Page 14: The view of Democrats as elitists perhaps began with the party's control over government planning during the New Deal era and was developed as a key theme by populist Republicans in the post-war period, including Richard Nixon, Barry Goldwater, and Ronald Reagan. Early in his career, Nixon was associated with a populist anti-communism, representing ordinary Americans in the battle against elite communist sympathizers. Barry Goldwater had pro-business policies (and came from a business-owning family himself), but in his campaign for the Republican nomination and then for the presidency in 1964, he and his followers were taking the position of insurgents against the liberal establishment.

For more on the populist appeal of Nixon and other mid-century Republicans, see, for example, *McCarthy and His Enemies* by William F. Buckley and Brent Bozell (1954); *Senator Joe McCarthy* by Richard Rovere (1959); *Suburban Warriors: The Origins of the New American Right* by Lisa McGirr (2001); *Before the Storm: Barry Goldwater and the Unmaking of the American Consensus* by Rick Perlstein (2002); and *Nixon's Shadow: The History of an Image* by David Greenberg (2003).

The Democratic Party, too, has had many prominent populists, from William Jennings Bryan over a hundred years ago and Huey Long in the Great Depression, through Harry Truman, Jimmy Carter, Al Gore ("the people versus the powerful"), and John Edwards, but this is less remarkable given its traditional role as the party of the lower classes.

Page 15: The "tax and tax, spend and spend" quote has been attributed to Harry Hopkins. For example, see E. J. Dionne's *New York Times* article "Let Democrats be Democrats" from 15 November 1987.

Page 15: James Carville is reported to have put a sign reading "The economy, stupid" in Bill Clinton's office to remind him to focus on economic issues during his presidential campaign.

Page 17: David Brooks's description of zip code areas with affluent professionals appeared in his *New York Times* column under the title "Bitter at the top" on 15 June 2004.

Page 17: Matt Bai wrote about Bush's red zones in a *Newsweek* article analyzing the 2000 election.

Page 18: The graph of votes by income within Mississippi, Ohio, and Connecticut is based on exit poll data from 2004, smoothed using a statistical model whose details are described in our "What's the matter with Connecticut?" article. Academic work proceeds slowly: we began the project in 2003 with an analysis of the 2000 election. It took us about a year to get all our data together, and then we were held up for another year because we couldn't get the varying-slopes model to fit our data. By the time we were satisfied enough with our model to submit the paper to an academic journal, it was 2005. The review process took another year or so, and then it took us several months to make our changes, which included cleaning our model and fitting to new data including polls from 2004. The article was finally published in late 2007.

CHAPTER 3: HOW THE TALKING HEADS CAN BE SO CONFUSED

Page 24: Nicholas Kristof wrote about the yuppification of the Democratic Party in a column, "Living poor, voting rich," in the *New York Times* on November 3, 2004.

Page 24: Michael Barone's remarks appear in his article "The trustfunder left" at http://www.realclearpolitics.com on 21 March 2005. His *Almanac of American Politics* has been published every two years since 1973.

Page 24: See page 144 for some data on the voting patterns of the richest Americans.

Page 25: For more on the distinction between individual and group-level analyses of elections, see Gerald Kramer's article "The ecological fallacy revisited: Aggregate- versus individual-level findings on economics and elections, and sociotropic voting," which appeared in the *American Political Science Review* in 1983.

Page 25: For more on political participation by different groups, see the 1995 book, *Voice and Equality*, by Sidney Verba, Kay Lehman Schlozman, and Henry Brady.

Page 26: Eleanor Rosch and Carolyn Mervis's article "Family resemblances: Studies in the internal structure of categories," which appeared in *Cognitive Psychology* in 1975, is an important work on people's understanding of typicality. We are not aware of research on stereotypes of states within the United States, but there must be a huge literature on views of typical people of different nationalities.

Political journalists have long explored the psychological effects of the branding of political parties and candidates. Thomas Edsall's 2004 book *Building Red America* discusses the efforts of the two parties to associate themselves with popular attitudes.

Academics such as linguist George Lakoff and psychologist Drew Westen have attributed some of the Republicans' political successes during the 1990s and early 2000s to framing. Westen wrote in his 2007 book *The Political Brain* that "a substantial minority of Americans hold authoritarian, intolerant ideologies driven by fear, hate and prejudice that are fundamentally incompatible with Democratic (and democratic) principles." In a review of Westen's book, David Brooks criticized these "cliches of the Why Democrats Lose genre" as neglecting the substance of politics. In Brooks's words, "Could it be that Democrats won in the middle part of the 20th century because they were right about the big issues—the New Deal and the civil rights movement? Is it possible Republicans won in the latter part of the century because they were right about economic growth and the cold war? Is it possible Democrats are winning now because they were right about whether to go to war in Iraq?"

Our point in this chapter is that psychological associations can be affecting journalists' perceptions of Democrats and Republicans beyond whatever effects these categorizations might be having on voting decisions.

Page 26: Thomas Fitzgerald wrote about microtargeting in the *Houston Chronicle* on 29 October 2006; see also political consultant Mark Penn's 2007 book *Microtrends*.

Page 27: Our graphs of voting by occupation use data from the National Election Study, extending an analysis by Clem Brooks and Jeff Manza in their 1999 book *Social Cleavages and Political Change*. See also the discussion of occupation, income, social class, and voting in Paul

Abramson, John Aldrich, and David Rohde's 2002 book *Change and Continuity in the 2000 Election*.

Page 28: E. J. Dionne's comments on income and class appear in his analysis of 2004 exit poll results, "Polarized by God: American politics and the religious divide," in *Red and Blue Nation*.

Page 28: We compiled the counts of news mentions using Nexis.

Page 29: Nixon described his wife's coat while defending himself against charges of corruption during the famous press conference in which he also mentioned his children's dog, Checkers. The speech was broadcast live on television on 23 September 1952.

Page 30: We got the Wal-Mart data from http://www.walmartstores .com/FactsNews/StateByState/ and Starbucks data from its Web site. We're not trying to draw any deep conclusions from these maps; it's just interesting to see some data, given all the talk about the political leanings of latte drinkers and so forth. The number of Wal-Marts per capita is highly correlated with statewide Republican voting, but the number of Starbucks shows no particular correlation with statewide vote margins for either party. We attribute this more to geography than anything else—Wal-Mart began in Arkansas, at the center of a highly Republican part of the country, whereas Starbucks expanded south from Seattle to the Democratic states of Oregon and California but also eastward to the Republican states of the mountain West.

Page 31: Dan Quayle described his middle-American upbringing in his acceptance speech delivered at the Republican National Convention on 20 August 1992.

Page 31: Toni Morrison is an African American novelist and Nobel Prize winner whose description of Bill Clinton's cultural "blackness" appeared in the *New Yorker* on 5 October 1998. In August of that year, comedian Chris Rock was quoted as calling Clinton "the first black president" in an article by David Kamp in *Vanity Fair*.

Page 32: Dan Quayle made the "rubber ducky" comment at a campaign stop in Milwaukee on 13 September 1988.

Page 32: The survey on attitudes about racial groups was reported by Richard Morin, "A distorted image of minorities; poll suggests that what whites think they see may affect their beliefs" in the *Washington Post* on 8 November 1995.

Page 34: The results on public opinion about immigrants come from the unpublished article "How large the huddled masses? The causes and consequences of public misperceptions about immigrant populations" by John Sides and Jack Citrin.

Page 34: The opinions on foreign aid are presented in the report "Americans on foreign aid," published by the Program on International Policy Attitudes in 1995.

Page 34: Michael Finnegan's analysis of Bustamante's weight loss appeared in the *Los Angeles Times* article "Election 2006: The California vote" on 9 November 2006.

Page 35: For our thoughts on the predictability of voters, see the paper "Why are American presidential election campaign polls so variable when votes are so predictable?" by Andrew Gelman and Gary King, published in the *British Journal of Political Science* in 1993.

Page 35: Matt Franklin prepared a map of the 2004 election with a red dot for every 2,500 Bush voters and a blue dot for for every 2,500 Kerry voters; see http://www.stat.columbia.edu/~cook/movabletype/archives/2007/07/voting_map_with.html.

Page 36: Apparently, Pauline Kael never made the celebrated statement of surprise at Nixon's victory; see Steven Rubio's discussion: http://begonias.typepad.com/srubio/2004/12/kaelnixon_updat.html.

Page 36: Michael Barone's statement about the superaffluent people of fashion appeared in a *U.S. News and World Report* column from 14 September 2005 entitled "Adam Smith, political pundit."

Page 36: For more on the availability bias and the belief that others are similar to oneself, see "The false consensus effect: An egocentric bias in social perception and attribution process" by Lee Ross, David Green, and Pamela House, from the *Journal of Experimental Social Psychology* in 1977, and "The truly false consensus effect: An ineradicable and egocentric bias in social perception" by Joachim Krueger and Russell Clement, from the *Journal of Personality and Social Psychology* in 1994. See also the critique "The false consensus effect and overconfidence: Flaws in judgment or flaws in how we study judgment?" by Robyn Dawes and Matthew Mulford, which appeared in *Organizational Behavior and Human Decision Processes* in 1996.

Page 36: The survey of journalists was a Poynter survey, "The face and mind of the American journalist," conducted at Indiana University and reported at Quicklink A28235, 10 April 2003; see here: http://www.poynter.org/content/content_view.asp?id=28235.

Page 36: We use the term "second-order" because this bias does not involve inference about a frequency (that is what we refer to as first-order availability bias; for example, thinking that muggings are more likely if you have been mugged, or thinking that cancer is rare because you don't know anyone with cancer) but rather inference about a correlation (for example, that richer people are more likely to vote for the Democrats). Correlation, or more precisely covariance, is a second moment in statistical terms, as compared with simple frequencies, which are first moments. What we have termed the "second-order availability bias" is related to the systematic errors in estimation of covariation that have been found by cognitive psychologists; see, for example, chapter 5 of the book *Human Inference: Strategies and Shortcomings of Social Judgment* by Richard Nisbett and Lee Ross, from 1980.

For more general discussions of psychological biases, see the classic collection of articles *Judgment Under Uncertainty: Heuristics and Biases*, edited by Daniel Kahneman, Paul Slovic, and Amos Tversky, from 1982, and the recent book *Predictably Irrational*, by Dan Ariely.

Page 38: The Pew survey on happiness is described here: http://pewresearch.org/pubs/301/are-we-happy-yet.

Page 38: The Gallup survey on party identification and mental health is described here: http://www.gallup.com/poll/102943/Republicans-Report-Much-Better-Mental-Health-Than-Others.aspx.

Arthur Brooks discusses these and similar poll findings in his recent book *Gross National Happiness: Why Happiness Matters for America, and How We Can Get More of It*. In their unpublished article, "Why are conservatives happier than liberals," Jaime Napier and John Jost attribute these differences to different attitudes about economic inequality.

Page 38: Geoffrey Wheatcroft's quote is from his fascinating book *The Strange Death of Tory England*.

Page 39: In his notorious "malaise" speech on 15 July 1979, Jimmy Carter referred to "a crisis of confidence … that strikes at the very heart and soul and spirit of our national will."

Page 39: The 2007 book *Why Do Welfare States Persist?* by Jeff Manza (reviewed by Andrew Gelman in 2008 in *Political Science Quarterly*) discusses reasons for the longstanding stable differences in welfare policy in Europe and the United States.

Page 39: G. K. Chesterton's discussion of happiness in the twelfth and twentieth centuries appears on the final page of his book *Bernard Shaw* from 1910.

CHAPTER 4: INCOME AND VOTING OVER TIME

Page 43: Mark Twain's *Life on the Mississippi* is a book-length development of the theme that what seems eternal is often ephemeral.

Page 44: If you plot presidential election returns for each state *without* first subtracting the national vote, you'll just see the lines jumping up and down with national swings, and the relative patterns of the states will be obscured. Also, in this graph we grouped Indiana among the border south states, Colorado in the southwest, and Alaska in the mountain west, in order to classify states according to their political trends.

Page 45: We exclude third party votes except for 1948, where we count the Republican vote share as votes for Thomas Dewey divided by votes for Harry Truman plus votes for Dixiecrat Strom Thurmond (to account for Truman not being on the ballot in several southern states).

From 1948 onward, our estimates of voting and income for individuals come from the National Election Study cumulative data file. Rich Americans are classified as those in the upper third of family income (greater than or equal to the 68th percentile), with the poor as the lower third (less than or equal to the 33rd percentile). For 1940 and 1944, we use Gallup Poll data compiled by Adam Berinsky and Tiffany Washburn.

Page 47: In their article "Class polarization in partisanship among native Southern whites, 1952–1990," published in the *American Journal of Political Science* in 1993, Richard Nadeau and Harold Stanley discuss how, in recent years, rich and poor people vote more differently in the South than in the rest of the country. See also their 2004 follow-up, written with Richard Niemi and Jean-Francois Godbout, "Class, party, and South/non-South differences: An update," in *American Politics Research.*

Page 47: In *The Responsible Electorate,* V. O. Key analyzes voting and income data from the 1930s through 1960 and finds that the gap between how rich and poor voted increased during the New Deal period and declined in the 1950s.

Page 47: In *Race and the Decline of Class in American Politics,* Robert Huckfeldt and Carol Kohfeld discuss the importance of class-based voting during the New Deal period.

Page 50: The estimates for the states are based on exit poll data fitted to multilevel logistic regression models in each year, as described in our "What's the matter with Connecticut?" paper. The 2000 graph differs slightly from the Mississippi/Ohio/Connecticut superplot on page 18 because we used slightly different income categories here to maintain compatibility with past polls.

The sizes of the circles on the graph on page 50 are based on Census estimates of the proportion of each state's families that were in each of the income categories, compared to the number of families in each category in the entire United States in that year.

Pages 51 and 52: We compute the level and slope for each state based on the fitted logistic regression model for each election year. The level is simply the logistic probability curve evaluated at the mean level of income for the survey respondents in that year, and the slope is computed as the logistic regression slope divided by 4 to transform to the probability scale, as described in chapter 5 of our *Applied Regression and Multilevel Modeling* book.

Page 53: For our historical comparisons of rich and poor, we pool National Election Study data for each pair of decades. The sample size varies from survey to survey, and we reweight so as to count each election year equally.

Page 54: The 2006 U.S. House exit poll data broken down by region are available at http://www.cnn.com/ELECTION/2004/pages/results/states/US/P/00/epolls.0.html

Pages 55–56: Our estimates of historical trends in the House and the Senate come from the National Election Study.

CHAPTER 5: INEQUALITY AND VOTING

Page 58: The graph on income inequality in the United States and other countries comes from "The evolution of top incomes: A historical and international perspective," by Thomas Piketty and Emmanuel Saez, appearing in the *American Economic Review, Papers and Proceedings* in 2006.

Page 59: In "The South will fall again: The South as leader and laggard in economic growth," published in the *Southern Economic Journal*, Mancur Olson attributes the economic growth of the South to the lack of anti-growth distributional coalitions such as are found in many cities in the North. For a recent review, see Edward Glaeser and Kristina Tobio's unpublished article "The rise of the sunbelt," which argues that, from the 1950s through the 1970s, southern economic growth was driven by increasing productivity, with growth since 1980 being supported by a more elastic housing supply.

Page 62: The Tax Foundation study of tax receipts and federal spending in the states appears at http://www.taxfoundation.org/research /show/266.html.

Page 63: Edward Glaeser and Bryce Ward's comment about rural and urban states comes from their article "Myths and realities of American political geography," which appeared in the *Journal of Economic Perspectives* in 2006.

Page 64: We use the revised 2004 version of the cost of living index developed by William Berry, Richard Fording, and Russell Hanson and described in the paper "An annual cost of living index for the American states, 1960–95," which appeared in the *Journal of Politics* in 2000. The cost of living index can change dramatically depending on what it includes. For example, a state-level aggregation of the city-level Accra index (used for estimating cost of living for relocations of corporate employees) gives California a level of 151, compared to 100 in Minnesota. In contrast, the Berry, Fording, and Hanson index that we use gives Minnesota a 105 and California a 109. The difference may lie in how the indexes account for housing costs; further discussion appears at http:// www.stat.columbia.edu/~cook/movabletype/archives/2007/09/ update_on_cost.html.

Page 64: Todd Wasserman's comparison of incomes in different states comes from his article "Divided we brand" in the advertising trade magazine *Brandweek* on 17 June 2002.

Page 65: Michael Barone's remarks are taken from his aforementioned article "The trustfunder left."

Pages 68–70: For each presidential election year, we fit a linear regression of Republican vote on county income in each year with a multilevel model allowing the intercept and slope to vary by state. County incomes were standardized (as described in the 2008 *Statistics in Medicine* paper "Scaling regression inputs by two standard deviations" by Andrew Gelman) so that the slope within each state can be interpreted as the difference in Republican vote between rich and poor counties in that state. Alaska is excluded from this graph because its income and election returns are reported in different geographical units.

Page 70: The saying about Pennsylvania including Alabama within it is also attributed to many people in politics; see, for example, the article

"The 10 regions of US politics" by Robert Sullivan, in the *Boston Globe* on 18 January 2004.

Jonathan Rodden discusses some of the implications of the political differences between rural, suburban, and urban areas in America and elsewhere in his forthcoming book *Political Geography and Electoral Rules: Why Single-Member Districts Are Bad for the Left*; see http://web.mit.edu/ polisci/research/rodden/ucsd_07.pdf.

Page 71: Thomas and Mary Edsall's description of how the Democratic Party is viewed comes from their 1991 book *Chain Reaction.*

Page 71: In their 1996 *American Journal of Political Science* paper "Will the real Americans please stand up: Anglo and Mexican-American support of core American political values," Rodolfo de la Garza, Angelo Falcon, and F. Chris Garcia discuss the relation between cultural values and voting among these groups.

Page 72: For each county, congressional district, state, and region, we compute the difference in Republican share, comparing the rich and poor respondents in the 2000 Annenberg pre-election survey. We then average these within each region, weighting by the sample size for each comparison.

Also relevant to the discussion of local comparisons of income is Jacob Vigdor's unpublished paper "Fifty million voters can't be wrong: Economic self-interest and redistributive politics," which sets up a model in which people support left or right parties based on their income relative to their neighbors.

Page 72: See Matthew Lassiter's 2007 book *The Silent Majority: Suburban Politics in the Sunbelt South,* for more on that region's transition from the Democratic to the Republican Party.

Chapter 6: Religious Reds and Secular Blues

Page 76: George H. W. Bush's statement about atheists was reported by Robert Sherman of the *American Atheist* news journal on 27 August 1987.

Page 76: John Podesta was quoted by Gail Russell Chaddock in the *Christian Science Monitor* on 9 June 2004.

Page 76: In the 1992 book *The Churching of America, 1776–1990: Winners and Losers in Our Religious Economy,* Roger Finke and Rodney Stark study "how and why America shifted from a nation in which most people took no part in organized religion to a nation in which nearly two-thirds of American adults do."

Page 77: There is a large literature comparing the United States to other less religious developed countries. The graph of religiosity and income across countries is adapted from the Pew Global Attitudes Project report of 4 October 2007, http://pewglobal.org/reports/display.php?ReportID=258. Religiosity is measured by survey responses to three questions involving faith in God, the importance of religion, and daily prayer. Some of the country names on the scatterplot have been moved slightly to avoid overplotting.

Page 78: Robert Putnam told us about the frequent pattern of people changing their church attendance to fit their political views.

Page 78: The statistics on divorces come from a *New York Times* article "To avoid divorce, move to Massachusetts" by Pam Belluck, 14 November 2004.

Page 78: We estimated the probability of voting for Bush given religion and religious attendance using a multilevel logistic regression fit to the 2004 Annenberg pre-election survey. Polls from 2000 gave similar results except that the line for Jews was flat, with essentially no correlation between synagogue attendance and vote for Bush or Gore.

Page 79: Alan Wolfe's comment about lifestyles in red and blue America comes from his article "Myths and realities of religion in politics" in *Red and Blue Nation*.

Page 79: Jean Baudrillard's quote about joggers appears in his book *America*, translated by Chris Turner.

Page 80: We pool the 2000 and 2004 Annenberg surveys to estimate the average religious attendance within each state. Polls typically do not survey enough people in small states to get representative samples in each state—they aim for the whole country. This creates a challenge for us, which we deal with by statistical modeling and, in figures 6.3 and 6.7, by pooling data from 2000 and 2004 to get a reasonably large sample size within each state. Another measure of religiosity, which gives similar results to ours, is provided by Robert Putnam, who combines state-level data on church adherents, number of religious organizations per person, and average responses to survey questions on religious attendance and the importance of religion.

Page 80: Alan Wolfe's statement about bowling alone but praying together comes from his aforementioned article "Myths and realities of religion in politics."

Page 80: For more on people overreporting church attendance, see http://www.stat.columbia.edu/~cook/movabletype/archives/2006/07/counting_church.html.

Page 81: The time series on church attendance comes from the National Election Study cumulative data file. Through 1968, the question was a five-category response: regularly, often, seldom, never, or no religious preference. Starting in 1970, the question became a six-category response: every week, almost every week, once or twice a month, a few times a year, never, or no religious preference. We combined both questions into a three-category response. Through 1968, we code "regularly" as regular attendance, "often" and "seldom" as occasional attendance, and "never" and "no religious attendance" as nonattendance. For the surveys since 1970, we code "every week" and "almost every week" as regular, "once or twice a month" and "a few times a year" as occasional, and "never" and "no religious preference" as nonattendance. (We use the terms "church attendance" and "religious attendance" interchangeably throughout.) Survey respondents are told not to include weddings and funerals when counting attendance at religious services.

In their paper "Why more Americans have no religious preference: Politics and generations," published in 2002 in the *American Sociological Review*, Michael Hout and Claude Fisher attribute the increase in the rate of religious nonattachment to demographic shifts, including delayed marriage and parenthood, and report that "Most people with no preference hold conventional religious beliefs, despite their alienation from organized religion....The increase in 'no religion' responses was confined to political moderates and liberals; the religious preferences of political conservatives did not change."

Page 82: We constructed the graphs of income and church attendance and born-again status from the 2004 Annenberg survey. The born-again question was asked only of survey respondents who had described themselves as Protestant.

Page 83: We took the data on prayer and the importance of religion from the World Values Survey, pooling data from 1980 through 2004. A similar graph appears in Pippa Norris and Ronald Inglehart's 2005 book *Sacred and Secular: Religion and Politics Worldwide*.

Page 84: E. J. Dionne made this statement about the paradox of the Religious Right in his book *Why Americans Hate Politics*.

Page 84: In computing the correlations of religious attendance and income, we pooled the responses from the 2000 and 2004 Annenberg surveys.

Page 85: In his 1997 autobiography, Jerry Falwell wrote of *Roe v. Wade:* "The Supreme Court had just made a decision by a seven-to-two margin that would legalize the killing of millions of unborn children. In one terrible act they struck down all the state laws against abortion and legalized infanticide across the land. I could not believe that seven justices on the nation's highest court could have so little regard for the value of human life. Apparently, there were others who shared my disbelief." (Quoted by Michael Foust in the *Baptist Press*, 15 May 1997.)

Pages 85 and 86: The time trends in voting by religion come from the National Election Study, which has asked about religious denomination and religious attendance from the beginning.

Pages 88 and 92: We computed Bush's vote by income and religious attendance from the 2004 Annenberg survey.

Page 89: E. J. Dionne's analysis of geography and religious voting appear in his article "Polarized by God" in *Red and Blue Nation*.

Page 90: We construct estimates for individual states using a multilevel linear model fit separately to each of the four sets of correlations, with economic and social issues scales that we constructed from the following questions in the 2000 Annenberg survey. *Economic*: are tax rates a problem, favor cutting taxes or strengthening Social Security, federal government should reduce the top tax rate, federal government should adopt flat tax, federal government should spend more on Social Security, favor investing Social Security in stock market, is poverty a problem, federal government should reduce income differences, federal government should spend more on aid to mothers with young children, federal government should expend effort to eliminate many business regulations. *Social*: federal government should give school vouchers, federal government should restrict abortion, federal government should ban abortion, favor death penalty, favor handgun licenses, federal government should expend effort to restrict gun purchases, are underpunished criminals a problem, is immigration a problem, favor gays in military, federal government should expend effort to stop job discrimination against gays, federal government should expend effort to stop job discrimination against blacks, federal government should expend effort to stop job discrimination against women, federal government should allow school prayer. We recode each question so that lower numbers indicate liberal responses and higher numbers conservative ones. We then add the responses and rescale. Unfortunately, the 2004 version of this survey did not ask a full range of economic and social issue questions and so we were not able to construct good scales for that year.

Page 91: A fuller version of the Karl Marx quote, from his *Critique of Hegel's Philosophy of Right,* has been translated as, "Religion is the sigh of the oppressed creature, the heart of a heartless world, just as it is the spirit of a spiritless situation. It is the opium of the people."

Page 93: Linguist Mark Liberman writes, "I suspect that it remains true in the U.S. that on average, lower-income people are more likely to have local accents." Liberman cites the following passage from Jenny Cheshire and Peter Trudgill's article "Dialect and education in the United Kingdom," which appeared in the 1989 book *Dialect and Education:* "In Great Britain and Northern Ireland, as in many other countries, the relationship between social and regional language varieties is such that the greatest degree of regional differentiation is found among lower working-class speakers and the smallest degree at the other end of the social scale, among speakers from the upper middle class." See http://www.stat.columbia.edu/~cook/movabletype/archives/2008/03/who_talks_like.html

CHAPTER 7: THE UNITED STATES IN COMPARATIVE PERSPECTIVE

Page 94: Denise Dresser wrote about the close election in the article "Ocho lecciones" in *Reforma,* 3 July 2006.

Page 94: James McKinley's overview of Mexico's political geography appeared in "Mexico faces its own red-blue standoff," in the *New York Times,* 9 July 2006.

Page 96: A good sample of works studying the variation in voting behavior in recent Mexican elections are the edited volume by Jorge Domínguez and Chappell Lawson, *Mexico's Pivotal Democratic Election: Candidates, Voters, and the Presidential Campaign of 2000;* the book by Domínguez and James McCann, *Democratizing Mexico: Public Opinion and Electoral Choices;* Alejandro Moreno's *El Votante Mexicano: Democracia, Actitudes Políticas y Conducta Electoral;* and *México 2006: Los Ciudadanos Ante las Urnas,* edited by Ulíses Beltrán from Mexico's Centro de Investigación y Docencia Económicas.

Page 96: We give state-level GDP in purchasing-power-parity 2000 U.S. dollars; see *Informe sobre desarrollo humano: Mexico 2002*, published in 2003 by Programa de las Naciones Unidas para el Desarrollo.

Page 98: Ricardo Alemán's conclusions about the reality of social polarization appeared in *El Universal*, "Itinerario político: no gana pero arrebata," 3 July 2006.

Page 98: Adapting Joseph Klesner's 2004 article "The structure of the Mexican electorate" in *Mexico's Pivotal Democratic Election: Candidates, Voters, and the Presidential Campaign of 2000*, we define the regions of Mexico as follows. *North*: Baja California, Baja California Sur, Coahuila, Chihuahua, Durango, Nuevo León, San Luis Potosí, Sinaloa, Sonora, Tamaulipas, Zacatecas. *Center-west*: Aguascalientes, Colima, Guanajuato, Jalisco, Michoacán, Nayarit, Querétaro. *Center*: Estado de México, Hidalgo, Morelos, Puebla, Tlaxcala. *South*: Campeche, Chiapas, Guerrero, Oaxaca, Quintana Roo, Tabasco, Veracruz, Yucatán. For our analyses, we consider the Federal District (México, D.F.) as its own state and region, distinct from the rest of the Estado de México.

Page 98: Juan Linz and Alfred Stepan write in their 1996 book *Problems of Democratic Transition and Consolidation*: "A democratic transition is complete when sufficient agreement has been reached about political procedures to produce an elected government, when a government comes to power that is the direct result of a free and popular vote, when this government de facto has the authority to generate new policies, and when the executive, legislative and judicial power generated by the new democracy does not have to share power with other bodies de jure."

Page 99: Our central model is a varying-intercept, varying-slope logistic regression predicting vote choice from individual income and GDP per capita, which we fit to data from Mitofsky International for 1994, Consulta Mitofsky-Televisa for 2000, and BGC Ulíses Beltrán y Asocs. for 2006, excluding those respondents who did not report for whom they voted or who supported parties other than the PAN, PRI, or PRD. This left us with 4,213 responses for 1994, 24,584 for 2000, and 3,709 for 2006, with sample sizes within states ranging from 23 in Quintana Roo in the year 1994 to 3,947 in Guanajuato in 2000. The multilevel model allows us to estimate the income–voting relation in each state, with the estimates for the larger states coming largely from their own data and the estimates for smaller states relying more on the state-level regression model. (More specifically, each estimated state-level coefficient in a multilevel model is a weighted average of the unpooled estimate for the state and the completely pooled estimate using individual and state-level predictors.) Further analysis appears in our unpublished paper "One vote, many Mexicos: Income and vote choice in the 1994, 2000, and 2006 presidential elections" by Jeronimo Cortina, Andrew Gelman, and Narayani Lasala.

Page 101: Our data on income, religious attendance, and voting come from the Comparative Study of Electoral Systems, a collaborative program of cross-national research among election studies conducted in over fifty countries. Our analysis is adapted from John Huber and Piero Stanig's unpublished article "Why do the poor support right-wing parties? A cross-national analysis." The sample of countries includes modules covering a time period from 1996 to 2006. We used the most recent election for each country in the sample. Some of the classification of parties as left and right came from the Party Policy in Modern Democracies dataset, constructed by Kenneth Benoit and Michael Laver. Huber and Stanig define parties as right- or left-wing based on their positions on economic redistribution. For our analyses, we classify parties as left (including center-left) or right (including center-right), excluding votes for parties that could not be easily classified on the left–right scale.

In the unpublished article "Religious belief, religious participation, and social policy attitudes across countries," Huber studies the relations between religious belief, participation, and attitudes on economic and social issues, finding that "church attenders become relatively more conservative than non-attenders as GDP increases, corruption declines, and abortion policy becomes more liberal."

Page 101: William Gibson is the author of *Neuromancer* and other science fiction books. His statement about the future being unevenly distributed has been much quoted, for example in the article "The future catches up with novelist William Gibson" by Fiona Morrow in the *Toronto Globe and Mail*, 3 October 2007.

Page 103: Within each country, we collapse the five income categories of the Comparative Study of Electoral Systems into three and then take the difference of conservative vote in the highest and lowest of the three income categories.

Page 104: We fit a multilevel logistic regression model with varying intercepts and varying slopes for income, religious attendance, and their interaction. The graphs include fewer countries than in figure 7.4 because not all the surveys asked about religious attendance. We display the fitted model in each country, which can be misleading because the actual pattern is not always smooth; for example, in some countries, middle-income people vote more conservatively than the rich or the poor. The purpose of this figure is to quickly show overall patterns of richer or more religious people voting conservatively in different countries.

Page 105: In his 2002 book *Citizen Politics: Public Opinion and Political Parties in Advanced Industrial Democracies*, Russell Dalton contrasts politics in predominantly Catholic countries with those of mixed religions.

Page 107: The Democratic and Republican Parties' positions have shifted over the years. The Republicans traditionally favored tariffs, with the Democrats supporting free trade, with Franklin Roosevelt lowering tariffs during his presidency. By 1993, Bill Clinton pushed for the ratification of the North American Free Trade Agreement against the opposition of organized labor and a majority of the Democrats in Congress, and free trade is now more strongly associated with the Republicans. In the article "Activists and partisan realignment in the United States," published in the *American Political Science Review* in 2003, Gary Miller and Norman Schofield trace in general terms the changing bases of support of the two parties during the twentieth century, considering positions in the economic and social dimensions.

CHAPTER 8: POLARIZED PARTIES

Page 111: Barry Goldwater is a conservative icon today, but back when he was running for president he was notorious for his seemingly effortless ability to offend large segments of the American population. Richard Rovere's 1965 book *The Goldwater Caper* has many more examples.

Page 111: Rodney King made his famous statement after the 1992 Los Angeles riots. For more on King and how his quote has been remembered, see http://www.time.com/time/specials/2007/la_riot/article/0,28804,1614117_1614084,00.html.

Page 111: In a CNN poll from January 2005, 49% of respondents thought Bush was a "uniter," 49% thought he was a "divider," and 2% had no opinion: http://www.cnn.com/2005/ALLPOLITICS/01/19/poll/. For a whole book on the topic, see Gary Jacobson's book *A Divider, Not a Uniter: George Bush and the American People*.

Page 112: The much-emailed Jesusland map was created by G. Webb on 3 November 2004.

Page 113: The "feeling thermometer" series come from the National Election Study.

Page 113: The idea that voters have sorted by party is developed by Matthew Levendusky in the article "Sorting, not polarization: The changing nature of party ID and ideology in the U.S. electorate," presented at the 2004 meeting of the American Political Science Association, and by Morris Fiorina, Samuel Abrams, and Jeremy Pope in the 2005 book *Culture War? The Myth of Polarized America*. In their 2006 *American Journal of Political Science* article, "Changing sides or changing minds? Party identification and policy preferences in the American electorate," Thomas Carsey and Geoffrey Layman have found that for issues that are not particularly salient, people may change their issue stances to conform with their existing partisan preferences rather than the reverse.

Page 114: McCarty, Poole, and Rosenthal, in their *Polarized America* book, and David Brady and Hahrie Han, in their article "Polarization then and now," in *Red and Blue Nation*, provide evidence that members of single-issue-based interest groups tend to hold extreme positions. See also James Campbell's discussion of Brady and Han in that same volume.

Page 115: The data on opinions about Iraq come from the *Washington Post*/ABC News Poll, as reported by Robert Shapiro and Yaeli Bloch-Elkon in their 2006 paper "Political polarization and the rational public," which was prepared for the Center for American Progress and The Century Fund's Conference on Power and Superpower: Global Leadership in the Twenty-first Century.

Furthermore, as Alan Abramowitz and Bill Bishop write in their column "The myth of the middle" in the *Washington Post* from 1 March 2007, "the divisions between the parties weren't limited to Iraq....For example, 69 percent of Democratic voters chose the most strongly pro-choice position on the issue of abortion, compared with 20 percent of Republican voters; only 16 percent of Democratic voters supported a constitutional amendment to ban same-sex marriage, while 80 percent of Republican voters did; and 91 percent of Democratic voters favored governmental action to reduce global warming, compared with 27 percent of Republican voters. When we [Abramowitz and Bishop] combined voters' answers to the 14 issue questions to form a liberal-conservative scale (answers were divided into five equivalent categories based on overall liberalism vs. conservatism), 86 percent of Democratic voters were on the liberal side of the scale while 80 percent of Republican voters were on the conservative side. Only 10 percent of all voters were in the center."

Page 115: Partisan differences in political perceptions are not new. For example, in their article "Misperceptions about perceptual bias," from the 1999 *Annual Review of Political Science*, Alan Gerber and Donald Green note the striking finding from V. O. Key's *Public Opinion and American Democracy*: "Early survey researchers noted in 1936 that 83% of Republicans felt that President Roosevelt's policies were leading the country down the road to dictatorship, a view shared by only 9% of Democrats." Gerber and Green connect this to psychological research on cognitive dissonance and stability of attitudes.

Page 116: The poll data from Korea and Vietnam come from the American Institute of Public Opinion surveys and were reported by Shapiro and Bloch-Elkon, who got the data from John Mueller's 1973 book, *War, Presidents, and Public Opinion*.

Page 117: The data on perceptions of inflation come from the 1988 National Election Study, as reported by Larry Bartels in his article "Beyond the running tally: Partisan bias in political perceptions," published in *Political Behavior* in 2002. It was not just Democrats who misperceived or misremembered economic statistics—even among strong Republicans, only half thought inflation had gotten much better during Reagan's term—but the gap between the parties is disturbing.

Another mysterious pattern in these surveys is that respondents of both parties thought more favorably about trends in unemployment than inflation. For example, among strong Democrats, 30% thought that unemployment had improved, but less than 25% said this about inflation; among strong Republicans, the corresponding numbers were 85% for unemployment and only 70% for inflation. Actually, though, unemployment declined only slightly during Reagan's time in office (from 7.1% to 5.5%), compared to inflation falling by more than two thirds.

Page 117: Senator Santorum made his famous statement about "man on dog" in an Associated Press interview on 7 April 2003.

Page 118: The trends on abortion attitudes come from the National Election Study and are reported in Joseph Bafumi and Robert Shapiro's unpublished article "A new partisan voter." The four possible responses to the question are:

1. By law, abortion should never be permitted.
2. The law should permit abortion only in case of rape, incest, or when the woman's life is in danger.

3. The law should permit abortion for reasons other than rape, incest, or danger to the woman's life, but only after the need for the abortion has been clearly established.

4. By law, a woman should always be able to obtain an abortion as a matter of personal choice.

Page 118: The survey on 9/11 conspiracies was conducted by the Rasmussen survey group in May, 2007. As noted, Republicans overwhelmingly disagreed with the claim that George W. Bush knew about the attacks in advance. Among Democrats, 35% thought that Bush knew, while 39% did not agree (26% were not sure); details are at http://www.rasmussenreports.com/public_content/politics/current_events/general_current_events/president_bush/22_believe_bush_knew_about_9_11_attacks_in_advance.

Given what we know about perceptual screens induced by polarization, we would expect the converse would hold true about agreement with the notion that President Clinton's missile attacks on Sudan and Afghanistan in August 1998 were instances of "wagging the dog" or done as distractions from the Lewinsky scandal. And this is in fact the case. From a *Los Angeles Times* poll in August, 1998, 68% of Democrats agreed with the idea that the strikes were for legitimate, national security reasons. On the other hand, only 50% of Republicans felt the same way; see http://www.latimes.com/news/nationworld/timespoll/la-980823raidpoll-415pa1an,1,7942692.htmlstory.

Page 119: Edward Glaeser and Bryce Ward recount geographic variation in opinions in their article "Myths and realities of American political geography." In their unpublished paper "Public opinion and policy responsiveness: Gay rights in the states" Jeffrey Lax and Justin Phillips connect state-by-state variation in attitudes to differences in state policies.

Page 119: The material on voters' perceptions of economic issues is taken from Joseph Bafumi's unpublished article "The decline of economic retrospections." This is part of a literature showing evidence for the increasing importance of partisan lenses during the current era of partisan polarization. For example, Shapiro and Bloch-Elkon find that foreign policy stances are more painted by partisan allegiances than ever before, and Gary Jacobson shows this for a variety of issues in *A Divider, Not a Uniter*. Also relevant to this discussion is Morris Fiorina's 1981 book *Retrospective Voting in American National Elections*.

Page 119: Carl Cannon presents his views on excess partisanship in his article in *Red and Blue Nation*.

Page 123: The data and graphs on ideological positions of congress-members come from McCarty, Poole, and Rosenthal's book *Polarized America*, which itself draws upon earlier work of these researchers on aligning legislators using roll call votes. Brady and Han further discuss historical patterns of polarization in their article "Polarization then and now."

Page 123: Claudia Goldin and Robert Margo published the paper "The Great Compression: The wage structure in the United States at mid-century" in the *Quarterly Journal of Economics* in 1992. In *The Conscience of a Liberal*, Paul Krugman draws upon that work in giving his perspective on the trends in political and economic inequality over the past half century.

In "The American wage structure, 1920–1947," published in the journal *Research in Economic History* in 1999, Thomas Ferguson and James Galbraith discuss the roles of unionization and Keynesian economic policies in setting America up for a period of full employment.

Page 124: Richard Nixon's statement about the universality of Keyenesian economics is mentioned in *Time* magazine's profile of John Maynard Keynes at http://www.time.com/time/time100/scientist/profile/keynes03.html.

Page 124: The issues used here to scale opinions of voters and members of Congress are based on roll call votes in the House and Senate. These issues include stem cell research, the minimum wage, the appropriate use of the military, immigration, international trade agreements, the capital gains tax, the partial birth abortion ban, the Patriot Act, gun control, medical malpractice legislation, Internet gambling, bankruptcy protection, funding overseas abortions, several first amendment cases, and many other issues. Questions asking about vote choices and ideological and partisan self-placement were also used. The questions were asked of a random sample of 8,223 respondents from the Cooperative Congressional Election Study, an Internet survey conducted by Polimetrix and organized by the Massachusetts Institute of Technology and involving several universities around the country. The sample used for this research stems from the extended Dartmouth, MIT, and UCSD pools of respondents.

Pages 125 and 131: The graphs showing simultaneous positions of voters and politicians are adapted from the 2007 paper "Preference aggregation, representation, and elected American political institutions" by

Joseph Bafumi and Michael Herron. That paper also presents estimates for the positions of Congress before and after the 2006 election and for the estimated median voter in individual states.

Page 125: The claim that citizens who are more politically involved tend to be more extreme than the electorate comes from Bafumi and Herron, who estimate the ideological positions of the survey respondents who have contributed financially to political campaigns.

Page 126: We estimate the rate of split-ticket voting using responses to the National Election Study in each presidential election year.

Page 126: The statement about "liberal voters leaving the Republican party and conservatives leaving the Democrats" is supported by an analysis by Bafumi and Shapiro, who fit a logistic regression predicting party identification from self-declared ideology (on a liberal–conservative scale) and several demographic predictors, fitting separately to pre-election poll data from each election since 1972. The coefficient for ideology has steadily increased, more than doubling in size over the period, ending up being the most important predictor in the model, except for race and religion. The analysis is described in Bafumi and Shapiro's paper "A new partisan voter."

Page 127: Half a year after his celebrated convention address, Barack Obama said, "Since that election, that gay couple I knew in the red states? They've moved back to the blue states," in a speech at the Gridiron Club in Washington, D.C.

Page 127: The data on the diversity of partisan opinions in multiple dimensions come from the National Election Study. Social scientists have a long tradition of debate about the level of incoherence in American opinions, dating back at least to Angus Campbell, Philip Converse, Warren Miller, and Donald Stokes's 1960 book *The American Voter*, and Philip Converse's paper "The nature of belief systems in mass publics" in the 1964 volume *Ideology and Discontent*. Since then, important research in this area includes Christopher Achen's 1975 *American Political Science Review* article "Mass political attitudes and the survey response"; Robert Erikson's 1979 *British Journal of Political Science* article "The SRC panel data and mass political attitudes"; Norman Nie, Sidney Verba, and John Petrocik's 1979 book *The Changing American Voter*; John Zaller and Stanley Feldman's 1992 *American Journal of Political Science* article "A simple theory of the survey response: Answering questions versus revealing preferences"; Zaller's 1992 book *The Nature and Origins of Mass Opinion*; Diana Mutz's 1998 book *Impersonal Influence:*

How Perceptions of Mass Collectives Affect Political Attitudes; and much other work.

Page 129: Robert Erikson, Gerald Wright, and John McIver demonstrate the sorting of voters by party in their 1993 book *Statehouse Democracy*.

Page 129: Our analysis of issue polarization using time trends in correlations follows the article "Partisans without constraint: Political polarization and trends in American public opinion" by Delia Baldassarri and Andrew Gelman, to appear in the *American Journal of Sociology*.

Page 130: Alan Abramowitz and Kyle Saunders wrote about the differences between red and blue state voters in the article "Is polarization a myth?" in the *Journal of Politics* in 2006.

Page 133: We estimate the trends in correlations of issue attitudes using the National Election Study. Not all questions were asked in all years, so we compute correlations where possible and then fit a varying-intercept, varying-slope model to allow a different linear time trend for each pair of responses.

In looking at correlations among issues, we also consider the approach of aggregating survey items to create a single measure for each issue domain. Following this strategy, we confirm the findings of Stephen Ansolabehere, Jonathan Rodden, and James Snyder in their unpublished 2006 paper "Issue preferences and measurement error": when we look at averages and when the number of items increases, we see higher constraint between issue domains.

Page 134: John Kenneth White's comment about parallel universes was quoted in the article "Democrats are slow to connect with voters" by Bill Lambrecht in the *St. Louis Post-Dispatch*, 14 August 2005.

Page 134: In their paper, "Dynamics of political polarization," forthcoming in the *American Sociological Review*, Delia Baldassarri and Peter Bearman set up a model in which people can overestimate the amount of polarization because they unwittingly limit their political discussions to topics on which they agree.

Page 135: The summaries of Bush voters knowing Bush voters and Gore voters knowing Gore voters are based on data from a special set of questions asked in the 2000 National Election Study. First, each respondent was asked about up to four people with whom they "discuss government, elections, and politics." Then, for each of the names that was given as a discussion partner, the survey respondent was asked, "How do you think _____ voted in the election? Do you think he/she voted for Al Gore, George Bush, some other candidate, or do you think _____ didn't vote?" We computed proportions by combining the information from all respondents, excluding those contacts whose vote preferences were unknown.

Page 135: Stephen Ansolabehere, Jonathan Rodden, and James Snyder wrote that most Americans are ideological moderates in their article "Purple America," which appeared in the *Journal of Economic Perspectives* in 2006. Here, they "put issue cleavages and electoral maps into historical perspective and demonstrate that over the course of the twentieth century there has been a noteworthy political convergence between the states. Compared to the past, the political geography of the United States today is purple."

Page 136: Paul DiMaggio, John Evans, and Bethany Bryson discuss trends in distributions of attitudes is their 1986 article "Have Americans' social attitudes become more polarized?" published in the *American Journal of Sociology*, and updated by John Evans in *Social Science Quarterly* in 2003. Also see chapter 7 of Benjamin Page and Robert Shapiro's 1992 compendium *The Rational Public: Fifty Years of Trends in Americans' Policy Preferences*.

Page 136: In "How polarization affects political engagement," from *Red and Blue Nation*, Marc Hetherington argues that "elite polarization has stimulated participation at the mass level even though the masses remain relatively moderate."

Page 136: We generally agree with Fiorina's claims about moderate voters and polarized politics, but there is some dispute over this topic in political science; see, for example, the discussion of Fiorina and Levendusky's article in *Red and Blue Nation*, Abramowitz and Saunders's aforementioned "Is polarization a myth?" and Gary Jacobson's *A Divider, Not a Uniter*.

CHAPTER 9: COMPETING TO BUILD A MAJORITY COALITION

Page 137: The *Los Angeles Times* editorial on the red–blue schism appeared on 4 November 2004.

Page 137: Tom DeLay gave his thoughts on partisanship in his farewell speech upon his retirement from the House of Representatives; the scene is described in Ronald Brownstein's 2007 book, *The Second Civil War: How Extreme Partisanship Has Polarized Washington and Polarized America*.

Page 139: Will Rogers's statement about the Republicans is included in his posthumous collection *Never Met a Man I Didn't Like*.

Page 139: Clare Boothe Luce was a playwright, congresswoman, and Republican Party activist. Her description of Democrats as troubadours of trouble has been dated to the 1952 Republican national convention (in Colin Bingham's 1982 book *Wit and Wisdom: A Public Affairs Miscellany*) and the 1956 convention (in William Safire's "On language" column in the *New York Times*, 21 June 1992).

Page 139: A striking example of the majority of voters supporting conservative economic policies was the debate over the repeal of the inheritance tax, a repeal that would largely benefit people in the top 1% of incomes. Larry Bartels wrote a paper, "Homer Simpson gets a tax cut," analyzing survey data and coming to the conclusion that most people who supported repealing the inheritance tax expected that they would personally benefit from the repeal, even though realistically a great majority will never amass enough assets for the tax to apply to them. The Homer Simpson paper has been incorporated into Bartels's new book *Unequal Democracy: The Political Economy of the New Gilded Age*. For more on the politics behind the inheritance tax battle, see Michael Graetz and Ian Shapiro's 2005 book *Death by a Thousand Cuts*.

Page 141: Larry Bartels's graph of income growth under Democratic and Republican presidents appears in *Unequal Democracy* and is reproduced here courtesy of the Russell Sage Foundation. The graph here shows pre-tax income; Bartels also presents post-tax comparisons.

In their 2002 book *Partisan Hearts and Minds: Political Parties and the Social Identities of Voters*, Donald Green, Brad Palmquist, and Eric Shickler discuss how Republicans could dominate presidential voting during the forty-year period where Democrats were the majority in congressional voting and party identification.

Page 141: The discussion of economic growth under Democratic and Republican presidents is related to the political business cycle theory in economics and political science. In their paper "Political parties and the business cycle in the United States, 1948–1984," published in the *Journal of Money, Credit, and Banking* in 1988, Alberto Alesina and Jeffrey Sachs wrote:

The most famous attempt to model the relationship between political and economic cycles is the "political business cycle" theory formulated by Nordhaus (1975) and MacRae (1977). Three crucial assumptions underlie this approach: (i) the parties care only about winning the elections, as in Downs (1957); (ii) the voters have short memories and can be systematically fooled; and (iii) the economy is described by an exploitable Phillips curve and the rational expectations critique is not taken into account. The results derived by Nordhaus from these assumptions are well known. The incumbent stimulates the economy close to election time in order to increase its chances of reelection. At the beginning of the new term, the inflationary effects of the pre-electoral expansion are eliminated with a recession. The behavior of the two parties is identical, and a cycle results in equilibrium.

The references here are William Nordhaus, "The political business cycle" (*Review of Economic Studies*, 1975), Duncan MacRae, "A political model of the business cycle" (*Journal of Political Economy*, 1977), and Anthony Downs, *An Economic Theory of Democracy* (1957). An "exploitable Phillips curve" means that the government has the ability to contract the economy (reducing inflation but raising unemployment) or to pursue an expansionary policy (with the reverse effect). Alesina and Sachs go on to discuss the asymmetrical model proposed by Douglas Hibbs in his 1977 *American Political Science Review* paper "Political parties and macroeconomic policy," which proposes that Democratic administrations are more motivated to reduce unemployment, whereas Republicans view controlling inflation as a higher priority.

For a recent review of the research in this area, see Allan Drazen's article "The political business cycle after 25 years" (with accompanying discussion by Alberto Alesina and Carl Walsh) in the *NBER Macroeconomics Annual 2000*.

Page 142: Douglas Hibbs's work on economic performance and incumbent party vote for president has appeared in his 1982 paper with Douglas Rivers and Nicholas Vasilatos "On the demand for economic outcomes: Macroeconomic performance and mass political support in the United States" in the *Journal of Politics*, his 2000 article "Bread and peace voting in U.S. presidential elections" in *Public Choice*, and his recent update "Implications of the 'bread and peace' model for the 2008 U.S. presidential election."

Steven Rosenstone's 1984 book *Forecasting Presidential Elections* remains an excellent overview of the topic. For some more recent discussions of election forecasting, see the symposium published in the October 2004 issue of the journal *PS: Political Science and Politics*.

Page 143: George Bush made his joke about the "haves and the have-mores" at the Al Smith memorial dinner in New York City on 19 October 2000.

Page 143: Bill Clinton's statement on Marc Rich was quoted from a *New York Times* op-ed, "My reasons for the pardons," 18 February 2001.

Page 143: Thomas Frank made this point about upper-class conservatives in his article "Class dismissed."

Page 144: We are grateful to Thomas Ferguson for summarizing his research results for us here. Some of Ferguson's work on political contributions appears in "Blowing smoke: Impeachment, the Clinton presidency, and the political economy" in the 2000 volume *The State of Democracy in America* and "Globalization, religion, and politics in the 2004 election" in the 2005 volume *A Defining Election: The Presidential Race of 2004*. A longer version of the latter article is available at the University of Texas Inequality Project.

Page 144: Verba, Schlozman, and Brady's *Voice and Equality* presents data showing that higher-income people participate more in politics.

Page 145: Thomas Edsall quotes labor leader Andy Stern in his article, "Party hardy" in the *New Republic*, 25 September 2006.

Page 146: The advice to move to the extreme in the primary and the center in the general election has also been attributed to many others.

Page 146: George H. W. Bush made his notorious "no new taxes" pledge at the 1988 Republican national convention.

Page 146: John Kerry's statements on the Iraq War are collected in "Kerry's top ten flip-flops": http://www.cbsnews.com/stories/2004/09/29/politics/main646435.shtml. ("Bush's top ten flip-flops" are at http://www.cbsnews.com/stories/2004/09/28/politics/main646142.shtml.)

Page 146: The median voter theorem dates back to Harold Hotelling's 1929 paper "Stability in competition" in the *Economic Journal,* was elaborated upon by Anthony Downs in his 1957 book *An Economic Theory of Democracy,* and has been studied extensively since then. Particularly relevant to our discussion here are "Valence politics and equilibrium in spatial election models" by Stephen Ansolabehere and James Snyder, published in *Public Choice* in 2000; "A model of candidate location when one candidate has a valence advantage" by Tim Groseclose, published in the *American Journal of Political Science* in 2001; and the 2004 article "Beyond the median: Voter preferences, district heterogeneity, and political representation" by Elisabeth Gerber and Jeffrey Lewis, from the *Journal of Political Economy.* Important earlier references include Gerald

Kramer's 1971 article "Short-term fluctuations in U.S. voting behavior, 1896–1964" and Robert Erikson and David Romero's 1990 article "Candidate equilibrium and the behavioral model of the vote," both of which appeared in the *American Political Science Review*.

Page 148: The analysis reported here comes from the article "Should the Democrats move to the left on economic policy?" by Andrew Gelman and Jeff Cai and appearing in the *Annals of Applied Statistics* in 2008. The questions we use to measure social attitudes are opinions about the role of women, gun-control policy, and government aid to African Americans. The economic issues are opinions about the level of spending that the government should undertake in the economy, the role of the government in providing an economic environment where there is job security, and the level at which the government should spend on defense. Replicating our analysis removing the defense spending question (which is arguably on a different dimension than economics) yields similar results.

In our analysis, we are assuming that ideological stances reflect real policy issues—or to put it another way, we are assuming that the candidates have already performed whatever ideological posturing they can and that changes in their spatial locations can be effected only by changes in policy positions. Reasoning based on median voters also becomes more complicated with constraints on candidate positions, multiple issue dimensions, and variation among voters in perceptions of candidates.

Page 149: The correlation between political attitudes and views of the candidates can be understood in terms of the assimilation and contrast effects, which have been studied in social psychology; see, for example, the article "Assimilation and contrast effects in voter projections of party locations: Evidence from Norway, France, and the USA" by Samuel Merrill, Bernard Grofman, and James Adams, published in the *European Journal of Social Research* in 2004.

Page 150: In their aforementioned "Purple America" article, Stephen Ansolabehere, Jonathan Rodden, and James Snyder also find economic issues to be more important than social issues in predicting vote choice.

Page 150: To perform our simulation of what would have happened if Kerry or Bush had shifted their positions, we alter the constant terms in the regression models we fit to voters' impressions of the candidates' economic and social issue positions; for example, shifting Kerry by one point to the right on the −9 to +9 economic scale. We then run the models of vote choice forward, first simulating random estimated issue positions, then computing estimated ideological distances and simulating vote preferences from our already fitted logistic regressions. This represents a replicated election outcome under the hypothetical position shift. For each hypothesized shift, we take the average of 100 simulations to get the predicted election outcome.

We fit our model to national survey data and predict popular vote. The mapping to electoral vote is not perfect—recall Florida in 2000—but, at the margin, a popular vote gain will generally translate into a higher probability of winning the electoral vote.

Page 153: We do not discuss voter turnout here, but it can make a difference. In their 2001 article "The political implications of higher turnout" in the *British Journal of Political Science*, Benjamin Highton and Raymond Wolfinger estimate that under 100% turnout, the Democrats would receive about three percentage points more of the national vote—not a lot, but enough to have swung the Bush–Gore and Bush–Kerry contests. Beyond this, election campaigns are not static. In their paper "Who votes now? And does it matter?" presented at the 2007 meeting of the Midwest Political Science Association, Jonathan Nagler and Jan Leighley show that nonvoters care about different issues than voters, and they conjecture that increased turnout would raise the profiles of these issues in the campaign.

Page 153: At the 1964 Republican national convention, Barry Goldwater said, "I would remind you that extremism in the defense of liberty is no vice. Let me remind you also that moderation in the pursuit of justice is no virtue."

Page 153: Steven Levitt, in his 1996 paper "How do senators vote?" in the *American Economic Review*, and Robert Erikson and Gerald Wright, in their paper "Representation of constituency ideology in Congress" (which appeared in 2000 in the volume *Continuity and Change in House Elections*), provide evidence that congressmembers balance their goals and their constituents' preferences.

Page 153: In his article "The polarization of American parties and mistrust of government," from the 1997 book *Why People Don't Trust Government*, David King discusses the increasing polarization in political debate.

Page 153: In their article "Toward depolarization" in *Red and Blue Nation*, Pietro Nivola and William Galston write, "the most conspicuous losers in 2006 were not the perpetrators of a 'radical experiment' but the GOP's moderates." The general phenomenon of moderates losing in swing elections is no surprise, given that moderates are more likely to be representing marginal districts where both parties are competitive. Congressmembers with more extreme ideologies are more likely to sit in safer seats.

Pages 155–156: In their 2002 book *Elbridge Gerry's Salamander: The Electoral Consequences of the Reapportionment Revolution*, Gary Cox and Jonathan Katz discuss the connections between political competition, ideological polarization, and incumbency in Congress.

Page 156: We estimated the benefits of moderation by fitting a linear regression to predict the vote shares of congressmembers running for reelection in each year. The summaries here average over parties and election years in each decade.

Page 157: Hubert Humphrey delivered his speech on states' rights and human rights at the 1948 Democratic national convention.

Page 158: Ansolabehere and Snyder discuss the switch to the one-person, one-vote system in their book *The End of Inequality*.

Page 158: Benjamin Page and Robert Shapiro's defense of public opinion comes from their 1992 book *The Rational Public: Fifty Years of Trends in Americans' Policy Preferences*.

Page 159: Here is a list of all the U.S. presidential elections that were decided by less than 1% of the vote: 1880, 1884, 1888, 1960, 1968, 2000. We have been living in an unusual period of partisan balance.

Page 160: Nicholas Kristof wrote about Democrats and the heartland in his *New York Times* column from 3 November 2004, "Living poor, voting rich."

Page 160: Some discussion of the idea that parties reward their supporters as well as compete for swing voters appears in the articles "Electoral politics as a redistributive game" by Gary Cox and Matthew McCubbins in the *Journal of Politics* in 1986; "The determinants of success of special interests in redistributive politics" by Avinash Dixit and John Londregan in that same journal and year; and "Vote buying or turnout buying? Machine politics and the secret ballot" by Simeon Nichter in the *American Political Science Review* in 2008. In the unpublished article "Republican vote buying in the 2004 U.S. presidential election" Jowei Chen argues that disaster aid from the Federal Emergency Management Agency after the Florida hurricanes in 2004 increased turnout among Republican homeowners in the affected areas of the state.

Page 160: An example of a Democrat supporting rich voters in a rich state is Senator Charles Schumer's opposition to a tax on hedge funds;

see Raymond Hernandez and Stephen Labaton's article "In opposing tax plan, Schumer breaks with party" in the *New York Times* on 30 July 2008.

Page 164: In their unpublished article "State parties, polarization, and representation of the poor," Elizabeth Rigby and Gerald Wright analyzed the positions of 16,000 state legislative candidates from the Project Vote Smart surveys and found that these politicians' attitudes on economic redistribution were highly correlated with their general liberal–conservative positions.

Page 164: The asymmetry between the two parties in their appeals to rich and poor is not new. In *The Second Civil War*, Ronald Brownstein, recounting the politics of the first half of the twentieth century, writes that, when Republicans controlled the government, they "offered little to labor, slighted middle-class reformers uneasy about the rise of corporate power, and slowly alienated farmers squeezed by the high-tariff, tight-money policies demanded by the party's Eastern industrial base." In contrast, Democrats when in power "could not be quite so insular. Typically, their coalition always contained more diverse and contradictory elements: Northern liberals and Southern racists, ardent progressives and corporate lawyers. That required them to juggle more complex demands than the Republicans; Wilson and Roosevelt, for example, could never dismiss the leaders of business as thoroughly as McKinley or Coolidge could dismiss the critics of business."

CHAPTER 10: PUTTING IT ALL TOGETHER

Page 165: As of this writing, we still have mechanical lever voting machines in New York State.

Page 168: The Ansolabehere, Rodden, and Snyder quote on the growing culture war is taken from their paper "Purple America."

Page 169: To get at regional differences more directly, political scientist Peter Rentfrow and psychologists John Jost and Samuel Gosling conducted a national survey over the Internet in which people were asked to fill out personality assessment forms as well as to answer some political and demographic questions. The researchers found that "'blue states' are disproportionately high in Openness, and 'red states' are disproportionately high in Conscientiousness." Rentfrow, Jost, and Gosling's study is described in their unpublished article with the descriptive title "Regional differences in personality predict voting patterns in 1996–2004 U.S. presidential elections." In "The end of the end of ideology," which appeared in the *American Psychologist* in 2006, Jost reviews research correlating political attitudes with personality traits. See also Jost's paper with Jaime Napier "The 'anti-democratic personality' revisited: A cross-national investigation of working class authoritarianism," to appear in the *Journal of Social Issues*.

Page 169: Migration by choice was studied by Charles Tiebout in his article "A pure theory of local expenditures" in the *Journal of Political Economy* in 1956.

Page 169: James Gimpel and Jason Schuknecht report their findings on moving and politics in "Interstate migration and electoral politics," which appeared in the *Journal of Politics* in 2001. See also "Regional shifts in America's voting-aged population," a research report by demographer William Frey published by the Population Studies Center at the University of Michigan.

As Alison Stein Wellner wrote in 2006 in her article "The mobility myth" in *Reason* magazine, America is often described as an increasingly mobile society, but, actually, based on current U.S. trends, "a person born today is more likely to remain near his birthplace than a person born in the 19th century." Some recent research in this area is summarized in Claude Fischer's "Ever-more rooted Americans," published in the journal *City and Community* in 2002; Patricia Kelly Hall and Steven Ruggles's 2004 article, "'Restless in the midst of their prosperity': New evidence on the internal migration of Americans, 1850–2000," in the *Journal of American History*; and Joseph Ferrie's unpublished 2005 paper "The end of American exceptionalism? Mobility in the U.S. since 1950." When reading this literature, be careful to distinguish claims about moves between counties, states, and regions of the country.

Page 170: The differences in income between people who move to red and blue states are not large: it's the forty-eighth percentile of income compared to the fifty-second percentile.

Page 170: Steve Sailer wrote about his affordable family formation hypothesis in an article, "Values voters" in *The American Conservative* on 11 February 2008. He adds, "'family values' voters would thus tend to move to states where they could more easily afford a house with a yard in a satisfactory public school district, painting the Red States redder," and he speculates that "young people of middle-of-the-road tendencies might be more susceptible to starting down the path to conservatism in a state where family formation is quite affordable, such as Texas, than in an expensive state, such as California."

In a related article, "Why do gay men live in San Francisco," from the *Journal of Urban Economics* in 2002, Dan Black, Gary Gates, Seth Sanders, and Lowell Taylor argue that gay men disproportionately move to more attractive cities because they are less likely to have children and thus are more able to afford high housing prices. Also relevant to this discussion is Richard Florida's latest book, *Who's Your City?* on the topic of how people are now choosing where to live.

Page 171: Edward Glaeser and Bruce Sacerdote's model appears in their unpublished paper "Aggregation reversals and the social formation of beliefs."

Page 171: David Brooks's comments on the influence of the upper middle class come from his article "The Democratic party gets a brain—and loses its mind" in the *Weekly Standard* on 26 January 1998. E. J. Dionne discusses the perspectives of Brooks and others in his article "Polarized by God" in *Red and Blue Nation*.

Page 172: In the *International Political Science Review* in 1985, Ferdinand Muller-Rommel wrote, "According to Inglehart, it is possible to hold that the left–right dimension no longer adequately describes modern patterns of political conflicts, because 'new' issues can no longer be regarded solely as expressions of left–right conflicts. The need, for example, to combat environmental pollution and the need for a peace policy are not, at least overtly, questioned by either conservatives or left-wing parties." Muller-Rommel was referring to the 1976 article "Party identification, ideological preferences, and left–right dimension among western publics" by Ronald Inglehart and Hans-Dieter Klingemann, published in the volume *Party Identification and Beyond*.

Scholars such as Raghuram Rajan and Luigi Zingales (in their 2003 paper "The great reversals: The politics of financial development in the twentieth century" in the *Journal of Financial Economics*) and Thomas Piketty attribute the postwar European economic consensus to the fact that the continent was starting from scratch after the devastation of two world wars.

Page 172: For more on the increasing importance of both class and culture in voting, see Mark Brewer and Jeffrey Stonecash's 2007 book *Split*.

Page 173: Ansolabehere, Rodden, and Snyder's quote is from their article "Purple America."

Page 173: Matthew Fellowes, Virginia Gray, and Davie Lowery's discussion of post-materialist politics appears in their article, "What's on the table? The content of state policy agendas," published in *Party Politics* in 2006.

Page 175: A key book on race and postwar American politics is Edward Carmines and James Stimson's *Issue Evolution: Race and the Transformation of American Politics* from 1989.

Page 175: In their unpublished article "International polarity and domestic polarization: Explaining American disunity," Joseph Parent and Joseph Bafumi present the unipolarity theory, arguing that the end of the Cold War around 1990 and the associated removal of an external threat reduced the incentives for political leaders to coordinate and allowed for a new era of polarization that persists today.

Page 175: The effects of the new ideological media are discussed in Gary Jacobson's 2007 book *A Divider, Not a Uniter*, and three articles in the *Red and Blue Nation* volume: "Polarizing the House of Representatives: How much does gerrymandering matter?" by Thomas Mann, "Disconnected: The political class versus the people" by Morris Fiorina and Matthew Levendusky, and "How the mass media divide us" by Diana Mutz. Markus Prior provides a thorough treatment of these issues in his 2007 book *Post-Broadcast Democracy: How Media Choice Increases Inequality in Political Involvement and Polarizes Elections*.

Page 176: As Carl Cannon points out in his article in *Red and Blue Nation*, recent political polarization is all the more striking considering the general economic prosperity of the past few decades.

AFTERWORD: THE 2008 ELECTION

We thank Michael McDonald for turnout numbers, Nate Silver for summaries of pre-election forecasts, Eric Rauchway and Cosma Shalizi for county-level data, and Ben Lauderdale for making the county-level maps. We used Voter News Service exit polls (available from cnn.com) and Pew Research pre-election surveys (for which we thank Scott Keeter and Leah Christian) for most of our calculations, and we thank Yair Ghitza for assistance in the statistical analysis.

Page 182: In estimating vote by state and income level, we used five categories of family income: $0–$20,000, $20,000–$40,000, $40,000–$75,000, $75,000–$150,000, and over $150,000. We fit a multilevel logistic regression of vote preference (including only those survey respondents who reported supporting either Obama or McCain and said they were sure they were registered to vote) given five categories of income, four ethnic categories (non-Hispanic whites, blacks, Hispanics, and others), and state. We used average income, 2004 election outcome, and region of the country as state-level predictors. Our model gave us estimates for each income and ethnic category in each state (excluding Alaska and Hawaii, which were not covered by the Pew surveys); we then aggregated these using voter turnout numbers estimated from the Current Population Survey post-election supplement across the five income categories to get estimated aggregate vote shares for Obama and McCain in each state. Finally, we computed the difference between our estimates and the actual election outcomes for each state and shifted our estimates within each income and ethnic category by this amount within each state.

Page 185: Ansolabehere and Stewart made their comment about race and voting in an article in the *Boston Review* in January/February 2009. Mark Penn's remark about the voting of young people appeared in the *New York Times*'s "Campaign Stops" blog on 5 November 2008. Allen Gathman pointed out the similarity between vote swings and cotton production on 6 November 2008; see http://cstl-csm.semo.edu/gathman/cottonvote.htm.

Page 191: To estimate Obama's vote share among nonblacks within each county, we used the following calculation:

Obama got 96% of the black vote. If he got 96% in every county, which cannot be far from the truth, simple algebra will show his share of the nonblack vote in every county. If B is the proportion black in the county and X is the (unknown) Obama vote share among nonblacks, then, for each county:

$$\text{Obama's vote share} = 0.96B + X(1 - B).$$

And so, under these assumptions,

$$X = (\text{Obama's vote share} - 0.96B)/(1 - B).$$

Page 195: Douglas Hibbs's summary of his 2008 forecast is at http://douglas-hibbs.com/Election2008/2008Election-MainPage.htm. Our own analysis combining early polls and past election results appears in the unpublished article "Bayesian combination of state polls and election forecasts," by Kari Lock and Andrew Gelman. Related ideas appear in Aaron Strauss's unpublished article, "Florida or Ohio? Forecasting presidential state outcomes using reverse random walks."

COLOR SECTION

Plates 1 and 2: For compactness, we do not display Alaska and Hawaii on our maps. Since their admission as states, Alaska has supported the Republicans in every presidential election except for Lyndon Johnson's landslide in 1964, and Hawaii has supported the Democratic candidate in every election except for Ronald Reagan's landslide in 1984. We also exclude Alaska and Hawaii from many of our graphs because several otherwise national surveys do not include them. We also exclude Washington, D.C., which has overwhelmingly supported the Democrats every year, from our state-level analyses and maps.

The consistent coloring of states as red for the Republicans and blue for the Democrats dates only from 2000. The history of the coloring is reported in Tom Zeller's *New York Times* article "One state, two state, red state, blue state" from 8 February 2004, and in Phil Patton's 24 September 2004 article, "One fate, two fates, red states, blue states" in *Voice*, the online journal of the American Institute of Graphic Arts. As Patton writes, "In many ways the link goes against tradition. Red has long stood for the left and one has to suspect that the first usage of it to represent Republicans was inspired by an effort to seem non-prejudicial."

Plate 3: The maps and scatterplots of estimated winners among upper-, middle-, and lower-income voters come from our multilevel analysis based on 2000 exit polls. The three income categories are 0–16th percentile, 33–67th percentile, and 95–100th percentile, as determined by the national distribution of family incomes.

Plates 4 and 5: Robert Vanderbei presents and discusses various purple maps in his unpublished report "On graphical representations of voting results."

Plate 6: The distorted maps were created by Michael Gastner, Cosma Shalizi, and Mark Newman. For more detail and several other maps, see their Web page, http://www-personal.umich.edu/~mejn/election/, and their article "Maps and cartograms of the 2004 U.S. presidential election results," which appeared in *Advances in Complex Systems* in 2005.

Plate 7: The three categories correspond to attending religious services more than once per week, once or twice per month, and never (excluding weddings and funerals).

Plate 8: These ideological polarization graphs come from the 2004 Annenberg Election Survey. We recode the survey response as follows:

liberal $= -1$, somewhat liberal $= -0.5$, moderate or no answer $= 0$, somewhat conservative $= +0.5$, conservative $= +1$. A difference of 0.5 thus corresponds to the difference between moderate and somewhat conservative, for example. For the first of the three graphs, we determine Democrat and Republican based on the party identification question in the survey. For the second graph, we define high and low as the upper and lower thirds of income. For the third graph, we compare people who report attending religious services at least once per week to those who say they never attend (not counting weddings and funerals).

Plate 9: The blue, yellow, and green colors of Mexico's political parties are filled with political and historic symbolism. The official colors of the PAN are white and blue, which signify the purity of the vote. The PRI uses the colors of the Mexican flag—green, white, and red—which, according to the PRI, represent the historical involvement of the party on Mexico's political history. Finally, the official color of the PRD is yellow from its logo, which is a stylized version of the Aztec sun.

Plates 10 and 11: We constructed these social and economic ideology scores based on several questions asked in the 2000 Annenberg survey. For details, go to page 213 and see the note for page 90.

Plates 12–15: See the notes for the afterword.

Acknowledgments

One of the great things about teaching at Columbia is the opportunity to work with students who know so much more than I do. Three of these students have become coauthors on this book.

When we started on this project, the four of us had, between us, one Ph.D. and one child. We now have four doctorates and seven children, some of whom have not always been completely appreciative of this project:

Zacky: Papi, it's not a school day. Why are you going to work?
AG: I'm working on the book.
Zacky: When the book is done, you'll be able to play with me all the time, right?

We thank Steve Ansolabehere, Kevin Arcenaux, Joseph Bafumi, Susan Baker, Delia Baldassarri, Larry Bartels, Joel Beal, Bernd Beber, Tom Belin,

Ulíses Beltrán, Adam Berinsky, Dan Bial, Clem Brooks, Jeff Cai, Ernesto Calvo, Bob Carpenter, Stephen Carter, Andres Centeno, Jamie Chandler, Abigail Charles, Lauren Cowles, Amanda Czerniawski, Stephen Dee, Rodolfo de la Garza, Tom DiPrete, Jorge Domínguez, David Epstein, Bob Erikson, Doug Erwing, Henry Farrell, Thomas Ferguson, Maryann Fiebach, Morris Fiorina, Claude Fischer, Mitchell Flax, Brian Fogarty, James Galbraith, Reuven Garrett, Jane Gelman, Robert Gelman, Susan Gelman, Edward Glaeser, Sharad Goel, Lucy Goodhart, Lucas Graves, Gabor Halasz, Lewis Herrera, Michael Herron, Douglas Hibbs, Shigeo Hirano, Scott Holcomb, Yu-Chieh Hsu, Thomas Huang, John Huber, Iris Hui, Paula Hurtado, Aleks Jakulin, Alison Jones, Stuart Jordan, John Jost, Elizabeth Kaplan, Noah Kaplan, Dimitri Karetnikov, John Kastellec, Jonathan Katz, Ira Katznelson, Vickie Kearn, Luke Keele, Jouni Kerman, Georgia Kernell, Eunseong Kim, Walter Kim, Dave Krantz, Narayani Lasala, Jeff Lax, David Leal, Jan Lee, Mark D. Lew, Mark Liberman, Rob Lieberman, Christian Logan, Josh Luger, Bruce Mannheim, Jeff Manza, Nolan McCarty, Tyler McCormick, Carrie McLaren, Diana McNally, José Ramón Montero, Jonathan Nagler, Amy Nazer, Craig Newmark, Virginia Oliveros, Terri O'Prey, Bob Pees, Justin Phillips, Nancy Pines, Pablo Pinto, Maria Grazia Pittau, Aldo Ponce, Keith Poole, Phillip Price, Robert Putnam, Kevin Quinn, Rozlyn Redd, Jason Reifler, Seth Roberts, Jonathan Rodden, Caroline Rosenthal Gelman, Bruce Sacerdote, Steve Sailer, Matt Salganik, Cyrus Samii, Alex Scacco, Bill Schenker, Matt Schofield, Melissa Schwartzberg, Jasjeet Sekhon, Cosma Shalizi, Bob Shapiro, Andrea Siegel, Juli Simon Thomas, Jim Snyder, Piero Stanig, Annie Stilz, Kevin Stolarick, Yu-Sung Su, Brian Sung, Julien Teitler, Milan Vaishnav, Robert Vanderbei, Howard Wainer, Tiffany Washburn, Duncan Watts, Greg Wawro, David Weaver, Elke Weber, Rebecca Weitz-Shapiro, Bruce Western, Bill Wetzel, Matt Winters, Masanao Yajima, Tian Zheng, Boliang Zhu, Al Zuckerman, and various blog commenters, seminar participants, and anonymous reviewers for their extremely helpful contributions and suggestions at various stages of this work; the Roper Center and the Inter-university Consortium for Political and Social Research for poll data; and the U.S. National Science Foundation, National Institutes of Health, and Columbia University Applied Statistics Center for financial support.

Most importantly, we thank our families for their love, support, and advice during the writing of this book.

ABOUT THE AUTHORS

Andrew Gelman is a professor of statistics and political science at Columbia University. His previous books include *Bayesian Data Analysis and Teaching Statistics: A Bag of Tricks.* His research has won several awards, including the Presidents of Statistical Societies Award for outstanding contributions to statistics by a person under the age of 40. David Park is an assistant professor in political science at George Washington University. His research focuses on the linkages between the public and their elected representatives. Boris Shor is an assistant professor at the Harris School for Public Policy Studies at the University of Chicago. He is currently studying the links between public opinion, elite ideology, and policy. Jeronimo Cortina is an assistant professor of political science at the University of Houston. His research focuses on immigration, public opinion, and the connections between the United States and Latin America.

Index

abortion, 117, 118, 124, 127, 128, 213, 218, 219
Abramowitz, Alan, 130, 200, 218, 223, 224
Abrams, Samuel, 199, 218
Abramson, Paul, 204
academic work, slowness of, 202
Accra index of cost of living, 209
Achen, Christopher, 222
Adams, James, 228
aerospace, political contributions of, 144
affordable family formation hypothesis, 170, 232
African Americans
    percentage in U.S., 32
    whites' misperception of economic status of, 33
Alaska, not on maps, 236
Aldrich, John, 204
Alemán, Ricardo, 98, 215
Alesina, Alberto, 225, 226
Alford, Robert, 199
Almanac of American Politics, 24, 202
Annenberg Election Survey, 197, 210–213, 236
Ansolabehere, Stephen, 72, 135, 158, 168, 173, 199, 223, 224, 227, 228, 230
apple pie, mom and, 31
Ariely, Dan, 206
Asians, percentage in U.S., 33
assimilation effect, 228
atheists, 76, 210

Austin, Texas, 12, 13
availability bias, 36–37, 205
    second-order, 206
average American, most people think Democratic Party looks out for, 14
Aztec sun, 237

Bafumi, Joseph, 117, 120, 121, 219, 222, 234
Bai, Matt, 17, 202
Baker v. Carr, 72
Baldassarri, Delia, 223
Barone, Michael, 24, 25, 36, 65, 202, 205, 209
Bartels, Larry, 140, 141, 174, 200, 219, 225
baseball cap, Michael Moore's, 31
Bates, Doug, 198
battleground states, our definition of, 198
Baudrillard, Jean, 79, 211
Bearman, Peter, 223
Bell, Daniel, 175
Bell Labs, 199
Belluck, Pam, 211
Beltrán, Ulíses, 214, 215
Benoit, Kenneth, 216
Benz-driving, not used as symbol of Republicans' inauthenticity, 145
Berinsky, Adam, 207
Berry, William, 209
Bertin, Jacques, 197
Bingham, Colin, 225
Bishop, Bill, 218
Black, Dan, 233

241